ASSESSING PROGRESS on the Institute of Medicine Report *THE FUTURE OF NURSING*

Committee for Assessing Progress on Implementing the
Recommendations of the Institute of Medicine Report
The Future of Nursing: Leading Change, Advancing Health

Stuart H. Altman, Adrienne Stith Butler, Lauren Shern, *Editors*

Institute of Medicine

The National Academies of
SCIENCES · ENGINEERING · MEDICINE

THE NATIONAL ACADEMIES PRESS
Washington, DC
www.nap.edu

THE NATIONAL ACADEMIES PRESS   500 Fifth Street, NW   Washington, DC 20001

This study was supported by Contract/Grant No. 72309 from the Robert Wood Johnson Foundation. Any opinions, findings, conclusions, or recommendations expressed in this publication do not necessarily reflect the views of any organization or agency that provided support for the project.

International Standard Book Number-13:   978-0-309-38031-7
International Standard Book Number-10:   0-309-38031-6
Library of Congress Control Number: 2016931586

Additional copies of this report are available for sale from the National Academies Press, 500 Fifth Street, NW, Keck 360, Washington, DC 20001; (800) 624-6242 or (202) 334-3313; http://www.nap.edu.

Suggested citation: National Academies of Sciences, Engineering, and Medicine. 2016. *Assessing Progress on the Institute of Medicine Report* The Future of Nursing. Washington, DC: The National Academies Press.

The National Academies of
SCIENCES · ENGINEERING · MEDICINE

The **National Academy of Sciences** was established in 1863 by an Act of Congress, signed by President Lincoln, as a private, nongovernmental institution to advise the nation on issues related to science and technology. Members are elected by their peers for outstanding contributions to research. Dr. Ralph J. Cicerone is president.

The **National Academy of Engineering** was established in 1964 under the charter of the National Academy of Sciences to bring the practices of engineering to advising the nation. Members are elected by their peers for extraordinary contributions to engineering. Dr. C. D. Mote, Jr., is president.

The **National Academy of Medicine** (formerly the Institute of Medicine) was established in 1970 under the charter of the National Academy of Sciences to advise the nation on medical and health issues. Members are elected by their peers for distinguished contributions to medicine and health. Dr. Victor J. Dzau is president.

The three Academies work together as the **National Academies of Sciences, Engineering, and Medicine** to provide independent, objective analysis and advice to the nation and conduct other activities to solve complex problems and inform public policy decisions. The Academies also encourage education and research, recognize outstanding contributions to knowledge, and increase public understanding in matters of science, engineering, and medicine.

Learn more about the **National Academies of Sciences, Engineering, and Medicine** at **www.national-academies.org**.

v

Consultants

RONA BRIERE, Consultant Editor
ERIN HAMMERS FORSTAG, Consultant Writer

Reviewers

This report has been reviewed in draft form by individuals chosen for their diverse perspectives and technical expertise. The purpose of this independent review is to provide candid and critical comments that will assist the institution in making its published report as sound as possible and to ensure that the report meets institutional standards for objectivity, evidence, and responsiveness to the study charge. The review comments and draft manuscript remain confidential to protect the integrity of the deliberative process. We wish to thank the following individuals for their review of this report:

David Auerbach, Massachusetts Health Policy Commission
Elizabeth H. Bradley, Yale School of Public Health
Patrick H. DeLeon, Uniformed Services University of the Health Sciences
Catherine Dower, Kaiser Permanente
Kathleen Gallo, North Shore–Long Island Jewish Health System
Ann Hubbard, Indian River State College
Judith R. Kunisch, Yale School of Nursing
Salimah H. Meghani, University of Pennsylvania School of Nursing
Wayne J. Riley, Vanderbilt University
John W. Rowe, Columbia University Mailman School of Public Health
William M. Sage, University of Texas at Austin
Richard Sorian, FleishmanHillard
Antonia M. Villarruel, University of Pennsylvania School of Nursing

Although the reviewers listed above provided many constructive comments and suggestions, they were not asked to endorse the report's conclusions or recommendations, nor did they see the final draft of the report before its release. The review of this report was overseen by **Bobbie Berkowitz,** Columbia University School of Nursing and Columbia University Medical Center, and **Mark R. Cullen,** Stanford University. They were responsible for making certain that an independent examination of this report was carried out in accordance with institutional procedures and that all review comments were carefully considered. Responsibility for the final content of this report rests entirely with the authoring committee and the institution.

Preface

In 2010, the Institute of Medicine (IOM) released a landmark report titled *The Future of Nursing: Leading Change, Advancing Health.* In the preface to the report, the chair and vice chair of the committee, Donna Shalala and Linda Burnes Bolton, stated that the passage of the Patient Protection and Affordable Care Act, also in 2010, would require that the U.S. health care system expand to accommodate a significant increase in demand for services, particularly those needed to manage patients with chronic conditions or mental health conditions or to provide basic primary care. They noted that nurses were in a unique position to take on a leadership role in helping the nation attain these goals. They stated that "nurses have a key role to play as team members and leaders for a reformed and better integrated patient-centered health care system."

The Future of Nursing was sponsored by the Robert Wood Johnson Foundation (RWJF), and senior staff of RWJF helped the IOM gather material for the 2-year study. Following the publication of the report, RWJF supported the creation of the Future of Nursing: Campaign for Action (the Campaign) and its 51 state Action Coalitions. The efforts of outside groups devoted to the implementation of the IOM report's recommendations have been extraordinary.

It has now been 5 years since *The Future of Nursing* was issued, and RWJF asked the IOM to assess the progress made toward implementing the report's recommendations and to identify areas that should be emphasized over the next 5 years to help the Campaign fulfill the recommendations. The committee convened to carry out this study was not asked to reexamine the merits of or amend the recommendations of *The Future of Nursing*. I was delighted when the new president of the now National Academy of Medicine, Dr. Victor Dzau, asked me to chair the committee and take on this task. The field of nursing has been of special interest to me since I published my first book—*Present and Future Supply of Registered Nurses*—in the early 1970s. After reviewing *The Future of Nursing* and analyzing the information collected as part of the present study, it is clear to me that the nursing profession is a far more important component of the U.S. health care system than it was 45 years ago.

The committee conducted three public workshops and met as a group four times. In addition, it held three full-committee and several smaller subcommittee phone meetings. I am especially appreciative of the time commitment and pursuit of excellence of the 11 other members of our committee. Without their expertise, their experience, and their knowledge of the information that could be used to assess the changes that have occurred in the health care system, this report could not have been completed. We also are indebted to the staff of RWJF for their help in assembling this information. We appreciate as well the efforts of the three IOM staff members and the consultant writer who guided us through the study and the writing of this report. In particular, the dedication and drive of our study director, Adrienne Stith Butler, were irreplaceable.

Clearly much has been accomplished by the Campaign and other stakeholders, and it is readily apparent that *The Future of Nursing* was a catalyst for a number of new activities and accelerated several trends that had begun before the report was completed. The present report is timely in that it allows for reflection on the progress that has been achieved over the past 5 years in implementing the recommendations of *The Future of Nursing*, while leaving time for the Campaign and others to adjust to the many changes occurring in nursing and the health care system. The committee worked diligently over a short period of time to assemble and review the available data and evidence to help in understanding the changes that have occurred in the field of nursing—the structure of its education system, who is entering the field and in which programs, where nurses are employed, the attitudes of others about the appropriate role of nurses, and, where possible, how the expanded use of nurses has impacted the quality of patient care. With the help of this assessment, the committee generated a number of recommendations, which we hope will assist the Campaign, its state Action Coalitions, and other groups and stakeholders in positively impacting the field of nursing and improving the U.S. health care system.

Stuart H. Altman, *Chair*
Committee for Assessing Progress on
Implementing the Recommendations of the
Institute of Medicine Report
The Future of Nursing: Leading Change, Advancing Health

Acknowledgments

Many individuals and organizations made important contributions to the study committee's process and to this report. The committee wishes to thank these individuals, but recognizes that attempts to identify all of them and to acknowledge their contributions would require more space than is available in this brief section.

To begin, the committee would like to thank the sponsor of this study; funds for the committee's work were provided by the Robert Wood Johnson Foundation. The committee also gratefully acknowledges the contributions of the many individuals and organizations that assisted in the conduct of the study. Their perspectives were valuable in understanding the work undertaken to implement the recommendations from the Institute of Medicine report *The Future of Nursing: Leading Change, Advancing Health*. The committee thanks those individuals who provided important presentations and oral testimony at its open workshops. Appendix A lists these individuals and their affiliations. Written testimony received from nearly 100 individuals and organizations also helped the committee understand the status of implementation of the recommendations. The committee is grateful for the time, effort, and valuable information provided by all of these dedicated individuals and organizations. We are immensely grateful for the organizations that provided the committee with data and other inputs: the Accreditation Commission for Education in Nursing (ACEN), the American Association of Colleges of Nursing (AACN), the Center to Champion Nursing in America (CCNA), the Commission on Collegiate Nursing Education (CCNE), the National League for Nursing (NLN), the Robert Wood Johnson Foundation (RWJF), and TCC Group.

Finally, many within the National Academies of Sciences, Engineering, and Medicine were helpful to the study staff. We would like to thank Clyde Behney, Laura DeStefano, Chelsea Frakes, Greta Gorman, Nicole Joy, Ellen Kimmel, Fariha Mahmud, Rebecca Morgan, Bettina Ritter, Jennifer Walsh, and Colleen Willis for their invaluable assistance.

Contents

Acronyms and Abbreviations

AACN	American Association of Colleges of Nursing
AAMC	Association of American Medical Colleges
AANP	American Association of Nurse Practitioners
ACA	Patient Protection and Affordable Care Act
ACCME	Accreditation Council for Continuing Medical Education
ACEN	Accreditation Commission for Education in Nursing
ACP	American College of Physicians
ACPE	Accreditation Council for Pharmacy Education
ACS	American Community Survey
ADN	associate degree in nursing
AMA	American Medical Association
ANA	American Nurses Association
ANCC	American Nurses Credentialing Center
AONE	American Organization of Nurse Executives
APIN	Academic Progression in Nursing
APRN	advanced practice registered nurse
ARRA	American Recovery and Reinvestment Act
BSN	bachelor of science in nursing
Campaign	Future of Nursing: Campaign for Action
CCNA	Center to Champion Nursing in America
CCNE	Commission on Collegiate Nursing Education
CDC	Centers for Disease Control and Prevention
CHC	Community Health Center, Inc.

CMA	California Medical Association
CMMI	Center for Medicare & Medicaid Innovation
CMS	Centers for Medicare & Medicaid Services
CNM	certified nurse midwife
CNO	chief nursing officer
CPS	Current Population Survey
CRNA	certified registered nurse anesthetist
DNP	doctor of nursing practice
FQHC	federally qualified health center
FTC	Federal Trade Commission
GNE	(Medicare) Graduate Nursing Education
HPAC	Health Professions Accreditors Collaborative
HRSA	Health Resources and Services Administration
INQRI	Interdisciplinary Nursing Quality Research Initiative
IOM	Institute of Medicine
IPE	interprofessional education
IPEC	Interprofessional Education Collaborative
IPEDS	Integrated Postsecondary Education Data System
LPN	licensed practical nurse
LVN	licensed vocational nurse
MDS	Minimum Data Set
MSN	master of science in nursing
NAMCS	National Ambulatory Medical Care Survey
NCES	National Center for Education Statistics
NCIN	New Careers in Nursing
NCIPE	National Center for Interprofessional Practice and Education
NCLEX	National Council Licensure Examination
NCSBN	National Council of State Boards of Nursing
NHIS	National Health Interview Survey
NLN	National League for Nursing
NMHC	nurse-managed health clinic
NMNEC	New Mexico Nursing Education Consortium
NP	nurse practitioner
NPI	National Provider Identifier
NSSNP	National Sample Survey of Nurse Practitioners

NSSRN   National Sample Survey of Registered Nurses

OHSU   Oregon Health & Science University

PA   physician assistant
PIN   Partners Investing in Nursing's Future

RN   registered nurse
RWJF   Robert Wood Johnson Foundation

SIP   State Implementation Program
SOC   Standard Occupational Classification

UHC   University HealthSystem Consortium

VA   U.S. Department of Veterans Affairs
VHA   Veterans Health Administration

Summary[1]

Nurses make up the largest segment of the health care profession; there are approximately 3 million registered nurses in the United States. Nurses work in a wide variety of settings, including hospitals, public health centers, schools, and homes, and provide a continuum of services involving direct patient care, health promotion, patient education, and coordination of care. They serve in leadership roles, are researchers, and work to improve health care policy. As the health care system undergoes transformation, in part as a result of the Patient Protection and Affordable Care Act, the nursing profession is having a wide-ranging impact by providing patient-centered, accessible, and affordable care. In 2010, the Institute of Medicine released *The Future of Nursing: Leading Change, Advancing Health*, offering recommendations for nursing in the new health care landscape. The present report assesses progress made toward implementing those recommendations. This report also identifies areas that should be emphasized over the next 5 years to advance the recommendations' implementation. The 10 recommendations offered in the present report are intended to help the Future of Nursing: Campaign for Action and the nursing profession effect change in the culture in which health care is provided by addressing scope of practice, education, collaborative leadership, and diversity in the nursing profession and improving the collection of nursing workforce data.

In the past decade, the changing climate of health care policy and practice has sharpened the national focus on the challenges of providing high-quality and affordable care to an aging and increasingly diverse population. The priorities of this changed climate will increasingly require the collaboration of health profes-

---

[1] This summary does not include references. Citations for the discussion presented in the summary appear in the subsequent report chapters.

1

BOX S-1
Key Areas Addressed by Recommendations from
The Future of Nursing: Leading Change, Advancing Health

1. Remove scope-of-practice barriers.
2. Expand opportunities for nurses to lead and diffuse collaborative improvement efforts.
3. Implement nurse residency programs.
4. Increase the proportion of nurses with a baccalaureate degree to 80 percent by 2020.
5. Double the number of nurses with a doctorate by 2020.
6. Ensure that nurses engage in lifelong learning.
7. Prepare and enable nurses to lead change to advance health.
8. Build an infrastructure for the collection and analysis of interprofessional health care workforce data.

---

sionals to provide patient-centered, coordinated, and community-based primary and specialty care services. Nurses, who are the largest group of health care professionals, are positioned to lead and partner in teams that provide services across the continuum of care (hospitals, ambulatory care, public health, schools, long-term care, and home health). Nurses also are positioned to provide leadership within a variety of health care systems and policy settings.

In 2008, the Robert Wood Johnson Foundation (RWJF) partnered with the Institute of Medicine (IOM) to establish an Initiative on the Future of Nursing, which convened a committee that in 2010 released the report *The Future of Nursing: Leading Change, Advancing Health.* This report offers a series of recommendations to advance nursing's contributions to the new health care environment (see Box S-1). Shortly after release of the report, AARP and RWJF launched the Future of Nursing: Campaign for Action (the Campaign) to shepherd the implementation of the report's recommendations. The Campaign, coordinated through the Center to Champion Nursing in America (CCNA), works nationally and through state Action Coalitions to advance its goals. The Campaign's efforts target six major areas, or "pillars":

- advancing education transformation,
- leveraging nursing leadership,
- removing barriers to practice and care,
- fostering interprofessional collaboration,
- promoting diversity, and
- bolstering workforce data.

Reports released by many other organizations (for example, the World Health Organization, the Carnegie Foundation, and the Tri-Council for Nursing) contemporaneously with *The Future of Nursing* call for similar changes. *The Future of Nursing* lent momentum to a movement that was under way, offering tangible and specific recommendations.

STUDY CHARGE AND APPROACH

In 2014, RWJF asked the IOM to convene a committee to assess progress made on implementing the recommendations of *The Future of Nursing* and identify areas that should be emphasized over the next 5 years to help the Campaign fulfill its aims. The committee considered the utilization of the report by the Campaign and other groups, the impact of the Campaign on areas peripheral to nursing, and the Campaign's use of traditional and new media in meeting its goals. The present report, the product of these efforts, is based, in part, on three workshops organized by the committee that focused on practice, education, leadership, diversity, collaboration, and health workforce data.

The committee's task did not include reexamining the merits of the recommendations of *The Future of Nursing*. Given the short time since the release of that report, the committee did not perform a comprehensive evaluation of the impact of the report's recommendations or of the Campaign, but instead focused on progress achieved on the report's goals. Further, the committee did not attribute progress or the lack thereof in areas of the report's recommendations directly to the report or to the Campaign, recognizing that other factors were at play in the environment. The committee examined how the current context of health care delivery, nursing education, and practice could affect implementation of the report's recommendations and identified barriers to and unintended consequences of their implementation. The committee also considered how the recommendations might yet be advanced.

STUDY CONTEXT

The Future of Nursing was produced at a propitious moment in health care in the United States, a time of growing awareness that dramatic changes in the care delivery system were needed to accomplish the "Triple Aim" of better patient experience, better health of the public, and lower costs. The committee that developed the report anticipated that passage of the Patient Protection and Affordable Care Act (ACA) would necessitate that nurses play a larger role in bridging the gap between coverage and access. New delivery models emphasize teamwork, care coordination for specialty care and chronic disease management, prevention, and greater focus on population health and community-based care. New payment models are moving away from fee-for-service and episodic payment to value-based payment. Rapid advances in information technology are changing the way health professionals and the public receive information and communicate with one another. Greater attention to preparing the health care workforce to meet growing and evolving needs has led to more emphasis on interprofessional education, teamwork training, and a better understanding of the roles of all health professionals in creating an optimal health care delivery system. While the committee that developed *The Future of Nursing* anticipated many of these changes, it could not have foreseen exactly how they would play out.

STUDY FINDINGS AND RECOMMENDATIONS

The present report's recommendations are intended to help the Campaign, as well as policy makers, payers, and health professions organizations, make further progress toward implementing the recommendations of *The Future of Nursing*. The committee found that the Campaign has made significant progress in many aspects of this effort. In a short period of time, it has galvanized the nursing community through its work at the national level and through the 51 state Action Coalitions it has organized. The committee found that the Campaign has met or exceeded expectations in many areas. However, given the changing health care culture, particularly the increasing importance placed on interprofessional collaboration, the Campaign needs to engage a broader network of stakeholders. The present report also recommends addressing challenges in the areas of scope of practice, education, diversity, collaboration, leadership, and data. The committee believes these contributions can change the impact of nurses on the health care system and on patient care and outcomes.

In the committee's view, the work of the Campaign and others would best be advanced if it were driven by the following three themes:

- the need to build a broader coalition to increase awareness of nurses' ability to play a full role in health professions practice, education, collaboration, and leadership;
- the need to continue to make promoting diversity in the nursing workforce a priority; and
- the need for better data with which to assess and drive progress.

The committee hopes that, taken together, the 10 recommendations presented in this report provide a blueprint for advancing implementation of the recommendations of *The Future of Nursing*.

Removing Scope-of-Practice Barriers

The Future of Nursing proposes that advanced practice registered nurses (APRNs) could help build the workforce necessary to meet the country's health care needs if permitted to practice to the full extent of their education and training.

In 2010, 13 states were classified as meeting criteria for full practice authority. Since then, 8 more states (Connecticut, Maryland, Minnesota, Nebraska, Nevada, North Dakota, Rhode Island, and Vermont) have changed their laws to give nurse practitioners (NPs) full practice and prescriptive authority. As of this writing, 17 states are categorized as having reduced practice authority and 12 as having restricted practice authority. Some states—for example, Kentucky, New York, Texas, and Utah—have made incremental improvements to their laws but are still categorized as having reduced or restricted practice authority for APRNs. These broad categorizations, while useful for classification purposes, mask a number of subtle differences among state laws. For example, Maine, a state with full practice authority, has legislative prohibitions against NP hospital privileges.

At the federal level, the Centers for Medicare & Medicaid Services in 2012 issued a final rule broadening the concept of medical staff, permitting hospitals to allow other practitioners (e.g., APRNs, physician assistants, and pharmacists) to perform all functions within their scope of practice. Despite this rule, medical staff membership and hospital privileges remain subject to existing state laws and business preferences. The Federal Trade Commission has engaged in competition advocacy for APRNs' scope of practice in many states, providing letters, comments, and/or testimony.

While there has been on-the-ground collaboration between medicine and nursing, opposition by some physicians and physician organizations has been noted as a barrier to expansion of APRNs' scope of practice. The health care environment continues to evolve and demand greater team-based and value-based care. There is growing evidence that new models of practice in which all health professionals practice to the full extent of their education and training offer greater efficiency and quality of services. Several studies have shown, moreover, that these care models enhance satisfaction among health care providers. This is an important contextual change since the release of *The Future of Nursing*, one that offers potential common ground for that report's goals regarding scope-of-practice expansion.

***Recommendation 1: Build Common Ground Around Scope of Practice and Other Issues in Policy and Practice.* The Future of Nursing: Campaign for Action (the Campaign) should broaden its coalition to include more diverse stakeholders. The Campaign should build on its successes and work with other health professions groups, policy makers, and the community to build common ground around removing scope-of-practice restrictions, increasing interprofessional collaboration, and addressing other issues to improve health care practice in the interest of patients.**

Achieving Higher Levels of Education

According to *The Future of Nursing*, transformation in the health care system and practice environments requires a corresponding transformation in nursing education. If nurses are to be prepared to meet increasingly complex patient needs, function as leaders, and advance the science of care, they need to achieve higher levels of education upon entering the workforce and throughout their careers.

Baccalaureate Education

In 2010, approximately half of the nation's 3 million nurses held a baccalaureate or higher degree. *The Future of Nursing* recommends that this proportion be increased, suggesting an ambitious goal of 80 percent by 2020.

Baccalaureate program enrollment has increased substantially since 2010: entry-level baccalaureate enrollment increased from 147,935 in 2010 to 172,794 in 2014; accelerated baccalaureate enrollment increased from 13,605 to 16,935; and baccalaureate completion enrollment (so-called RN [registered nurse] to bachelor of science in nursing [BSN]) increased from 77,259 to 130,345.

The number of nursing programs, particularly 4-year college programs, grew significantly over the past decade. There is also an increasing preference for hiring BSNs; however, a majority of employers do not require a BSN. The increase in the quantity of baccalaureate programs is commendable; however, attention to the educational quality of these programs is essential to ensure that nurses—and patients—are reaping the assumed benefits of the additional education. The committee is concerned that the funding for nursing education has been relatively flat for the past decade, creating logistical problems for students (e.g., taking time away from work to pursue education) that are identified as barriers to obtaining a baccalaureate degree.

Transition-to-Practice Residency Programs

The Future of Nursing notes a high turnover rate among newly graduated nurses; some nurses leave their first job for a different care setting, but some leave the profession entirely. The report recommends that nurses be supported in their transition to practice through residency programs to help reduce attrition. *The Future of Nursing* focuses largely on residencies for postlicensure RNs but acknowledges that residencies would be useful for nurses transitioning to new care settings or entering practice as APRNs.

In 2011, the National Council of State Boards of Nursing (NCSBN) began to study transition-to-practice models for new nurse graduates in hospitals as well as in long-term care, home health, and other settings.

Transition-to-practice residencies appear to have some positive outcomes, including improved ability to organize, manage, and communicate, as well as higher retention. These residencies vary considerably, and comprehensive data are sparse. It is difficult to gauge growth in programs overall, within particular settings, and for nurses of different educational levels. Despite their positive benefits, cost and a lack of data on the value of these programs remain barriers to broader implementation. This committee believes that residencies for both RNs and APRNs are beneficial and need to be encouraged, and that attention to residency programs for outpatient care is insufficient.

Doctoral Education

The small number of doctorate-trained nurses, who are needed to teach, perform research, and serve as leaders in clinical practice and health policy, remains a substantial barrier. In 2010, fewer than 1 percent of nurses held a doctoral degree. *The Future of Nursing* recommends doubling this number by 2020, but is not specific about types of doctoral programs (doctor of nursing practice [DNP], PhD in nursing, PhD in another field). Because doctoral degrees typically take years to complete, the committee was unable to assess progress on this recommendation.

Since fall 2010, enrollment in DNP programs has more than doubled, from 7,034 to 18,352 students (a 161 percent increase). Meanwhile, enrollment in PhD programs has increased by 15 percent over the past 5 years, with 5,290 students now pursuing the research-focused doctorate. An assessment of the mix of doctorally prepared nurses is needed, and more emphasis on PhD program expansion, incentives for nurses to return to school, and more scholarships for baccalaureate-to-PhD programs is warranted.

Many schools need more faculty, especially nurses with doctorates, to increase enrollment at all levels. Barriers cited to meeting this challenge include insufficient faculty expansion and funding, faculty recruiting difficulty, and the limited number of doctorally prepared nurses.

Lifelong Learning

After nurses obtain their degrees, lifelong learning is necessary to provide quality care. Continuing education and competence have not kept pace with the needs of the increasingly complex, team-based health care system. Nurses and other providers will increasingly need to update skills for providing care in both hospital and community-based settings. One obstacle to progress on this recommendation of *The Future of Nursing* is a lack of data on continuing education for nurses, as well as on whether nurse certification and credentialing lead to better patient outcomes. Greater understanding of the impact of nurse certification and credentialing has implications not only for advancing lifelong learning but also for scope of practice and care delivery and for collaboration and leadership to improve the design of the health care system and care delivery.

Recommendation 2: Continue Pathways Toward Increasing the Percentage of Nurses with a Baccalaureate Degree. **The Campaign, the nursing education community, and state systems of higher education should continue efforts aimed at strengthening academic pathways for nurses toward the baccalaureate degree—both entry-level baccalaureate and baccalaureate completion programs.**

- **Efforts to expand and encourage partnerships between community colleges and 4-year universities, as well as other models for establishing these pathways, should continue to be promulgated. Employers play a critical role in promoting educational progression and should be encouraged to provide financial and logistical support for employees pursuing a baccalaureate degree.**
- **In addition, the quality of new programs should be monitored to ensure consistency in effective educational practices and to ensure the ability of nursing graduates to qualify to attend other accredited schools as they pursue advanced studies. This monitoring could be conducted through a national accrediting body such as the Commission on Collegiate Nursing Education or the American Commission for Education in Nursing.**

Recommendation 3: Create and Fund Transition-to-Practice Residency Programs. **The Campaign, in coordination with health care providers, health care delivery organizations, and payers, should lead efforts to explore ways of creating and funding transition-to-practice residency programs at both the registered nurse and advanced practice registered nurse levels. Such programs are needed in all practice settings, including community-based practices and long-term care. These efforts should include determining the most appropriate program models; setting standards for programs; exploring funding and business case models; and creating an overarching structure with which to track and evaluate the quality, effectiveness, and impact of transition-to-practice programs. With respect to funding models,**

- **government agencies, philanthropic organizations, and foundations should support these programs on a temporary basis to help better understand how the programs should be designed; and**
- **health care organizations should support these programs on a permanent basis as they can be beneficial in the evolving value-based payment system.**

Recommendation 4: Promote Nurses' Pursuit of Doctoral Degrees. **The Campaign should make efforts, through incentives and expansion of programs, to promote nurses' pursuit of both the doctor of nursing practice (DNP) and PhD degrees so as to have an adequate supply of** nurses for clinical care, research, faculty, and leadership positions. More emphasis should be placed on increasing the number of PhD nurses in particular. To maximize the potential value of their additional education, nurses should be encouraged to pursue these degrees early in their careers. DNP and PhD programs should offer coursework that prepares students to serve as faculty, including preparing them to teach in an evolving health care system that is less focused on acute care than has previously been the case.

Recommendation 5: Promote Nurses' Interprofessional and Lifelong Learning. The Campaign should encourage nursing organizations, education programs, and professional societies, as well as individual nurses, to make lifelong learning a priority so that nurses are prepared to work in evolving health care environments. Lifelong learning should include continuing education that will enable nurses to gain, preserve, and measure the skills needed in the variety of environments and settings in which health care will be provided going forward, particularly community-based, outpatient, long-term care, primary care, and ambulatory settings. Nurses should work with other health care professionals to create opportunities for interprofessional collaboration and education. The Campaign could serve as a convener to bring together stakeholders from multiple areas of health care to discuss opportunities and strategies for interdisciplinary collaboration in this area.

Need for Diversity in the Nursing Workforce

African Americans make up 13.6 percent of the general population aged 20 to 40, but 10.7 percent of the RN workforce, 10.3 percent of associate's degree graduates, and 9.3 percent of baccalaureate graduates. The disparity is even greater for Hispanics/Latinos, who make up 20.3 percent of the general population aged 20 to 40, but only 5.6 percent of the RN workforce, 8.8 percent of associate's degree graduates, and 7.0 percent of baccalaureate graduates. Men make up just 9.2 percent of the RN workforce, 11.7 percent of baccalaureate nursing students, and 11.6 percent of graduates.

While *The Future of Nursing* does not offer a specific recommendation on this topic, it does identify lack of diversity as a challenge for the nursing profession and indicates that a more diverse workforce will better meet current and future health care needs and provide more culturally relevant care. Associate's degree nursing programs and community colleges appear to provide entry into the nursing profession for underrepresented populations. Initiatives to retain diverse and underrepresented students in nursing education programs include financial support, mentorship, social and academic support, and professional counseling.

Only 5 years after the release of *The Future of Nursing,* it is too soon to see significant changes in the diversity of the national nursing workforce that may be attributable to the report's recommendations or the activities of the Campaign and others. Changing the diversity of the overall nurse workforce is a slow process because only a small percentage of the workforce leaves and enters each year.

To be successful, any effort to improve the diversity of the nursing workforce must focus on each step along the professional pathway from recruitment to educational programs, retention and success within those programs, graduation and placement in a job, and retention and advancement within a nursing career.

Recommendation 6: Make Diversity in the Nursing Workforce a Priority. **The Campaign should continue to emphasize recruitment and retention of a diverse nursing workforce as a major priority for both its national efforts and the state Action Coalitions. In broadening its coalition to include more diverse stakeholders (see Recommendation 1), the Campaign should work with others to assess progress and exchange information about strategies that are effective in increasing the diversity of the health workforce. To that end, the Campaign should take the following actions:**

- **Develop a comprehensive, specific diversity plan with actionable steps that can be taken by state Action Coalitions and by nursing and other health professions stakeholders, including trade organizations and educational institutions.**
- **To assist planning and policy making at the state level, use the Campaign's dashboard infrastructure to develop and publish annual data reports on the diversity of nursing and other health professions graduates and enrollees by state, and compare the representation of minorities in each state with their representation in the state's general population.**
- **Convene an advisory group to identify best practices from both within and outside of the Campaign that are improving the diversity of the nursing and other health professions workforce to reflect that of the general population. Areas for research and assessment might include barriers that prevent individuals from diverse backgrounds from entering the nursing profession and from achieving higher levels of education, modes of academic progression to promote diversity in nursing programs at all levels, and the use of holistic admissions policies and need-based aid to support students from underrepresented and economically challenged backgrounds in obtaining nursing degrees. Results of these studies could be disseminated to key relevant stakeholders, including schools of nursing and employers.**
- **Assist state Action Coalitions in obtaining funds available for the development of new, innovative, targeted programs and strategies aimed at increasing the diversity of nursing students and the nurs-**

ing workforce and/or for the identification and tailoring of those programs that have been shown to be effective.

- Collect data to ensure that the call for higher educational attainment among nurses has positive implications for diversity (including economic, racial/ethnic, geographic, and gender diversity). The Campaign should research the opportunities for and barriers to utilization of baccalaureate completion programs by underrepresented minorities and economically and educationally disadvantaged individuals so that the Campaign and other stakeholders can more effectively implement programs to advance the educational attainment of African Americans, Hispanics/Latinos, and other underrepresented groups in nursing.
- Encourage state Action Coalitions to work with their state nursing workforce centers and state boards of nursing to collect and make available data on variables that can be used to assess progress toward increasing the diversity of the nurse workforce, the nursing student population, and nursing faculty.

Collaboration, Leadership, and Communication

The Future of Nursing includes recommendations for nurses to lead and disseminate collaborative improvement efforts and to lead change to advance health. Nurses are needed to lead and participate in the ongoing reforms to the system, to direct research on evidence-based improvements to care, to translate research findings to the practice environment, to be full partners on the health care team, and to advocate for policy change.

Collaboration

Expansion in the area of collaboration has been supported by the Campaign and state Action Coalitions, and by organizations such as the Josiah Macy Jr. Foundation and the Interprofessional Education Collaborative (IPEC). Going forward, the scope of *The Future of Nursing* recommendation to expand opportunities for nurses to lead and diffuse collaborative improvement efforts will need to be broadened to acknowledge that no profession can lead and expand interprofessional collaboration alone. Collaboration requires all members of a team working to their full potential on behalf of the patient and with respect for the contributions of other professions to the work. The Campaign acknowledged that this shift was needed in 2013 when it asked its state Action Coalitions to look beyond nursing as they worked to improve health and health care for individuals and families.

Leadership

According to *The Future of Nursing,* nurses are needed in leadership positions to contribute their unique perspective and expertise on such issues as health care delivery, quality, and safety. A 2011 survey of 1,000 hospitals found that nurses account for only 6 percent of board membership, compared with 20 percent for physicians; in 2014, the percentage of physician board members remained the same, while the percentage of board members that are nurses decreased to 5 percent.

Opportunities in leadership have been established and expanded by nursing education programs, nursing associations, and private organizations. While some progress has been observed in nurses appointed to health-related boards, there is a lack of data on nurses serving as leaders in other areas, and the data that are available are fragmented and incomplete. There is no single source of information about nurse training in leadership, entrepreneurship, or innovation.

Campaign Communication

Effective communication with groups within and outside of the nursing profession is critical to collaboration and leadership efforts. The Campaign has engaged targeted audiences through strategic communication initiatives that have leveraged both traditional media and new media platforms. The Speakers Bureau has sent Campaign representatives and leaders to various conferences across the country to raise awareness of and inform key audiences about the recommendations of *The Future of Nursing* and to gather relevant data and information to advance Campaign goals. Online communication tools provide Campaign volunteers with comprehensive materials with which to engage media, policy makers, and interested stakeholders.

The Campaign acknowledges that the capacity and ability of state Action Coalitions to communicate about their efforts vary greatly. Further, while the goal is to engage a wide range of stakeholders, the Campaign acknowledges that its efforts have been focused largely on engaging nurses. Strong relationships are needed with health policy and business reporters; editors and columnists at national, state, and local news outlets; and bloggers who cover related issues.

Recommendation 7: Expand Efforts and Opportunities for Interprofessional Collaboration and Leadership Development for Nurses. As the Campaign broadens its coalition (see Recommendation 1), it should expand its focus on supporting and promoting (1) interprofessional collaboration and opportunities for nurses to design, implement, and diffuse collaborative programs in care and delivery; and (2) interdisciplinary development programs that focus on leadership. Health care professionals from all disciplines should work together in the planning

and implementation of strategies for improving health care, particularly in an interprofessional and collaborative environment. Interdisciplinary development programs and activities should:

- Feature content in leadership, management, entrepreneurship, innovation, and other skills that will enable nurses to help ensure that the public receives accessible and quality health care. Courses could be offered through or in partnership with other professional schools. The Campaign should monitor nursing programs that offer these types of courses and programs and track nurses' participation, if possible, in order to assess progress.

- Include interprofessional and collaborative development or continuing competence in leadership skills—for example, through the participation of nurses in spokesperson and communication programs designed to teach persuasive communication skills that will facilitate their leading and managing collaborative efforts.

Recommendation 8: Promote the Involvement of Nurses in the Redesign of Care Delivery and Payment Systems. The Campaign should work with payers, health care organizations, providers, employers, and regulators to involve nurses in the redesign of care delivery and payment systems. To this end, the Campaign should encourage nurses to serve in executive and leadership positions in government, for-profit and nonprofit organizations, health care delivery systems (e.g., as hospital chief executive officers or chief operations officers), and advisory committees. The Campaign should expand its metrics to measure the progress of nurses in these areas. Types of organizations targeted by this recommendation could include

- health care systems;
- insurance companies and for-profit health care delivery systems (e.g., Minute Clinic);
- not-for-profit organizations that work to improve health care (e.g., the National Quality Forum);
- the National Academy of Medicine and other professional membership groups; and
- federal, state, and local governmental bodies related to health (e.g., the Veterans Health Administration, U.S. Department of Defense, Centers for Medicare & Medicaid Services).

Recommendation 9: Communicate with a Wider and More Diverse Audience to Gain Broad Support for Campaign Objectives. The Campaign should expand the scope of its communication strategies to connect with a broader, more diverse, consumer-oriented audience and galvanize support at the grassroots level. The Campaign, including its state Action

Coalitions, should bolster communication efforts geared toward the general public and consumers using messages that go beyond nursing and focus on improving health and health care for consumers and their families. The Campaign should recruit more allies in the health care community (such as physicians, pharmacists, and other professionals, as well as those outside of health care, such as business leaders, employers, and policy makers) as health care stakeholders to further demonstrate a collaborative approach in advancing the recommendations of *The Future of Nursing*.

Need for Better Data for Assessing and Driving Progress

Major gaps exist in understanding the numbers and types of health professionals, where they are employed, and what roles they fill. This knowledge is critical to support new models of health care delivery. *The Future of Nursing* report recommends that an infrastructure be built and led by the National Health Care Workforce Commission to improve the collection and analysis of data on the health care workforce. Because the National Health Care Workforce Commission has not been funded by Congress, this recommendation cannot be implemented as it was written. Nonetheless, progress has been made over the past 5 years in the collection and analysis of workforce data for both the nursing workforce and other health professions.

Barriers to the collection of data on the nursing workforce include the lack of national indicators providing consistent information from states, lag time in the collection and reporting of data, the lack of standardized databases with which to track ideal indicators of progress, and the need to use proxy measures to assess progress toward this recommendation of *The Future of Nursing* (given the short time frame for seeing progress in the outcomes of the report's recommendations). Little progress has been made on building a national infrastructure that could integrate the diverse sources of the necessary data, identify gaps, and improve and expand usable data not just on the nursing workforce but on the entire health care workforce.

Recommendation 10: Improve Workforce Data Collection. **The Campaign should promote collaboration among organizations that collect workforce-related data. Given the absence of the National Health Care Workforce Commission, the Campaign can use its strong brand and partnerships to help improve the collection of data on the nursing workforce.**
- **The Campaign should play a role in convening, supporting, and promoting collaboration among organizations and associations to consider how they might create more robust datasets and how various datasets can be organized and made available to researchers,**

policy makers, and planners. Specifically, the Campaign should encourage

- organizations and agencies to build national databases that could be shared and accessed by the Health Resources and Services Administration (HRSA) and researchers;
- states to implement the Minimum Data Set (MDS) and to share their data with the National Council of State Boards of Nursing (NCSBN) so they can build a national dataset on practicing nurses; and
- nursing organizations that currently engage in independent data collection efforts (such as American Association of Colleges of Nursing, the National League for Nursing, NCSBN, and the American Association of Nurse Practitioners) to collaborate and share their data to build more comprehensive datasets. Other organizations representing providers that employ nurses and other health professionals, such as the American Heart Association, should be invited to participate in this collaboration.

- The federal government and states should expand existing data collection activities to better measure and monitor the roles of registered nurses and advanced practice registered nurses. This expansion should include the collection of data on current and former licensees in the American Community Survey and a sampling of services provided by nurse practitioners and physician assistants for their own patient panels and outside of physician offices in the National Ambulatory Medical Care Survey.
- HRSA should undertake a combined National Sample Survey of Registered Nurses and National Sample Survey of Nurse Practitioners that can be administered more frequently than once every 4 years. This effort should include the involvement of national and state nursing organizations. HRSA should continue to promote the use of the MDS and assist in and support its implementation.

CONCLUSION

The Future of Nursing includes a number of recommendations aimed at ensuring that nurses, who represent the largest segment of the health care profession, are prepared to help fill the need for quality health care in a delivery system that is shifting rapidly and fundamentally. The release of the report in 2010 and the launch of the Campaign were timely, coinciding with the ACA's creation of new models of care to accommodate the large numbers of people previously without access to health insurance. These models focus on teamwork, care coordination, and prevention—models in which nurses can contribute a great deal of knowledge and skill.

The committee found that continued progress will require greater focus and effort in certain specific areas. Continued work is needed to remove scope-of-practice barriers; pathways to higher education need to be strengthened, with specific emphasis on increasing diversity; avenues for continuing competence need to be strengthened; and data on a wide range of outcomes are needed—from the education and makeup of the workforce to the services nurses provide and ways in which they lead. A major and overarching need is for the nursing community, including the Campaign, to build and strengthen coalitions with stakeholders outside of nursing. Nurses need to practice collaboratively; continue to develop skills and competencies in leadership and innovation; and work with other professionals, as no one profession alone can meet the complex needs of the future of health care. The committee hopes that its recommendations will be helpful to the Campaign and other organizations as they work to improve access to quality health care for all.

1

Introduction

In the past decade, the changing climate of health care policy and practice has sharpened national focus on the challenges of providing high-quality and affordable care to an aging and increasingly diverse population. In this era, population health needs assessment and management require the collaboration of health professionals to provide patient-centered, coordinated, and community-based primary and specialty care services. Nurses, who make up the largest segment of the health care professional workforce, are in a position to lead and partner in teams that provide services across the continuum and settings of care (hospitals, ambulatory care, public health, schools, long-term care, home care, and community health).

In 2010, the Institute of Medicine (IOM) released *The Future of Nursing: Leading Change, Advancing Health*, which offers a series of recommendations pertaining to roles for nurses in the new health care landscape (IOM, 2011). Shortly after the report's prepublication release in 2010, AARP and the Robert Wood Johnson Foundation (RWJF) launched the Future of Nursing: Campaign for Action (the Campaign) to help implement the report's recommendations. The present report provides an assessment of progress made by the Campaign and other initiatives and identifies areas that need to be emphasized as work continues to pursue recommendations from *The Future of Nursing*.

CONTEXT

The Future of Nursing was produced at a propitious moment in health care in the United States, a time of growing awareness that dramatic changes in the care delivery system were needed to accomplish the "Triple Aim" of better patient experience, better health of the public, and lower costs. The increasing burden of chronic disease, changing demographics, and demands for greater access to care lent added urgency to the calls for change. *The Future of Nursing* in many ways anticipated these trends in its recommendations. Now, 5 years later, one can appreciate how prescient and appropriately timed these recommendations were. But many changes have occurred since that report was released, and these changes have created both new opportunities and new challenges in achieving the goals laid out in the report.

As described in *The Future of Nursing*, it was anticipated that with the passage of the Patient Protection and Affordable Care Act (ACA), nurses would play a larger role in delivering health care, facilitating efforts that would increasingly emphasize health promotion and disease prevention, and helping to bridge the gap between coverage and access (IOM, 2011). As the report notes, "by virtue of their regular, close proximity to patients, and their scientific understanding of care processes across the continuum of care, nurses have a considerable opportunity to act as full partners with other health professionals and to lead in the improvement and redesign of the health care system and its practice environment" (IOM, 2011, p. 23). It is precisely because nurses practice in various health care settings and across the continuum of care and enter the profession through different pathways and achieve varying levels of education that they are poised to affect health and health care delivery at every level.

As a result of the ACA, more than 16 million previously uninsured people have gained health insurance coverage (HHS, 2015). To fulfill the promise of access to care for these newly insured people, as well as more affordable, better-coordinated care for all, incentives have been created for new delivery and payment models. The new delivery models emphasize teamwork, care coordination for specialty care and chronic disease management, prevention, and a greater focus on population health and community-based care. The new payment models are moving from fee-for-service and episodic payment to more comprehensive payment based on value.

At the same time, there has been growing awareness of the need for more attention to a health professions workforce that must be appropriately prepared to work in this changing health care system. This awareness has led to greater emphasis on interprofessional education, teamwork training, and a better understanding of the roles of all health professionals in creating an optimal health care delivery system. Rapid advances in information technology, including mobile and digital health tools, also are changing the way health professionals and the public receive information and communicate with one another. Properly harnessed, these advances can enable greater engagement of patients in their own care, as well as support better teamwork and care coordination.

Thus, the context of health care in the United States in 2015 is dramatically different from what it was when *The Future of Nursing* was released in 2010. While the report anticipated many of these changes, it could not have foreseen exactly how they would play out. The terms of the ACA dictated many of these changes, but they also set a tone and direction for the health care system regarding how care should be delivered.

All of these changes are consistent with the key messages in *The Future of Nursing*, which call for enhanced education and greater roles for nurses in the health care system (IOM, 2011). While *The Future of Nursing* focuses on advanced practice registered nurses (APRNs) and registered nurses (RNs) with higher educational attainment, implications for nurses' roles are significant. The shift from individual providers to interprofessional teams, for example, has implications for the role of nurses in teams and the education and competencies needed to provide care and function within those teams. Similarly, the shift to delivering care in the community, including retail clinics and patient homes, has important implications for how and where nurses receive clinical training. The changing landscape may enable additional strategies for achieving these goals, including value-based care, interprofessional collaboration and education, patient engagement, and new technologies.

The Future of Nursing coincided with dramatic changes in the health care landscape, and many other organizations released reports shortly before or after that report calling for similar changes in nursing and health care. Examples include

- the World Health Organization's (2009) *Global Standards for the Initial Education of Professional Nurses and Midwives,* developed from 2005 to 2007 and published in 2009, which calls for raising the initial education requirements for professional nurses;
- the Carnegie Foundation report *Educating Nurses: A Call for Radical Transformation,* published in December 2009 (Benner et al., 2009);
- the consensus statement of the Tri-Council for Nursing (comprising the American Association of Colleges of Nursing [AACN], American Nurses Association [ANA], American Organization of Nurse Executives, and National League for Nursing) titled *Educational Advancement of Registered Nurses,* published in May 2010, which calls for all RNs to pursue further education in order to improve the quality and safety of care across all settings (AACN, 2010);
- Josiah Macy Jr. Foundation efforts around care delivery and interprofessional education (AACN and AAMC, 2010; Josiah Macy Jr. Foundation, 2010, 2012, 2013); and
- various position statements and issue briefs from professional and trade organizations related to advancing the educational preparation of nurses, interprofessional education, interprofessional collaboration and team-based care, and health workforce diversity (AACN, 2015; AONE, 2015b; NLN, 2015).

Building on the changing health care landscape and the release of *The Future of Nursing* and these other reports, many organizations have been working diligently to make changes in nursing and health care. Nursing organizations have long been active in addressing the issues identified by the report, which lent momentum to a movement that was already under way and gave stakeholders tangible and specific recommendations toward which to work. After the report was released, these organizations continued or advanced their efforts to implement the recommended changes. Their efforts ranged from simple statements of support for the IOM report's recommendations to the establishment of new and far-reaching initiatives, such as the Campaign.

For example, the ANA released a statement citing areas in which that organization and its members were actively pursuing change, such as the efforts of state nursing associations to make state-level changes to scope-of-practice laws (ANA, 2011). The AACN held a strategic planning session to identify areas in which its activities could align with the IOM report's recommendations and it developed a new tactical plan for moving forward (AACN, n.d.). The National Council of State Boards of Nursing (NCSBN) undertook several new efforts, including the Campaign for Consensus, designed to assist states in adopting the Consensus Model regulations regarding scope of practice for APRNs, and a pilot study on lifelong learning and continued competency (Alexander, 2011). And the Jonas Center for Nursing and Veterans Healthcare, which had been supporting doctoral education for nurses through its Jonas Scholars program since 2008, began requiring students to complete a leadership project that incorporates the IOM report's recommendations (Curley, 2015; see also Jonas Center for Nursing and Veterans Healthcare, 2015). In addition to such individual efforts, many organizations signed on to the Campaign's Champion Nursing Council, which gives the Campaign strategic guidance on fulfilling its goal of implementing the IOM report's recommendations to improve health care and to prepare nurses to be essential partners in addressing the nation's health care system challenges (CCNA, n.d.-c). *The Future of Nursing* and the Campaign helped accelerate these and other efforts to ensure that nurses are able to provide and lead efforts in health care delivery and system redesign.

STUDY SCOPE

In 2014, RWJF asked the IOM to convene a committee to assess progress made toward implementing the recommendations of *The Future of Nursing,* assess the progress of the Campaign toward meeting its goals, and issue a brief report including recommendations for the Campaign (see Box 1-1 for the committee's statement of task). To conduct this study the IOM assembled a committee of 12 experts from the fields of nursing, communications, public health, research and evaluation, and medicine. The committee held four meetings over the course of 5 months that included three public workshops, during which stakeholders

BOX 1-1
Statement of Task

An ad hoc committee under the auspices of the Institute of Medicine (IOM) will assess the changes in the field of nursing and peripheral areas over the last 5 years as a result of the IOM report on *The Future of Nursing: Leading Change, Advancing Health.* The role of the AARP and Robert Wood Johnson Foundation's (RWJF's) Future of Nursing: Campaign for Action (the Campaign) will be taken into consideration in assessing these field changes. The report will assess the Campaign's progress in meeting its stated goals, and identify the areas that should be emphasized over the next 5 years that will help the Campaign fulfill the recommendations of the IOM report.

This report will be based, in part, on a series of three workshops. Each workshop, organized by the committee and held in conjunction with each of three committee meetings, will invite speakers to help assess the field's progress of the adoption of *The Future of Nursing* report, in addition to the work of the Campaign. Specifically, the workshops will invite stakeholders representing nursing, medicine, health systems, consumer groups, business, and policy makers at the state and national levels to provide testimony to the committee on the following broad topics: practice, education, and leadership; with diversity, interprofessional collaboration, and needed data as cross-cutting issues. In addition to the three workshops the committee will, during its closed meetings, consider data collected and provided by RWJF and other inputs and literature gathered by the committee.

In its review of data and input from workshops, the committee will consider the following:

- Utilization and impact of the IOM's *The Future of Nursing: Leading Change, Advancing Health* report.
- The Campaign's areas of focus (education, leadership, scope of practice, interprofessional collaboration, diversity, and workforce data).
- Impact that the Campaign has had on areas peripheral to nursing (such as activities undertaken by individuals and organizations to adopt the recommendations outside the sphere of Campaign activities and that impact).
- The role of traditional and new media in the impact of the Campaign.
- Future near-term (5 years) goals for the Campaign.

The committee will author a brief report that will include conclusions and recommendations on what actions need to take place to ensure sustainable impact of the Campaign in its work to implement the recommendations of the IOM *The Future of Nursing* report and other activities, with an emphasis on future steps and areas of focus.

provided testimony on the nursing field's progress in the areas of practice, education, leadership, diversity, interprofessional collaboration, and data needs. The committee also considered data collected and provided by RWJF, as well as from other sources (see Appendix A for further information about the study methods).

The committee's task was not to reexamine the merits of or amend the recommendations of *The Future of Nursing.* The committee did not perform a comprehensive or formal evaluation of the impact of the report's recommendations or of the Campaign's impact on health outcomes or access to care—two of the broader goals of the report's recommendations—as 5 years is an insufficient amount of time over which to evaluate these outcomes. In addition, the committee did not perform a comprehensive assessment of the state of the nursing profession. Instead, the committee focused on how the field of nursing has been impacted by the Campaign and other such efforts. The committee reviewed how the current context of health care delivery and nursing education and practice may affect how the IOM report's recommendations are being implemented, and it identified barriers to and unintended consequences of their implementation. In the present report, the committee notes when it conducted original analyses. When data were provided by the Campaign, the committee attempted to cross-reference those data with outside sources.

Further, while the committee did assess progress in implementing the recommendations of *The Future of Nursing,* it was not able to attribute progress or the lack thereof directly to the report or the Campaign, given efforts by other organizations and trends in the field. Progress in the areas of education, practice, collaboration, leadership, diversity, and workforce data may be attributable to those other efforts (described below) and contemporary factors. Regardless, the committee considered how the recommendations of *The Future of Nursing* have been advanced and how they might continue to be advanced.

The next section of this chapter provides an overview of *The Future of Nursing* and its findings and recommendations. This is followed by a description of the Campaign's efforts to implement the recommendations over the past 5 years, as well as salient RWJF activities outside of the Campaign. Finally, this chapter lays out the content of remaining chapters of the report.

OVERVIEW OF *THE FUTURE OF NURSING: LEADING CHANGE, ADVANCING HEALTH*

The Future of Nursing[1] was the product of a 2-year Initiative on the Future of Nursing, established by RWJF and the IOM (IOM, 2011). The 18-person committee convened by the Initiative was led by Donna Shalala, former U.S. Secretary of Health and Human Services, and included experts in such arenas as nursing, business, education, research, and public health. The committee was asked to "ex-

---

[1] The full report is available at http://www.nap.edu/catalog/12956.

amine the capacity of the nursing workforce to meet the demands of a reformed health care and public health system" and to develop a set of recommendations for changes at the national, state, and local levels (IOM, 2011, p. xiii). Specifically, the committee was asked to identify vital roles for nurses in the design and implementation of a more effective and efficient health care system and to make recommendations on how to

- reconceptualize the role of nurses within the context of the entire health care system;
- expand the capacity of nursing education to produce an adequate number of well-prepared nurses to meet current and future demand;
- develop innovative solutions related to professional education and health care delivery by focusing on the delivery of nursing services; and
- attract and retain well-prepared nurses in multiple care settings.

The Future of Nursing identifies a variety of barriers that have limited the nursing profession's ability to contribute fully to the health care system. These barriers include an aging workforce, regulatory restrictions on nursing practice, fragmentation of health care, limited capacity of the nursing education system, and a lack of workforce data. The report is centered on four key messages.

Key Message #1: Nurses should practice to the full extent of their education and training. The study committee found that historical, regulatory, and policy barriers have prevented nurses from being able to perform the full range of activities for which their education and training have prepared them. For example, regulations on nurse practitioners (NPs) vary by state, and many states limit or deny an NP's ability to prescribe medications, assess patient conditions, order and evaluate tests, or admit a patient to the hospital. The committee formulated recommendations for Congress, state legislatures, and various federal agencies on actions that could help remove these scope-of-practice barriers. In addition, the committee found that newly graduated nurses could benefit from additional assistance in the transition to practice, and it recommended the development of residency programs to help nursing graduates further hone their skills.

Key Message #2: Nurses should achieve higher levels of education and training through an improved education system that promotes seamless academic progression. The committee observed that major changes in the health care system will require equally major changes in the education of nurses to prepare them to work with sophisticated technology, analyze and synthesize complex information to make critical decisions, and collaborate with a variety of other health professionals. To meet these advanced needs, the committee recommended that more nurses obtain higher degrees so that by 2020, 80 percent of nurses would have a baccalaureate degree and the number of nurses with a doctorate would double. The committee also recommended that nurses engage in lifelong learning throughout their careers, and that efforts be made to increase the diversity of the nursing workforce.

Key Message #3: Nurses should be full partners, with physicians and other health professionals, in redesigning health care in the United States. The committee found that for nurses to participate fully in the transformation of the health care system, they need to act in positions of leadership and work collaboratively with leaders from other health professions. The committee noted that these nurse leaders need to be full partners at all levels of the system—from bedside to boardroom—and to contribute actively to policy making by serving on committees, commissions, and boards. To develop this leadership capacity, the committee recommended that health care organizations, funders, and education programs provide, expand, and fund opportunities for nurses to develop leadership skills and assume leadership positions, and that health care decision makers ensure that nurses are represented in key leadership positions on boards and management teams.

Key Message #4: Effective workforce planning and policy making require better data collection and an improved information infrastructure. The committee determined that to plan and prepare for fundamental changes in the health care system, it is necessary to have reliable and granular data on the health care workforce. The needed data include the numbers and types of health professionals working in the field, where and in what roles they work, and what types of activities they perform. These data are necessary to plan for workforce needs and to establish a baseline upon which to improve. The committee recommended that the National Health Care Workforce Commission (mandated by the ACA) work with the Health Resources and Services Administration to improve research and the collection and analysis of data in this area.

From the foundation of these key messages, the committee developed eight recommendations for addressing the barriers that have prevented the nursing profession from realizing its full potential in leading the transformation of the health care system (see Box 1-2). *The Future of Nursing* acknowledges the growing diversity of the U.S. population and the concomitant need for an increasingly diverse nursing workforce, incorporating this critical and crosscutting issue into its recommendations relating to nurses' educational attainment (recommendations 4, 5, and 6). The study committee directed its recommendations not only at the nursing profession but also at other entities that play a role in improving the system, including government, businesses, health care organizations, professional associations, and the insurance industry.

THE FUTURE OF NURSING: CAMPAIGN FOR ACTION

Goals

The Campaign was launched in 2010, shortly after the release of *The Future of Nursing* (CCNA, n.d.-a). The Campaign is coordinated through the Center to Champion Nursing in America (CCNA), an initiative of AARP, the AARP Foundation, and RWJF. Its stated purpose is to implement the recommendations of the IOM report through actions at the national and state levels. Based on the report's recommendations, the Campaign focuses on six major areas, or "pillars" (CCNA, n.d.-b):

- advancing education transformation,
- leveraging nursing leadership,
- removing barriers to practice and care,
- fostering interprofessional collaboration,
- promoting diversity, and
- bolstering workforce data.

The Campaign aims to achieve its goals through a wide variety of activities, working with stakeholders, including consumers, nurses, insurers, educators, and policy makers. To support these efforts, 51 state Action Coalitions (one in each state and the District of Columbia) build grassroots networks of local stakeholders to effect change at the state and local levels (CCNA, n.d.-f). In its first 2 years, the Campaign focused its efforts on building an infrastructure (the state Action Coalitions) to convene and mobilize constituents and stakeholders around the messages and recommendations of the IOM report. In its third year, the Campaign "shifted to strategic activation and partnership development," asking the Action Coalitions to work on five "campaign imperatives" (TCC Group, 2014, p. 1):

- move beyond nursing and focus on improving health and health care for consumers and their families;
- deliver short-term results while continuing to develop long-term plans;
- have the courage to place the right leaders at the helm or remove weak, ineffective leaders;
- have funding to sustain the [Action Coalitions'] work; and
- not ignore the diverse stakeholders critical to the [Action Coalitions'] success.

BOX 1-2
Recommendations from
The Future of Nursing: Leading Change, Advancing Health*

Recommendation 1: Remove scope-of-practice barriers. Advanced practice registered nurses should be able to practice to the full extent of their education and training.

Recommendation 2: Expand opportunities for nurses to lead and diffuse collaborative improvement efforts. Private and public funders, health care organizations, nursing education programs, and nursing associations should expand opportunities for nurses to lead and manage collaborative efforts with physicians and other members of the health care team to conduct research and to redesign and improve practice environments and health systems. These entities should also provide opportunities for nurses to diffuse successful practices.

Recommendation 3: Implement nurse residency programs. State boards of nursing, accrediting bodies, the federal government, and health care organizations should take actions to support nurses' completion of a transition-to-practice program (nurse residency) after they have completed a prelicensure or advanced practice degree program or when they are transitioning into new clinical practice areas.

Recommendation 4: Increase the proportion of nurses with a baccalaureate degree to 80 percent by 2020. Academic nurse leaders across all schools of nursing should work together to increase the proportion of nurses with a baccalaureate degree from 50 to 80 percent by 2020. These leaders should partner with education accrediting bodies, private and public funders, and employers to ensure funding, monitor progress, and increase the diversity of students to create a workforce prepared to meeting the demands of diverse populations across the lifespan.

Activities

The Campaign operates at both the national and state levels. The national Campaign convenes leadership and advisory groups—including a Strategic Advisory Committee, Diversity Steering Committee, Champion Nursing Coalition, and Champion Nursing Council—to advance the goals of the IOM report and the Campaign (CCNA, n.d.-e). In addition, the Campaign convenes meetings around the major topics of the IOM report (including leadership, education, and scope of practice) and provides technical assistance to the state Action Coalitions, which, as noted, work to advance the recommendations of *The Future of Nursing* at the state and local levels (CCNA, 2015c).

Recommendation 5: Double the number of nurses with a doctorate by 2020. Schools of nursing, with support from private and public funders, academic administrators and university trustees, and accrediting bodies, should double the number of nurses with a doctorate by 2020 to add to the cadre of nurse faculty and researchers, with attention to increasing diversity.

Recommendation 6: Ensure that nurses engage in lifelong learning. Accrediting bodies, schools of nursing, health care organizations, and continuing competency educators from multiple health professions should collaborate to ensure that nurses and nursing students and faculty continue their education and engage in lifelong learning to gain the competencies needed to provide care for diverse populations across the lifespan.

Recommendation 7: Prepare and enable nurses to lead change to advance health. Nurses, nursing education programs, and nursing associations should prepare the nursing workforce to assume leadership positions across all levels, while public, private, and governmental health care decision makers should ensure that leadership position are available to and filled by nurses.

Recommendation 8: Build an infrastructure for the collection and analysis of interprofessional health care workforce data. The National Health Care Workforce Commission, with oversight from the Government Accountability Office and the Health Resources and Services Administration, should lead a collaborative effort to improve research and the collection and analysis of data on health care workforce requirements. The Workforce Commission and the Health Resources and Services Administration should collaborate with state licensing boards, state nursing workforce centers, and the Department of Labor in this effort to ensure that the data are timely and publicly accessible.

---

* Recommendations listed in this box are abbreviated. See Appendix B for the full version of each recommendation.
SOURCE: IOM, 2011.

The state Action Coalitions are considered "the driving force of the Campaign" because they are able to work as a network to effect change at the local level (CCNA, n.d.-f). The first state Action Coalitions—in California, Michigan, Mississippi, New Jersey, and New York—were formed in November 2010; within 1 year after the launch of the Campaign, 36 Action Coalitions were operating around the country; and by January 2013, all 51 Action Coalitions were active (CCNA, n.d.-g). The Campaign provides funding to some state Action Coalitions, mainly through the State Implementation Program (SIP), but it also encourages (and in the case of SIP grantees, requires) that the Action Coalitions find external funding (CCNA, 2011, 2012, 2014, 2015a). As of January 2015, only 9 Action Coalitions had not received external funding. The remainder were receiving vari-

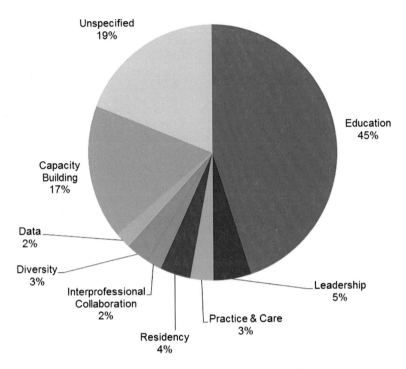

FIGURE 1-1 State Action Coalition funds by the Campaign pillar and/or imperative.
SOURCE: CCNA, 2015c.

ous amounts of funding (from a few thousand dollars to more than $1 million) from various sources, including foundations, government, colleges and universities, health and hospital systems, nursing organizations, and businesses (CCNA, 2015a). Figure 1-1 shows the allocation of total state Action Coalition funds to efforts relating to the recommendations of *The Future of Nursing*, the Campaign pillars, and Campaign imperatives.

Thirty-one state Action Coalitions currently receive funding from Campaign SIP grants (CCNA, 2015c). These Action Coalitions receive up to $150,000 from RWJF, but they also are required to secure $75,000 in matching funds from other sources (CCNA, 2011, 2012, 2014). All state Action Coalitions work to advance the recommendations of the IOM report, but SIP grantees are required to identify one or two recommendations from the report that they will work toward implementing at the state level using this funding.

A 2013 survey of all state Action Coalitions by the Campaign's external evaluator, TCC Group (see Evaluation section), asked respondents to indicate whether specific topics relating to the IOM report's recommendations were (1) a main focus for their efforts, (2) not a main focus but an issue on which they were working, or (3) not an issue on which they were working (TCC Group, 2013a). Figure 1-2 shows the attention paid to these priority areas of the IOM report and

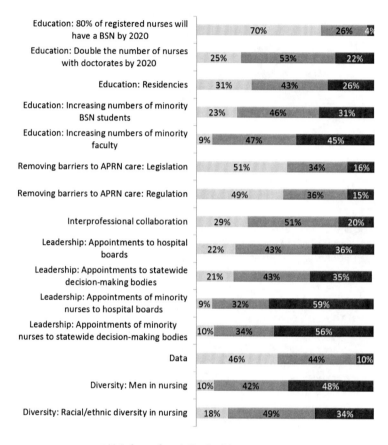

FIGURE 1-2 State Action Coalition members' focus on priority areas of *The Future of Nursing* and the Campaign.
NOTES: Data are based on responses of 1,100 survey respondents from 49 state Action Coalitions, including that of the District of Columbia. Scores were calculated for each state by aggregating and averaging all responses from that state. APRN = advanced practice registered nurse; BSN = bachelor of science in nursing.
SOURCE: Personal communication, K. Locke, TCC Group, September 3, 2015.

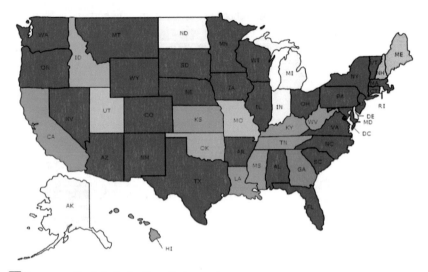

Diversity: Racial/ethnic diversity in nursing
Data
Removing barriers to APRN care: Regulation
Removing barriers to APRN care: Legislation
(Dual) Education: Residencies and Removing Barriers to APRN Care: Legislation
Education: 80% of registered nurses will have a BSN by 2020
Education: Double the number of nurses with doctorates by 2020

FIGURE 1-3 Priority focus area for each state Action Coalition.
NOTES: Survey respondents categorized the amount of focus given to each priority area.
State scores were aggregated, and the highest score was identified as the top priority. The
number of responses from Alaska, Delaware, Indiana, Michigan, and North Dakota was
insufficient for calculation of scores. APRN = advanced practice registered nurse; BSN =
bachelor of science in nursing.
SOURCE: TCC Group, 2013a.

the Campaign. Figure 1-3 shows the top priority area for each state, based on
aggregated scores for respondents from each state.

Measuring Progress

To track its progress toward implementation of the IOM report's recommendations, the Campaign developed dashboard indicators—specific, measurable
data points that approximate success for that recommendation (CCNA, 2015d)
(see Table 1-1). The Campaign also utilizes supplemental indicators for some
recommendations. In addition to the indicators and supplemental indicators for

TABLE 1-1 Recommendations from *The Future of Nursing* and Campaign Indicators

Recommendation	Indicator
#1: Remove scope-of-practice barriers.	State progress in removing regulatory barriers to care by nurse practitioners *Supplemental indicators:* • States that allow full practice authority for nurse-midwives by year • States that allow full practice authority for nurse practitioners by year • Number of hospitals in the United States with Magnet status • Number of nurse-led clinics in the United States • Number of nurse-led clinics located in medically underserved areas (MUAs)
#2: Expand opportunities for nurses to lead and diffuse collaborative improvement efforts.	Number of required clinical courses and/or activities at top nursing schools that include both RN students and other graduate health professional students *Supplemental indicator:* • Number of articles published in top 10 health services research journals co-authored by an RN and authors from other disciplines
#3: Implement nurse residency programs.	*None*
#4: Increase the proportion of nurses with a baccalaureate degree to 80 percent by 2020.	Percentage of employed nurses with a baccalaureate degree in nursing or higher degree *Supplemental indicators:* • New RN graduates by degree type, by race/ethnicity • New RN graduates by degree type, by gender • Number and percent of U.S.-educated, first-time NCLEX-takers with a BSN • Percent of hospitals that have new RN graduate residencies • Percentage of hospital employers that offer RNs tuition reimbursement • Number of RN-to-BSN graduates annually
#5: Double the number of nurses with a doctorate by 2020.	Total enrollment in nursing doctorate programs *Supplemental indicators:* • Number of employed nurses with a doctoral degree • Number of people receiving nursing doctoral degrees annually • Diversity of nursing doctorate graduates by race/ethnicity • Diversity of nursing doctorate graduates by gender
#6: Ensure that nurses engage in lifelong learning.	*None*
#7: Prepare and enable nurses to lead change to advance health.	Percent of hospital boards with RN members

continued

TABLE 1-1 Continued

Recommendation	Indicator
#8: Build an infrastructure for the collection and analysis of interprofessional health care workforce data.	Number of recommended nursing workforce data items collected by the states *Supplemental indicators:* • State boards of nursing that participate in the NCSBN Nursys Data System • States that collect race/ethnicity data about their nursing workforce

NOTE: BSN = bachelor of science in nursing; NCLEX = National Council Licensure Examination; NCSBN = National Council of State Boards of Nursing; RN = registered nurse.
SOURCE: CCNA, 2015d.

six of the eight recommendations from *The Future of Nursing,* the Campaign identified a supplemental indicator for progress on increasing the diversity of the nursing workforce: racial/ethnic composition of the RN workforce in the United States (CCNA, 2015d).

The Campaign recognized data limitations that hampered measuring progress toward implementation of the IOM report's recommendations (CCNA, n.d.-d; Spetz et al., 2014). For example, the IOM report calls for a doubling of the number of nurses with doctorates. Given that doctoral programs take 3 or more years to complete, however, the number of doctorally prepared nurses in the workforce would not show much progress due to efforts attributable to the report or the Campaign just 5 years after the report's release. Thus, the Campaign is looking at interim indicators to identify progress toward the report's goals, such as nurses' enrollment in doctoral programs. Further, the Campaign notes that "for national indicators, it is important to use a source of data that provides consistent information across states" (CCNA, n.d.-d, p. 3).

Communications Strategies

The Campaign undertakes a variety of communication activities and also provides communication support to state Action Coalitions (CCNA, 2015b). The Campaign has developed and maintains a website, social media presence, and speakers bureau, which it uses to communicate to stakeholders and the public. It also uses videos, email updates, listserv messages, and webinars to communicate with Action Coalitions and other stakeholder groups central to Campaign efforts. Further, leaders from the Campaign publish articles, stories, editorials, and blog posts in popular media and scholarly journals. Prior to the start of the Campaign, CCNA, which was founded in 2007, was building its communication network with organizations and individuals around the nation. CCNA has helped state Action Coalitions develop communication strategies and provided other communication support and technical assistance. The Campaign has stated that it has engaged as key stakeholders the nursing community, business leaders, payers, philanthropic organizations, policy makers, consumers, other health professionals, and the higher education community, "with an emphasis on community college leaders" (CCNA, 2015b, p. 2).

Evaluation

In 2011, the Campaign engaged an external company, TCC Group, to conduct an evaluation of its programs (Raynor and Locke, 2015). This evaluation is ongoing and is described as formative in focus and multilevel, including review of the efforts of the national Campaign, the state Action Coalitions, and the Academic Progression in Nursing program. The evaluation has included the following components:

- Interviews with key Campaign leaders and staff at RWJF and CCNA were conducted in 2012 to assess the effectiveness of collaboration between these two organizations; the roles and responsibilities of staff in each; and the benefits and challenges with respect to leadership, decision making, and communication that exist through this unique partnership (TCC Group, 2012a).
- Campaign partner interviews were conducted in September and October 2012 with a variety of Campaign stakeholders, as well as with members of the Campaign's Champion Nursing Council and Champion Nursing Coalition, to identify accomplishments in and barriers to implementing the goals of the Campaign that are based on the recommendations of the IOM report (TCC Group, 2012b).
- As discussed above, a national survey of the state Action Coalitions was conducted in fall 2013 to assess the implementation of Campaign activities, the use of Campaign services, the Action Coalitions' priority focus areas related to the IOM report's recommendations, and the outcomes of their efforts (TCC Group, 2013b).
- A formative evaluation of the Academic Progression in Nursing (APIN) program was conducted from October 2012 through October 2013 to assess the program's implementation and the results and outcomes each APIN grantee was able to accomplish within the 2 years since the start of the program. This evaluation also sought to identify aspects of models that appeared to be particularly successful with regard to advancing academic progression among nurses (TCC Group, 2013b).
- A survey was conducted in December 2013 among alumni of RWJF nursing programs (Executive Nurse Fellows, Partners Investing in Nursing's Future, and Nurse Faculty Scholars) to assess the engagement of program alumni in the Campaign (TCC Group, 2013c).

- An analysis focused on the Campaign imperatives (detailed earlier) was conducted in fall 2013 to determine the efforts and capacities of the state Action Coalitions with respect to making progress in the Campaign's strategic activation phase (TCC Group, 2014).

RWJF ACTIVITIES OUTSIDE OF THE CAMPAIGN

RWJF has a portfolio of work related to advancing the nursing profession that is separate from the work of the Campaign but still advances the messages and goals of *The Future of Nursing* and the Campaign. In many cases, these programs interface and collaborate with the Campaign at the national and state levels. These programs include the following:

- The APIN program was established in 2012 as an initiative of RWJF and the Tri-Council for Nursing, with program offices located in the American Organization of Nurse Executives. The program collaborates with and funds are distributed to state Action Coalitions and their stakeholders to establish models of seamless academic progression for nurses to further the IOM report's recommendation that 80 percent of nurses have a baccalaureate degree by 2020 (AONE, 2015a; RWJF, 2012) (see a more detailed description of this program in Chapter 3).
- The Future of Nursing Scholars program, established in 2013, supports nurses in obtaining their PhD and furthers the IOM report's recommendation that the number of nurses with a doctorate be doubled by 2020 (RWJF, 2015a) (see a more detailed description of this program in Chapter 3).
- Executive Nurse Fellows, established in 1997, is a 3-year program that provides leadership development and support to nurses in executive leadership positions, and includes leadership curriculum, coaching and mentoring, and team-based learning projects (RWJF, 2014b, 2015b).
- Nurse Faculty Scholars, established in 2008, provides career development awards to nurse faculty. The program requires that awardees have a doctorate in nursing or another related discipline, and that they be junior faculty in a tenure-track position. The 3-year award provides support for the scholar's research expenses and part of the scholar's salary. Scholars also receive leadership training and mentoring through the program. With the closing of the program scheduled for 2017, the 2014 call for proposals was this program's last (RWJF, 2014a, n.d.-e,g).
- The Nursing and Health Policy Collaborative at the University of New Mexico offers opportunities for PhD-prepared nurse fellows to engage in health policy through academic study in health policy; mentorship opportunities; and collaborative efforts with researchers, other health professionals, policy makers, and the community (RWJF, n.d.-f).

- The Interdisciplinary Nursing Quality Research Initiative (INQRI) was established in 2005 to fund research conducted by interdisciplinary teams that addresses gaps in knowledge relating to nursing and health care delivery and care quality, efficiency, and cost-effectiveness (RWJF, n.d.-a). Responding to the publication of the IOM report in 2010, RWJF created the Future of Nursing National Research Agenda, a research program coordinated by INQRI that supports studies specifically related to the report's recommendations (RWJF, n.d.-b,c).
- The New Careers in Nursing (NCIN) scholarship program (RWJF/ AARP) was established in 2008 to provide support for students returning to school to obtain baccalaureate and master's degrees in nursing (RWJF, 2013).
- Partners Investing in Nursing's Future (PIN) was established in 2006 as a partnership between RWJF and the Northwest Health Foundation to support local and regional foundations in advancing leadership in nursing. This program ended in June 30, 2015 (RWJF, n.d.-d).

In addition to the PIN program, four other nursing-related programs will be ending in the coming years as the result of RWJF's new focus on a "Culture of Health" and a review of its portfolio of human capital investments. These four programs are NCIN (closing in 2017), Executive Nurse Fellows (2017), Nurse Faculty Scholars (2017), and the Nursing and Health Policy Collaborative at the University of New Mexico (2018) (RWJF, 2014a, n.d.-h).

ORGANIZATION OF THE REPORT

Chapters 2 through 6 review the progress made in implementing the recommendations of *The Future of Nursing* in the areas of delivery of care, education, diversity, leadership and interprofessional collaboration, and data, respectively. These chapters include the committee's findings and conclusions in each of these areas, as well as its recommendations for how the Campaign and others should move forward in the next 5 years, considering the successes and challenges that have occurred over the past 5 years and the new context within which the recommendations of *The Future of Nursing* are being implemented.

REFERENCES

AACN (American Association of Colleges of Nursing). 2010. *Educational advancement of registered nurses: A consensus position.* http://www.aacn.nche.edu/education-resources/Tricouncil EdStatement.pdf (accessed September 22, 2015).

AACN. 2015. *Position statements.* http://www.aacn.nche.edu/publications/position-statements (accessed September 23, 2015).

AACN. n.d. *AACN strategic planning & the IOM report.* www.aacn.nche.edu/education-resources/ IOMStrategicPlanning.pdf (accessed November 23, 2015).

AACN and AAMC (Association of American Medical Colleges). 2010. *Lifelong learning in medicine and nursing: Final conference report*. Washington, DC: AACN and AAMC.

Alexander, M. 2011. Supporting the Future of Nursing. *Journal of Nursing Regulation* 2(2):3.

ANA (American Nurses Association). 2011. *ANA, CMA and OA activities reflected in the IOM recommendations*. http://www.nursingworld.org/ANA-Activities-IOM-Report (accessed November 23, 2015).

AONE (American Organization of Nurse Executives). 2015a. *Academic progression in nursing*. http://www.aone.org/resources/APIN/APIN_main.shtml (accessed September 23, 2015).

AONE. 2015b. *Position/policy statements*. http://www.aone.org/resources/leadership%20tools/policy stmnts.shtml (accessed September 23, 2015).

Benner, P., M. Sutphen, V. Leonard, and L. Day. 2009. *Educating nurses: A call for radical transformation* (Vol. 15). San Francisco, CA: Jossey-Bass.

CCNA (Center to Champion Nursing in America). 2011. *Future of Nursing: State Implementation Program 2012 request for proposals*. Washington, DC: CCNA.

CCNA. 2012. Future of Nursing: State Implementation Program 2013 request for proposals. Washington, DC: CCNA.

CCNA. 2014. *Future of Nursing: State Implementation Program 2014 request for proposals*. Washington, DC: CCNA.

CCNA. 2015a (unpublished). *Action coalition fundraising report, as of January 31, 2015*. Washington, DC: CCNA.

CCNA. 2015b. *Evaluation of the impact of the Institute of Medicine report "The future of nursing: Leading change, advancing health" communications report, July 20, 2015*. Washington, DC: CCNA.

CCNA. 2015c (unpublished). *Future of Nursing: Campaign for Action biannual operations report, August 1, 2014-May 31, 2015*. Washington, DC: The Center to Champion Nursing in America.

CCNA. 2015d. *Future of Nursing: Campaign for Action dashboard indicators*. http://campaignfor action.org/dashboard (accessed September 12, 2015).

CCNA. n.d.-a. *About us: Campaign history*. http://campaignforaction.org/about-us/campaign-history (accessed September 23, 2013).

CCNA. n.d.-b. *Campaign progress*. http://campaignforaction.org/campaign-progress (accessed September 23, 2015).

CCNA. n.d.-c. *Champion Nursing Council*. http://campaignforaction.org/whos-involved/champion-nursing-council (accessed November 23, 2015).

CCNA. n.d.-d. *Frequently asked questions about the Campaign for Action dashboard*. http://campaign foraction.org/sites/default/files/CFA%20Dashboard%20FAQ%20FINAL.docx (accessed October 26, 2015).

CCNA. n.d.-e. *Our partners*. http://campaignforaction.org/whos-involved (accessed November 23, 2015).

CCNA. n.d.-f. *State action coalitions*. http://campaignforaction.org/states (accessed September 23, 2015).

CCNA. n.d.-g (unpublished). *Growing the national campaign: Action coalition timeline*. Washington, DC: The Center to Champion Nursing in America.

Curley, D. 2015. Presentation to IOM Committee for Assessing Progress on Implementing the Recommendations of the Institute of Medicine Report *The Future of Nursing: Leading Change, Advancing Health*. Washington, DC, July 27, 2015.

HHS (U.S. Department of Health and Human Services). 2015. *Health insurance coverage and the Affordable Care Act*. http://aspe.hhs.gov/sites/default/files/pdf/83966/ib_uninsured_change.pdf (accessed October 22, 2015).

IOM (Institute of Medicine). 2011. *The future of nursing: Leading change, advancing health*. Washington, DC: The National Academies Press.

Jonas Center for Nursing and Veterans Healthcare. 2015. *Jonas Nurse Leaders Scholar Program.* http://www.jonascenter.org/program-areas/jonas-nurse-leaders-scholars (accessed September 23, 2015).

Josiah Macy Jr. Foundation. 2010. *Co-chairs' summary of the conference: Who will provide primary care and how will they be trained?* New York: Josiah Macy Jr. Foundation. http://macy foundation.org/docs/macy_pubs/jmf_ChairSumConf_Jan2010.pdf (accessed September 23, 2015).

Josiah Macy Jr. Foundation. 2012. *Conference on interprofessional education, April 1-3, 2012.* New York: Josiah Macy Jr. Foundation.

Josiah Macy Jr. Foundation. 2013. *Transforming patient care: Aligning interprofessional education with clinical practice redesign.* New York: Josiah Macy Jr. Foundation.

NLN (National League for Nursing). 2015. *Archived position statements.* http://www.nln.org/about/ position-statements/archived-position-statements (accessed September 23, 2015).

Raynor, J., and K. Locke. 2015. *The future of nursing: Leading change, advancing health.* Presentation to IOM Committee for Assessing Progress on Implementing the Recommendations of the Institute of Medicine Report *The Future of Nursing: Leading Change, Advancing Health.* Washington, DC, May 28, 2015.

RWJF (Robert Wood Johnson Foundation). 2012. *Robert Wood Johnson Foundation launches initiative to support academic progression in nursing.* http://www.rwjf.org/en/library/articles-and-news/2012/03/robert-wood-johnson-foundation-launches-initiative-to-support-ac.html (accessed September 18, 2015).

RWJF. 2013. *New careers in nursing program details.* http://www.newcareersinnursing.org/about-ncin/program-details (accessed September 23, 2015).

RWJF. 2014a. *Letter to the nursing field from Risa Lavizzo-Mourey: RWJF President and CEO describes transitions in the foundation's nursing programs.* http://www.rwjf.org/en/library/ articles-and-news/2014/02/letter-to-the-field.html?cq_ck=1392047707833 (accessed September 22, 2015).

RWJF. 2014b. *Robert Wood Johnson Foundation executive nurse fellows.* http://www.rwjf.org/content/ dam/farm/reports/program_results_reports/2014/rwjf69782 (accessed September 23, 2015).

RWJF. 2015a. *Future of Nursing Scholars: Strengthening nursing leadership of the health and health care systems.* http://futureofnursingscholars.org (accessed September 23, 2015).

RWJF. 2015b. *Robert Wood Johnson Foundation executive nurse fellows.* http://www.executivenurse-fellows.org (accessed September 23, 2015).

RWJF. n.d.-a. *Interdisciplinary nursing quality research initiative program overview.* http://www. inqri.org/about-inqri/program-overview (accessed September 23, 2015).

RWJF. n.d.-b. *INQRI and the future of nursing.* http://www.inqri.org/grants/agenda-studies (accessed October 26, 2015).

RWJF. n.d.-c. *National research agenda studies.* http://www.inqri.org/grants/agenda-studies/list (accessed October 26, 2015).

RWJF. n.d.-d. *Partners investing in nursing's future.* http://www.partnersinnursing.org (accessed September 22, 2015).

RWJF. n.d.-e. *Robert Wood Johnson Foundation Nurse Faculty Scholars frequently asked questions.* http://www.nursefacultyscholars.org/general (accessed September 22, 2015).

RWJF. n.d.-f. *Robert Wood Johnson Foundation Nursing and Health Policy Collaborative at the University of New Mexico.* http://nursinghealthpolicy.org/the-collaborative (accessed September 23, 2015).

RWJF. n.d.-g. *Robert Wood Johnson Foundation Nurse Faculty Scholars about.* http://www.nurse facultyscholars.org/about (accessed November 23, 2015).

RWJF. n.d.-h. *A bold new direction for leadership programs.* http://www.rwjf.org/en/library/ features/A-Bold-New-Direction-for-Leadership-Programs.html (accessed November 23, 2015).

Spetz, J., T. Bates, L. Chu, J. Lin, N. W. Fishman, and L. Melichar. 2014. Creating a dashboard to track progress toward IOM recommendations for the future of nursing. *Policy, Politics, & Nursing Practice* 14(3-4):117-124.

TCC Group. 2012a (unpublished). *Future of Nursing: Campaign for Action RWJF/CCNA collaboration report.* Philadelphia, PA: TCC Group.

TCC Group. 2012b (unpublished). *Future of Nursing: Campaign for Action campaign partner findings.* Philadelphia, PA: TCC Group.

TCC Group. 2013a (unpublished). *Future of Nursing: Campaign for Action coalition survey.* Philadelphia, PA: TCC Group.

TCC Group. 2013b (unpublished). *Evaluation of the Academic Progression in Nursing (APIN) initiative, year one report to the Robert Wood Johnson Foundation.* Philadelphia, PA: TCC Group.

TCC Group. 2013c (unpublished). *Future of Nursing: Campaign for Action RWJ alumni survey.* Philadelphia, PA: TCC Group.

TCC Group. 2014 (unpublished). *Robert Wood Johnson Foundation Future of Nursing Campaign imperative analysis.* Philadelphia, PA: TCC Group.

WHO (World Health Organization). 2009. *Global standards for the initial education of professional nurses and midwives.* Geneva, Switzerland: WHO Press.

2

Removing Barriers to Practice and Care

The Future of Nursing: Leading Change, Advancing Health observes that the changing landscape of health care and the changing profile of the U.S. population will require fundamental shifts in the care delivery system (IOM, 2011). In particular, the report notes concerns about a shortage of primary care health professionals in the United States, particularly given the expansion of insurance coverage under the Patient Protection and Affordable Care Act (ACA). It suggests that advanced practice registered nurses (APRNs), if permitted to practice to the full extent of their education and training, could help build the workforce necessary to meet the country's primary care needs and contribute their unique skills to the delivery of patient-centered, community-based health care. While the Institute of Medicine (IOM) report makes special mention of the role for APRNs in primary care (see Box 2-1), the report's recommendations are not limited to those settings, but encompass the full continuum of health services in many health organization and community settings.

The Future of Nursing notes that although APRNs are highly trained and able to provide a variety of services, they are prevented from doing so because of barriers, including state laws, federal policies, outdated insurance reimbursement models, and institutional practices and culture (IOM, 2011). The report includes several specific policy recommendations for overcoming these barriers and providing APRNs with licensure, privileges, and reimbursement consistent with their education and training.

In particular, the report encourages policy makers to be guided by the National Council of State Boards of Nursing's (NCSBN'S) Model Nursing Practice Act and Administrative Rules in efforts to change state scope-of-practice laws (NCSBN, 2009). An understanding of the provisions of this act may be useful

---

BOX 2-1
Recommendation 1 from *The Future of Nursing*:
Remove Scope-of-Practice Barriers

Advanced practice registered nurses (APRNs) should be able to practice to the full extent of their education and training. To achieve this goal, the committee recommends the following actions.

For Congress:
- Expand the Medicare program to include coverage of advanced practice registered nurse services that are within the scope of practice under applicable state law, just as physician services are now covered.
- Amend the Medicare program to authorize advanced practice registered nurses to perform admission assessments, as well as certification of patients for home health care services and for admission to hospice and skilled nursing facilities.
- Extend the increase in Medicaid reimbursement rates for primary care physicians included in the ACA to APRNs providing similar primary care services.
- Limit federal funding for nursing education programs to only those programs in states that have adopted the National Council of State Boards of Nursing Model Nursing Practice Act and Model Nursing Administrative Rules (Article XVIII, Chapter 18).

For state legislatures:
- Reform scope-of-practice regulations to conform to the National Council of State Boards of Nursing Model Nursing Practice Act and Model Nursing Administrative Rules (Article XVIII, Chapter 18).

---

for understanding how "full practice authority" has been defined and measured by NCSBN, the American Association of Nurse Practitioners (AANP), and the Future of Nursing: Campaign for Action (the Campaign) in their assessments of progress toward implementation of the report's recommendations. The NCSBN act includes a detailed set of guidelines. In summarizing the status of scope-of-practice authority in the U.S. states and territories, the Campaign (CCNA, 2015) and AANP (2015) track progress in three categories: full, reduced, and restricted practice (see Figure 2-1 for definitions).

ACTIVITY AND PROGRESS

The Campaign reports that since the release of the IOM report, 44 state Action Coalitions have worked on its recommendation to remove scope-of-practice barriers (see Box 2-1) (CCNA, 2014a). At the time the report was published,

- Require third-party payers that participate in fee-for-service payment arrangements to provide direct reimbursement to advanced practice registered nurses who are practicing within their scope of practice under state law.

For the Centers for Medicare & Medicaid Services:
- Amend or clarify the requirements for hospital participation in the Medicare program to ensure that advanced practice registered nurses are eligible for clinical privileges, admitting privileges, and membership on medical staff.

For the Office of Personnel Management:
- Require insurers participating in the Federal Employees Health Benefits Program to include coverage of those services of advanced practice registered nurses that are within their scope of practice under applicable state law.

For the Federal Trade Commission and the Antitrust Division of the Department of Justice:
- Review existing and proposed state regulations concerning advanced practice registered nurses to identify those that have anticompetitive effects without contributing to the health and safety of the public. States with unduly restrictive regulations should be urged to amend them to allow advanced practice registered nurses to provide care to patients in all circumstances in which they are qualified to do so.

SOURCE: IOM, 2011.

13 states were classified as meeting criteria for full practice authority. Since the Campaign began, 8 more states (Connecticut, Maryland, Minnesota, Nebraska, Nevada, North Dakota, Rhode Island, and Vermont) have changed their laws to give nurse practitioners (NPs) full practice and prescriptive authority, bringing the number of states with full authority to 21 (CCNA, 2015). Seventeen states are currently categorized as having reduced practice and 12 as having restricted practice (see Figure 2-1). Some states—for example, Kentucky, New York, Texas, and Utah—have made incremental improvements to their laws but are still categorized by AANP and the Campaign as having reduced or restricted practice for APRNs (AANP, 2015; CCNA, 2014b, 2015). The Campaign uses information from AANP's State Nurse Practice and Administrative Rules to track full practice authority, reduced practice, and restricted practice (AANP, 2015; CCNA, 2015).

These broad categorizations, while useful for classification purposes, mask a number of subtleties among state laws. Maine, for example, a state with full

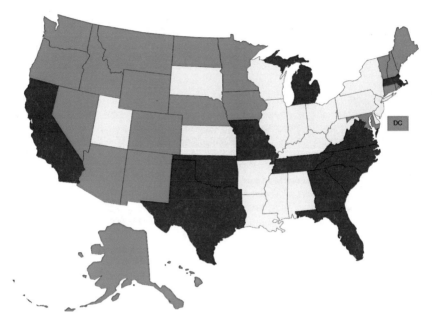

Full Practice: State practice and licensure law provides for nurse practitioners (NPs) to evaluate patients, diagnose, order and interpret diagnostic tests, initiate and manage treatments—including prescribing medications—under the exclusive licensure authority of the state board of nursing. This is the model recommended by the Institute of Medicine and National Council of State Boards of Nursing.

Reduced Practice: State practice and licensure law reduces the ability of NPs to engage in at least one element of NP practice. State requires a regulated collaborative agreement with an outside health discipline in order for the NP to provide patient care.

Restricted Practice: State practice and licensure law restricts the ability of an NP to engage in at least one element of NP practice. The state requires supervision, delegation, or team management by an outside health discipline for an NP to provide patient care.

FIGURE 2-1 State practice environment.
SOURCE: AANP, 2015. Reprinted, with permission, from the American Association of Nurse Practitioners. Copyright © 2015.

practice authority, has express legislative prohibitions against NP hospital privileges (Pearson, 2014). NPs in this state must be supervised when caring for patients in a hospital setting. In Ohio, a state without full practice authority, a bill was signed in 2014 that allows APRNs and physician assistants (PAs) to admit patients into hospitals.[1] Some states do not have legislative prohibitions per se, but other regulatory impediments exist. In Texas, for example, "hospital licensing law does not include APRNs as medical staff members who may admit and discharge patients; most hospitals grant privileges to APRNs as allied health providers" (Pearson, 2014, p. 255).

In addition to changes at the state level, several of the bulleted points under the IOM report's recommendation 1 (see Box 2-1) have been addressed through enacted or proposed legislative and regulatory changes at the federal level, as described below.

Congress

The ACA added a provision to the Public Health Service Act that prohibits health insurers from discriminating "against any health care provider who is acting within the scope of that provider's license or certification under applicable state law."[2] That is, if a plan covers a specific service, the plan cannot deny coverage for the service based solely on the practitioner's license or certification.

Centers for Medicare & Medicaid Services (CMS)

CMS issued a final rule in 2012 that broadens the concept of "medical staff," allowing hospitals to authorize "other practitioners . . . to practice in the hospital in accordance with State law" (CMS, 2012, p. 29034). CMS notes that this change "will clearly permit hospitals to allow other practitioners (e.g., APRNs, PAs, pharmacists) to perform all functions within their scope of practice" (p. 29034). Despite this rule, medical staff membership and hospital privileges remain subject to existing state law and business preferences. Another CMS rule, issued in 2014, clarifies that outpatient services may be ordered by any practitioner, regardless of whether he or she is on a medical staff, if the practitioner is acting within his or her scope of practice under state law (CMS, 2014). These rules apply to all hospitals that participate in Medicare or Medicaid programs; however, individual hospitals do have the option to restrict practice.

---

[1] Ohio. 130th General Assembly. H.B. 139. (2013-2014). See http://archives.legislature.state.oh.us/bills.cfm?ID=130_HB_139 (accessed September 23, 2015).

[2] 42 U.S.C. § 300gg-5 Non-discrimination in Health Care.

Federal Trade Commission (FTC)

The FTC has engaged in competition advocacy relating to APRNs' scope of practice in many states (CCNA, 2014a). Specifically, the FTC has provided letters, comments, and/or testimony related to removing barriers to APRNs' practicing to the full extent of their education and training in Connecticut (FTC, 2013b), Florida (FTC, 2011a), Illinois (FTC, 2013a), Kentucky (FTC, 2012b), Louisiana (FTC, 2012a), Massachusetts (FTC, 2014a), Missouri (FTC, 2012c, 2015a), South Carolina (FTC, 2015b), Texas (FTC, 2011b), and West Virginia (FTC, 2012d). No cases have been brought by the FTC relating to APRN scope-of-practice and anticompetition concerns[3]; however, the U.S. Supreme Court recently, in *North Carolina State Board of Dental Examiners v. Federal Trade Commission*,[4] sided with the FTC, which alleged that the Board's efforts to prevent nondentists from providing teeth-whitening services constituted an unfair method of competition under federal law.[5] The Board sought to dismiss the motion on grounds of state-action immunity. The Supreme Court ruling denied state-action immunity from federal trade laws to professional boards representing a majority of the regulated profession unless they are actively supervised by the state itself. The American Association of Nurse Anesthetists, American Nurses Association, AANP, American College of Nurse Midwives, National Association of Clinical Nurse Specialists, and Citizen Advocacy Center—understanding the potential implications of the case for nurse scope-of-practice regulation—filed an amicus brief in the case in support of the FTC.[6] In March 2014, the FTC released a paper stating that "physician supervision requirements may raise competition concerns because they effectively give one group of health care professionals the ability to restrict access to the market by another, competing group of health care professionals, thereby denying health care consumers the benefits of greater competition" (FTC, 2014b, pp. 1-2).

Veterans Health Administration (VHA)

The VHA proposed in 2012 that its APRNs be permitted to practice in-dependently throughout the VHA system, regardless of state scope-of-practice restrictions (VA, 2012). The proposal, which relies on the Supremacy Clause of

---

[3] Per a November 4, 2015, search of the FTC cases and proceedings (https://www.ftc.gov/enforcement/cases-proceedings/advanced-search).

[4] *North Carolina State Board of Dental Examiners v. Federal Trade Commission*, 574 U.S. ___ (2015).

[5] Federal Trade Commission Act. 15 U.S.C. §§ 45(a)(1).

[6] Brief of the American Association of Nurse Anesthetists, American Nurses Association, American Association of Nurse Practitioners, American College of Nurse Midwives, National Association of Clinical Nurse Specialists, and the Citizen Advocacy Center as Amici Curiae in Support of the Respondent, *North Carolina State Board of Dental Examiners v. Federal Trade Commission*, No. 13-534, Supreme Court of the United States, filed August 5, 2014.

the U.S. Constitution for authority, has not been finalized, although a bill was introduced in the U.S. Senate in 2015 that would give statutory authority to full APRN practice in the VHA.[7] This proposal was a direct result of *The Future of Nursing*, with VHA nursing officials saying that "the proposed change follows a 2010 Institute of Medicine recommendation that nurses should practice to the full extent of their education and training" (Beck, 2014).

DISCUSSION

APRN practice authority has been expanded considerably in the 5 years since the release of *The Future of Nursing*. Many organizations, in collaboration with or in addition to the Campaign and its state Action Coalitions, have worked to remove barriers that restricted APRNs from working to the full extent of their training and education. Twenty-one states now have full practice authority for APRNs, although several large states have not yet achieved that goal. APRNs now have prescribing authority in 49 states, albeit with some restrictions for certain classes of medication. In those states where new scope-of-practice proposals have met opposition, the major points of contention include requirements for APRN oversight by medical rather than nursing licensing boards; clinical oversight by or collaboration with physicians; and restrictions on APRNs' provision of a range of services, including hospital admitting privileges. Finding common ground on these points is a challenging process, as evidenced by, for example, recent debates in California and Virginia. Nonetheless, these debates and incremental steps still arguably represent progress, as exemplified by the successful resolution of a years-long process to remove scope-of-practice restrictions in Maryland.

In California, a bill[8] that would have authorized certified NPs who had practiced under the supervision of a physician for at least 4,160 hours to practice independently failed in 2013 after intense opposition from the California Medical Association (CMA). The CMA argued that, if passed, the bill would mean that "nurse practitioners will no longer need to work pursuant to standardized protocols and procedures or any supervising physician and would basically give them a plenary license to practice medicine" (California Medical Association, 2013). The bill did have the support of several other professional organizations and health insurers, but it was opposed by state and national physician organizations (Adashi, 2013).

In contrast, physician and NP groups collaborated to decrease restrictions in Virginia,[9] which is classified by AANP as a restrictive practice state (AANP,

---

[7] *Frontlines to Lifelines Act of 2015*, S. 297, 114th Cong.

[8] 2013 CA S.B. 491. See http://leginfo.legislature.ca.gov/faces/billNavClient.xhtml?bill_id=201320140SB491 (accessed September 23, 2015).

[9] 2012 VA H.B. 346. See https://lis.virginia.gov/cgi-bin/legp604.exe?121+ful+HB346 (accessed September 23, 2015).

2015; Iglehart, 2013). In 2012, the Virginia state legislature unanimously voted to approve a bill that was the result of negotiations between the Medical Society of Virginia and the Virginia Council of Nurse Practitioners. The bill requires NPs to work as part of a patient-care team that is led and managed by a physician, but permits the supervision to occur via telemedicine and expands the number of NPs who can be supervised by a physician from four to six. The American Medical Association (AMA) viewed the compromise reached in Virginia as a possible model for other states; however, AANP was disappointed in the outcome.

Finally, the incremental gains made over a number of years in Maryland demonstrate the progress that can be achieved through persistent efforts. In 2008, scope-of-practice restrictions were loosened slightly when legislation[10] was passed permitting APRNs to sign birth and death certificates, advance directives, and applications for handicapped license tags. In 2010, restrictions were further reduced when a decades-old collaborative agreement between the Boards of Nursing and Physicians was replaced by an attestation statement.[11] Finally, in 2015, the Certified Nurse Practitioners—Authority to Practice bill[12] was signed into law, removing the attestation requirement and giving NPs full practice authority.

Opposition by some physicians and physician organizations has been noted as a barrier to expansion of APRNs' scope of practice (Adashi, 2013; Hain and Fleck, 2014; Iglehart, 2013; Walters, 2015). Upon the release of *The Future of Nursing*, several national physicians' organizations raised concern about the report's recommendation regarding scope-of-practice expansion:

- American College of Physicians (ACP, 2010): "The IOM's emphasis on independent practice is at odds with the goal of ensuring that patients receive comprehensive and patient-centered care within the context of a health care team. . . . Today, no one clinician should practice independently of other clinicians."
- American Medical Association (AMA, 2010): "A physician-led team approach to care—with each member of the team playing the role they are educated and trained to play—helps ensure patients get high quality care and value for their health care spending. . . . Nurses are critical to the health care team, but there is no substitute for education and training."
- Council of Medical Specialty Societies (CMSS, 2010): "CMSS is concerned that the IOM report advocates for an expanded scope of nursing

---

[10] 2008 MD H.B. 1140. See http://mgaleg.maryland.gov/webmga/frmMain.aspx?ys=2008rs%2 fbillfile%2fhb1140.htm (accessed September 23, 2015).

[11] 2010 MD H.B. 319. See http://mgaleg.maryland.gov/webmga/frmMain.aspx?ys=2010rs/billfile/ hb0319.htm (accessed September 23, 2015).

[12] 2015 MD H.B. 999. See http://mgaleg.maryland.gov/webmga/frmMain.aspx?id=hb0999&stab=01 &pid=billpage&tab=subject3&ys=2015RS (accessed September 23, 2015).

practice without specifying the standard minimum amount of supervised clinical experience and documented clinical competency that must be achieved before an APN would be permitted to treat and prescribe without physician guidance."

In an effort to alleviate some of the tension between nurses and physicians, RWJF convened leaders of nurse and physician organizations in 2011 to develop a consensus document on interprofessional collaboration (Iglehart, 2013; RWJF, 2013). A draft report titled *Common Ground: An Agreement Between Nurse and Physician Leaders on Interprofessional Collaboration for the Future of Patient Care* was produced following a constructive dialogue. The draft report noted the shortage and maldistribution of primary care providers and emphasized the need for patient-centered care. It also acknowledged that nursing and medicine are not interchangeable professions and that the "captain-of-the-ship notion needs to be refined for the 21st century" (RWJF, 2013, p. 3). Efforts to refine and publish the report ended when a leaked early draft drew opposition from physician organizations.

Despite the failure of these efforts, participants—including representatives from AACN, the American College of Physicians (ACP), the American Nurses Association (ANA), the American Organization of Nurse Executives (AONE), the National League for Nursing (NLN), the Nurse Practitioner Roundtable, and other organizations—expressed hope that the focus would remain on how interprofessional collaboration is in the best interest of the patient. Further, participants noted that interprofessional collaboration already occurs in the health care system and that common ground is often found among health professionals, even if not among their associations. At the committee's May 2015 workshop, Steven Weinberger, Executive Vice President and CEO of ACP, continued to speak to the need for professional collaboration and for a focus on what is best for patients rather than professions:

> I think we need to change the perspective from which we're looking at this. We're looking at this from the perspective of "What does the physician population need?" "What does the nurse population need?" We have to look at this from the perspective of "What does the patient need?" And let's get it away from the professions and say that for this given patient and this point in time, the best person to provide care is x, y, or z.

Despite the political conflict between nursing and physician organizations and amid the wide array of scope-of-practice restrictions, APRNs and physicians most commonly are working collaboratively on the ground. A recent qualitative study conducted in Massachusetts, a restricted practice state, found that despite the state's scope-of-practice restrictions, some NPs described having a scope of practice similar to that of their physician colleagues, and the "supervision" mandated by written agreements was variably enforced (Poghosyan et al., 2013). However, testimony provided for the present study suggested that such administrative restrictions may adversely affect patients by causing delays in referrals, orders for medical equipment, discharges to home or hospice, and other services (Lamprecht, 2015).

The Future of Nursing does not call for nurses to replace doctors. It does recommend that "advanced practice registered nurses should be able to practice to the full extent of their education and training" (IOM, 2011, p. 278). In new collaborative models of practice, it is imperative that all health professionals practice to the full extent of their education and training to optimize the efficiency and quality of services for patients. The term "independent practice" has become a charged term for some physician groups, which view it as implying solo or competitive practice. However, considerable testimony provided for the present study supported viewing this term as meaning the full practice authority to use one's education and training. Full practice authority for APRNs, as for all health professionals, is ideally part of an organized, collaborative system of care.

Research conducted with NPs and physicians since The Future of Nursing was released provides perspectives of practicing clinicians on some of these issues. While state and federal efforts to reduce scope-of-practice restrictions were ongoing, the Health Resources and Services Administration (HRSA) conducted a national survey of NPs in 2012 (HRSA, 2014a). Among those surveyed, 11 percent were working without a physician on-site, and 84 percent indicated they were practicing "to the fullest extent of the state's legal scope of practice" (pp. 9-10). Another survey of primary care NPs conducted in the same year found that 75 percent were practicing to the "full extent of their education and training" (the key message of the IOM report) (Donelan et al., 2013, p. 1900), and 8 percent of NPs worked in a primary care practice without a physician and billed for all their services under their own National Provider Identifier (NPI) (Buerhaus et al., 2015). Fully 96 percent of primary care NPs and 76 percent of primary care physicians surveyed in 2013 agreed that NPs should be able to practice to the full extent of their education and training, reflecting a broad, if uneven, consensus around this core message (Donelan et al., 2013). Primary care NPs and physicians largely agreed that increasing the supply of NPs could enhance access to and the timeliness of primary care, but they disagreed about issues of reimbursement and quality of services provided.

Evidence published since the release of The Future of Nursing underscores previous research supporting removal of restrictions on scope of practice, showing that APRNs provide high-quality care with good patient outcomes (e.g., fewer avoidable hospitalizations, readmissions, and emergency room visits) in a wide variety of settings (Donald et al., 2013; Kilpatrick et al., 2014; Kuo et al., 2015; Lewis et al., 2014; Newhouse et al., 2011; Stanik-Hutt et al., 2013). APRNs continue to have an especially important role in delivering primary care services in rural areas and in medically underserved communities where primary care shortages are documented and physician oversight may not be locally available (Buerhaus et al., 2015; DesRoches et al., 2013). While APRNs often assume substantial responsibilities in delivering high-quality health care, regulatory and payment practices remain barriers to their being able to practice to the full extent of their education and training (Poghosyan et al., 2013; Stange, 2014; Yee et al., 2013). These findings suggest that further removal of scope-of-practice restrictions could have a positive impact on health care access and quality.

While *The Future of Nursing* places a strong emphasis on the importance of building the APRN workforce to meet the growing demands for primary care in a time of insurance expansion and shortages of primary care physicians, the 2012 HRSA National Sample Survey of Nurse Practitioners found that only 39.2 percent of all licensed NPs were working in primary care; the proportion was higher (47.4 percent) when calculated as the percentage of NPs who were currently employed in patient care roles (HRSA, 2014a). These estimates were consistent with those from the 2008 National Sample Survey of Registered Nurses (RNs) (HRSA, 2010) and research supported by the Agency for Healthcare Research and Quality (AHRQ, 2011). Among the NP respondents to the 2012 HRSA survey employed in patient care roles, 59 percent of those who had graduated in 1992 or earlier were working in primary care, compared with 42 percent of those who had graduated between 2003 and 2007. Among more recent graduates since 2008, the proportion in primary care was 47 percent. Despite the drop in the proportion of NPs who practice primary care, however, the percentage is still far higher than the percentage of physicians entering primary care (Chen et al., 2013), and the total number of primary care NPs is rising. Researchers have projected that by 2025, the number of primary care NPs in the United States will increase to 103,000 from the 60,407 measured in 2012 (Auerbach et al., 2013; HRSA, 2014a).

The committee that conducted the present study acknowledges that shortages of primary care providers, both nurses and physicians, remain a challenge in the United States (AHRQ, 2011; HRSA, 2013, 2014b; Petterson et al., 2012). However, the committee does not believe that the move toward specialty care detracts from the original intent of *The Future of Nursing* recommendations; rather, that it offers additional context for the value and implications of scope-of-practice expansion, and it also offers new focus for the Campaign. In addition, it reinforces the importance of collaborative practice among a full array of health professionals as the model for health care for the future in both primary and specialty care.

As discussed in Chapter 1, passage of the ACA and a number of transformations in the health care system have created a new context emphasizing the goal of providing value-based care and engaging in collaborative practice for all patients. Providers and health systems are increasingly being held accountable for patient outcomes, with a new emphasis on the "Triple Aim" for health care—improved health, improved health care, and reduced costs. While it should be noted that cost did not factor into the recommendation of *The Future of Nursing*, there is in this changing context of affordability and value a renewed focus on achieving higher quality at lower cost and with greater efficiency. Scope-of-practice expansion may contribute to the aim of lowering costs, particularly in the context of interdisciplinary teams (Sinsky et al., 2013). It makes sense that in several models of care, particularly in primary care settings, there is greater emphasis on team-based care to ensure that important services are provided through collaboration among all team members and a sharing of power and trust among the professionals involved (Gardner, 2005; Sinsky et al., 2013; Wen and Schulman, 2014). MacNaughton and colleagues (2013) argue that understanding one's contribution within a team and being able to perform that role autonomously, while recognizing the unique roles of other team members, facilitates collaboration. Several new initiatives in education and practice are part of national efforts both to foster interprofessional education and practice and to break down the barriers that exist when professionals are educated in silos (see Chapter 5).

Much research has been done on a "fourth aim" beyond the Triple Aim—to improve "the work life of health care providers, including clinicians and staff" (Bodenheimer and Sinsky, 2014). Burnout among health care providers is associated with lower patient satisfaction and worse patient outcomes, including higher mortality rates (Aiken et al., 2002; Leiter et al., 1998; Poghosyan et al., 2010; Shanafelt et al., 2012; Stimpfel et al., 2012; Vahey et al., 2004). Several studies have shown that expanded team scope and roles and support for high-functioning teams enhance satisfaction among providers. Sinsky and colleagues (2013) reinforced this association of "joy of practice" and expanded roles for all team members with enhanced team satisfaction and better outcomes in an intensive study of high-functioning practices. This fourth aim for health care, which research shows is increasingly associated with the goals of the Triple Aim, is an important contextual change since *The Future of Nursing* was released, and it offers potential common ground for that report's goals for scope-of-practice expansion. It also suggests that those goals need to be part of a larger effort to expand the scope and role of many clinical team members so as to improve outcomes and reduce burnout. In reaction to *The Future of Nursing*, ACP (2010) said, "today, no one clinician should practice independently of other clinicians" (p. 1). Accordingly, this may be an opportune time for discussions about how mutual support of scope expansion can support team-based care and reduce provider burnout.

FINDINGS AND CONCLUSION

Significant progress has been made toward reducing scope-of-practice restrictions nationwide. As the health care environment continues to evolve and to demand more value-based care, the full contribution of APRNs and other health care providers is critical. As health care reform expands access to care, states with restrictive laws for NPs are limiting access and the potential for APRNs to contribute fully to health care and to the optimal functioning of the health care team. More states are allowing NPs full practice authority as primary care providers. Moving forward, more efforts are needed to work with a broader coalition of stakeholders and providers to converge around issues of scope-of-practice restrictions and advocate for legislation that supports full practice authority for APRNs.

Findings

This study yielded the following findings on nursing care and scope of practice:

Finding 2-1. APRNs provide high-quality care to patients.

Finding 2-2. Progress has been made toward expanding scope of practice for APRNs, either fully or incrementally.

Finding 2-3. Physician organizations' opposition to expansion of scope of practice for APRNs remains a significant obstacle.

Finding 2-4. Health care is moving toward interdisciplinary, interdependent teams of health care professionals that are able to provide more comprehensive services.

Finding 2-5. Evidence demonstrates that expanded team scope and roles as well as high-functioning teams enhance satisfaction among health care providers. Provider burnout is associated with lower patient satisfaction and worse patient outcomes, including higher mortality rates.

Conclusion

The committee drew the following conclusion about progress toward removing barriers to practice and care:

Continued work is needed to remove scope-of-practice barriers. The policy and practice context has shifted since The Future of Nursing *was released. This shift has created an opportunity for nurses, physicians, and other providers to work together to find common ground in the new context of health care, and to devise solutions that work for all professions and patients.*

RECOMMENDATION

Recommendation 1: Build Common Ground Around Scope of Practice and Other Issues in Policy and Practice. The Future of Nursing: Campaign for Action (the Campaign) should broaden its coalition to include more

diverse stakeholders. The Campaign should build on its successes and work with other health professions groups, policy makers, and the community to build common ground around removing scope-of-practice restrictions, increasing interprofessional collaboration, and addressing other issues to improve health care practice in the interest of patients.

REFERENCES

AANP (American Association of Nurse Practitioners). 2015. *State practice environment.* http://www.aanp.org/legislation-regulation/state-legislation/state-practice-environment (accessed September 23, 2015).

ACP (American College of Physicians). 2010. *American College of Physicians response to the Institute of Medicine's report,* The Future of Nursing: Leading Change, Advancing Health. https://www.acponline.org/newsroom/future_nursing_release.pdf (accessed September 23, 2015).

Adashi, E. Y. 2013. *The JAMA forum: California dreamin'—the story of Senate (scope-of-practice) Bill 491.* http://newsatjama.jama.com/2013/09/25/the-jama-forum-california-dreamin-the-story-of-senate-scope-of-practice-bill-491 (accessed September 23, 2015).

AHRQ (Agency for Healthcare Research and Quality). 2011. *Primary care workforce facts and stats no. 2: The number of nurse practitioners and physician assistants practicing primary care in the United States.* http://www.ahrq.gov/sites/default/files/publications/files/pcwork2.pdf (accessed November 7, 2015).

Aiken, L. H., S. P. Clarke, D. M. Sloane, J. Sochalski, and J. H. Silber. 2002. Hospital nurse staffing and patient mortality, nurse burnout, and job dissatisfaction. *Journal of the American Medical Association* 288(16):1987-1993.

AMA (American Medical Association). 2010. *AMA responds to IOM report on future of nursing.* http://www.msv.org/DocumentVault/PDFs/101410-AMA-response-to-IOM-report-PDF.aspx (accessed September 25, 2015).

Auerbach, D. I., P. G. Chen, M. W. Friedberg, R. Reid, C. Lau, P. I. Buerhaus, and A. Mehrotra. 2013. Nurse-managed health centers and patient-centered medical homes could mitigate expected primary care physician shortage. *Health Affairs* 32(11):1933-1941.

Beck, M. 2014. The nurse will see you now. *Wall Street Journal,* January 26. http://www.wsj.com/news/articles/SB20001424052702304856504579340603947983912 (accessed September 21, 2015).

Bodenheimer T., and C. Sinsky. 2014. From triple to quadruple aim: Care of the patient requires care of the provider. *Annals of Family Medicine* 12(6):573-576.

Buerhaus, P. I., C. M. DesRoches, R. Dittus, and K. Donelan. 2015. Practice characteristics of primary care nurse practitioners and physicians. *Nursing Outlook* 63(2):144-153.

California Medical Association. 2013. *Issue detail: SB 491 (Hernandez): Nurse practitioners.* http://www.cmanet.org/issues/detail/?issue=sb-491-hernandez-nurse-practitioners (accessed September 23, 2015).

CCNA (Center to Champion Nursing in America). 2014a (unpublished). *Future of Nursing: Campaign for Action presentation, December 19, 2014.* Washington, DC: CCNA.

CCNA. 2014b (unpublished). *Progress on removing barriers to APRN practice and care.* Washington, DC: CCNA.

CCNA. 2015. *Future of Nursing: Campaign for Action dashboard indicators.* http://campaignforaction.org/dashboard (accessed September 12, 2015).

Chen, C., S. Petterson, R. L. Phillips, F. Mullan, A. Bazemore, and S. D. O'Donnell. 2013. Towards graduate medical education (GME) accountability: Measuring the outcomes of GME institutions. *Academic Medicine: Journal of the Association of American Medical Colleges* 88(9):1267-1280.

CMS (Centers for Medicare & Medicaid Services). 2012. Medicare and Medicaid programs; reform of hospital and critical access hospital conditions of participation. *Federal Register* 77(95): 29034-29076.

CMS. 2014. Medicare and Medicaid programs; regulatory provisions to promote program efficiency, transparency, and burden reduction; part II. *Federal Register* 79(91):27106-27157.

CMSS (Council of Medical Specialty Societies). 2010. *CMSS response to The Future of Nursing report.* http://www.cmss.org/uploadedfiles/site/cmss_policies/iom%20fon%20report%20 cmss%20response.pdf (accessed September 25, 2015).

DesRoches, C. M., J. Gaudet, J. Perloff, K. Donelan, L. Iezzoni, and P. Buerhaus. 2013. Using Medicare data to assess nurse practitioner-provided care. *Nursing Outlook* 61(6):400-407.

Donald, F., R. Martin-Misener, N. Carter, E. E. Donald, S. Kaasalainen, A. Wickson-Griffiths, M. Lloyd, N. Akhtar-Danesh, and A. DiCenso. 2013. A systematic review of the effectiveness of advanced practice nurses in long-term care. *Journal of Advanced Nursing* 69(10):2148-2161.

Donelan, K., C. M. DesRoches, R. S. Dittus, and P. Buerhaus. 2013. Perspectives of physicians and nurse practitioners on primary care practice. *New England Journal of Medicine* 368(20): 1898-1906.

FTC (Federal Trade Commission). 2011a. *FTC staff letter to the Honorable Daphne Campbell, Florida House of Representatives, concerning Florida House Bill 4103 and the regulation of advanced registered nurse practitioners (March 22, 2011).* https://www.ftc.gov/sites/default/ files/documents/advocacy_documents/ftc-staff-letter-honorable-daphne-campbell-florida-house-representatives-concerning-florida-house/v110004campbell-florida.pdf (accessed November 5, 2015).

FTC. 2011b. *FTC staff letter to the Honorable Rodney Ellis and the Honorable Royce West, the Senate of the State of Texas, concerning Texas Senate Bills 1260 and 1339 and the regulation of advanced practice registered nurses (May 11, 2011).* https://www.ftc.gov/sites/default/files/ documents/advocacy_documents/ftc-staff-letter-honorable-rodney-ellis-and-honorable-royce-west-senate-state-texas-concerning-texas/v110007texasaprn.pdf (accessed November 5, 2015).

FTC. 2012a. *FTC staff comment before the Louisiana House of Representatives on the likely competitive impact of Louisiana House Bill 951 concerning advanced practice registered nurses ("APRNs") (April 20, 2012).* https://www.ftc.gov/sites/default/files/documents/advocacy_ documents/ftc-staff-comment-louisiana-house-representatives-likely-competitive-impact-louisiana-house-bill-951/120425louisianastaffcomment.pdf (accessed November 5, 2015).

FTC. 2012b. *FTC staff letter to the Honorable Paul Hornback, Senator, Commonwealth of Kentucky State Senate concerning Kentucky Senate Bill 187 and the regulation of advanced practice registered nurses (March 26, 2012).* https://www.ftc.gov/sites/default/files/documents/ advocacy_documents/ftc-staff-letter-honorable-paul-hornback-senator-commonwealth-kentucky-state-senate-concerning/120326ky_staffletter.pdf (accessed November 5, 2015).

FTC. 2012c. *FTC staff letter to the Honorable Representative Jeanne Kirkton, Missouri House of Representatives, concerning Missouri House Bill 1399 and the regulation of certified registered nurse anesthetists (March 27, 2012).* https://www.ftc.gov/sites/default/files/documents/ advocacy_documents/ftc-staff-letter-honorable-representative-jeanne-kirkton-missouri-house-representatives-concerning/120327kirktonmissouriletter.pdf (accessed November 5, 2015).

FTC. 2012d. *FTC staff testimony before subcommittee of the WV legislature on laws governing the scope of practice for advanced practice registered nurses and possible revisions to remove practice restrictions (September 10-12, 2012).* https://www.ftc.gov/sites/default/files/documents/ advocacy_documents/ftc-staff-testimony-subcommittee-wv-legislature-laws-governing-scope-practice-advanced-practice/120907wvatestimony.pdf (accessed November 5, 2015).

FTC. 2013a. *FTC staff comment to the Honorable Heather A. Steans, Illinois State Senate, concerning Illinois Senate Bill 1662 and the regulation of certified registered nurse anesthetists (CRNAs) (April 19, 2013).* https://www.ftc.gov/sites/default/files/documents/advocacy_documents/ftc-staff-comment-honorable-heather.steans-illinois-state-senate-concerning-illinois-senate-bill-1662-and-regulation-certified/130424illinois-sb1662.pdf (accessed November 5, 2015).

FTC. 2013b. *FTC staff letter to the Honorable Theresa W. Conroy, Connecticut House of Representatives, concerning the likely competitive impact of Connecticut House Bill 6391 on advance practice registered nurses (March 19, 2013).* https://www.ftc.gov/sites/default/files/documents/advocacy_documents/ftc-staff-letter-honorable-theresa-w.conroy-connecticut-house-representatives-concerning-likely-competitive-impact-connecticut-house-bill/130319aprn conroy.pdf (accessed November 5, 2015).

FTC. 2014a. *FTC staff comment before the Massachusetts House of Representatives regarding House Bill 2009 (H.2009) concerning supervisory requirements for nurse practitioners and nurse anesthetists (January 17, 2014).* https://www.ftc.gov/sites/default/files/documents/advocacy_documents/ftc-staff-comment-massachusetts-house-representatives-regarding-house-bill-6-h.2009-concerning-supervisory-requirements-nurse-practitioners-nurse-anesthetists/1401 23massachusettnursesletter.pdf (accessed November 5, 2015).

FTC. 2014b. *Policy perspectives: Competition and the regulation of advanced practice nurses.* Washington, DC: FTC.

FTC. 2015a. *FTC staff comment to representative Jeanne Kirkton, Missouri House of Representatives, regarding the competitive impact of Missouri House Bill 633 on collaborative practice arrangements between physicians and advance practice registered nurses (April 21, 2015).* https://www.ftc.gov/system/files/documents/advocacy_documents/ftc-staff-comment-representative-jeanne-kirkton-missouri-house-representatives-regarding-competitive/150422missourihouse.pdf (accessed November 5, 2015).

FTC. 2015b. *FTC staff comment to South Carolina representative Jenny A. Horne regarding House Bill 3508 and 3078 on advanced practice registered nurse regulations (November 2, 2015).* https://www.ftc.gov/system/files/documents/advocacy_documents/ftc-staff-comment-south-carolina-representative-jenny.horne-regarding-house-bill-3508-3078-advanced-practice-registered-nurse-regulations/151103scaprn.pdf (accessed November 5, 2015).

Gardner, D. B. 2005. Ten lessons in collaboration. *Online Journal of Issues in Nursing* 10(1). http://gm6.nursingworld.org/MainMenuCategories/ANAMarketplace/ANAPeriodicals/OJIN/Tableof Contents/Volume102005/No1Jan05/tpc26_116008.aspx (accessed September 23, 2015).

Hain, D., and L. M. Fleck. 2014. Barriers to NP practice that impact healthcare redesign. *Online Journal of Issues in Nursing* 19(2). http://www.nursingworld.org/mainmenucategories/anamarket place/anaperiodicals/ojin/tableofcontents/vol-19-2014/no2-may-2014/barriers-to-np-practice. html#ACP (accessed September 23, 2015).

HRSA (Health Resources and Services Administration). 2010. *The registered nurse population: Findings from the 2008 National Sample Survey of Registered Nurses.* http://bhpr.hrsa.gov/healthworkforce/rnsurveys/rnsurveyfinal.pdf (accessed November 5, 2015).

HRSA. 2013. *Projecting the supply and demand for primary care practitioners through 2020.* Rockville, MD: U.S. Department of Health and Human Services.

HRSA. 2014a. *Highlights from the 2012 National Sample Survey of Nurse Practitioners.* Rockville, MD: U.S. Department of Health and Human Services. http://bhpr.hrsa.gov/healthworkforce/supplydemand/nursing/nursepractitionersurvey/npsurveyhighlights.pdf (accessed September 23, 2015).

HRSA. 2014b. *The future of the nursing workforce: national- and state-level projections, 2012-2025.* Rockville, MD: U.S. Department of Health and Human Services.

Iglehart, J. K. 2013. Expanding the role of advanced nurse practitioners—risks and rewards. *New England Journal of Medicine* 368:1935-1941.

IOM (Institute of Medicine). 2011. *The future of nursing: Leading change, advancing health.* Washington, DC: The National Academies Press.

Kilpatrick, K., S. Kaasalainen, F. Donald, K. Reid, N. Carter, D. Bryant-Lukosius, R. Martin-Misener, P. Harbman, D. A. Marshall, R. Charbonneau-Smith, and A. DiCenso. 2014. The effectiveness and cost-effectiveness of clinical nurse specialists in outpatient roles: A systematic review. *Journal of Evaluation in Clinical Practice* 20:1106-1123.

Kuo, Y., N. Chen, J. Baillargeon, M. A. Raji, and J. S. Goodwin. 2015. Potentially preventable hospitalizations in Medicare patients with diabetes: A comparison of primary care provided by nurse practitioners versus doctors. *Medical Care* 53(9):776-783.

Lamprecht, S. 2015. *The future of nursing: Leading change, advancing health.* Presentation to IOM Committee for Assessing Progress on Implementing the Recommendations of the Institute of Medicine Report *The Future of Nursing: Leading Change, Advancing Health.* Washington, DC, July 28, 2015.

Leiter, M. P., P. Harvie, and C. Frizzell. 1998. The correspondence of patient satisfaction and nurse burnout. *Social Science & Medicine* 47(10):1611-1617.

Lewis, S. R., A. Nicholson, A. F. Smith, and P. Alderson. 2014. Physician anaesthetists versus nonphysician providers of anaesthesia for surgical patients. *Cochrane Database of Systematic Reviews* 7.

MacNaughton, K., S. Chreim, and I. L. Bourgeault. 2013. Role construction and boundaries in interprofessional primary health care teams: A qualitative study. *BMC Health Services Research* 13(1):486. http://www.biomedcentral.com/1472-6963/13 (accessed September 23, 2015).

NCSBN (National Council of State Boards of Nursing). 2009. NCSBN Model Nursing Practice Act and Model Nursing Administrative Rules. http://www.apna.org/files/public/Model_Nursing_Practice_Act_December09_final%5B1%5D.pdf (accessed September 23, 2015).

Newhouse, R. P., J. Stanik-Hutt, K. M. White, M. Johantgen, E. B. Bass, G. Zangaro, R. R. Wilson, L. Fountain, D. M. Steinwachs, L. Heindel, and J. P. Weiner. 2011. Advanced practice nurse outcomes 1990-2008: A systematic review. *Nursing Economics* 29(5):1-21.

Pearson, L. 2014. *2014 Pearson Report.* Burlington, MA: Jones & Bartlett Learning, LLC.

Petterson, S. M., W. R. Liaw, R. L. Phillips, D. L. Rabin, D. S. Meyers, and A. W. Bazemore. 2012. Projecting US primary care physician workforce needs: 2010-2025. *Annals of Family Medicine* 10(6):503-509.

Poghosyan, L., S. P. Clarke, M. Finlayson, and L. H. Aiken. 2010. Nurse burnout and quality of care: Cross-national investigation in six countries. *Research in Nursing & Health* 33(4):288-298.

Poghosyan, L., A. Nannini, A. Smaldone, S. Clarke, N. C. O'Rourke, B. G. Rosato, and B. Berkowitz. 2013. Revisiting scope of practice facilitators and barriers for primary care nurse practitioners: A qualitative investigation. *Policy, Politics & Nursing Practice* 14(1):6-15.

RWJF (Robert Wood Johnson Foundation). 2013. *How to foster interprofessional collaboration between physicians and nurses? Incorporating lessons learned in pursuing a consensus.* http://www.rwjf.org/content/dam/farm/reports/program_results_reports/2013/rwjf403637 (accessed September 23, 2015).

Shanafelt, T. D., S. Boone, L. Tan, L. N. Dyrbye, M. Sotile, D. Satele, C. P. West, J. Sloan, and M. R. Oreskovich. 2012. Burnout and satisfaction with work-life balance among U.S. physicians relative to the general U.S. population. *Archives of Internal Medicine* 172(18):1377-1385.

Sinsky, C. A., R. Willard-Grace, A. M. Schutzbank, D. Margolius, and T. Bodenheimer. 2013. In search of joy in practice: A report of 23 high-functioning primary care practices. *Annals of Family Medicine* 11(3):272-278.

Stange, K. 2014. How does provider supply and regulation influence health care markets? Evidence from nurse practitioners and physician assistants. *Journal of Health Economics* 33:1-27.

Stanik-Hutt J., R. P. Newhouse, K. M. White, M. Johantgen, E. B. Bass, G. Zangaro, R. Wilson, L. Fountain, D. M. Steinwachs, L. Heindel, and J. P. Weiner. 2013. The quality and effectiveness of care provided by nurse practitioners. *Journal for Nurse Practitioners* 9(8):492-500.

Stimpfel, A. W., D. M. Sloane, and L. H. Aiken. 2012. The longer the shifts for hospital nurses, the higher the levels of burnout and patient dissatisfaction. *Health Affairs* 31(11):2501-2509.

VA (U.S. Department of Veterans Affairs). 2012. *VA Office of Nursing Services (ONS) annual report 2012.* http://www.va.gov/nursing/docs/2012onsAnnualRptweb.pdf (accessed September 21, 2015).

Vahey, D. C., L. H. Aiken, D. M. Sloane, S. P. Clarke, and D. Vargas. 2004. Nurse burnout and patient satisfaction. *Medical Care* 42(Suppl. 2):II57-II66.

Walters, D. 2015. California nurses lose bid to expand practices. *The Sacramento Bee.* http://www. sacbee.com/news/politics-government/capitol-alert/article25872118.html (accessed September 23, 2015).

Wen, J., and K. A. Schulman. 2014. Can team-based care improve patient satisfaction? A systematic review of randomized controlled trials. *PLoS ONE* 9(7):1-9.

Yee, T. E. Boukus, D. Cross, and D. Samuel. 2013. *Primary care workforce shortages: Nurse practitioner scope-of-practice laws and payment policies.* NIHCR Research Brief no. 13. Washington, DC: National Institute for Health Care Reform.

3

Achieving Higher Levels of Education

According to *The Future of Nursing*, the current transformation of the health care system and practice environments requires a corresponding transformation of nursing education (IOM, 2011). The report notes that the goals of nursing education will remain the same—preparing nurses to meet patient needs, function as leaders, and advance science. The report suggests, however, that to work collaboratively and effectively as partners with other professionals in a complex and changing system, nurses need to achieve higher levels of education, both at the time of entry into the profession and throughout their careers. The report offers four recommendations that have implications for the education and preparation of nurses throughout their careers:

- recommendation 4: Increase the proportion of nurses with a baccalaureate degree to 80 percent by 2020;
- recommendation 3: Implement nurse residency programs;
- recommendation 5: Double the number of nurses with a doctorate by 2020; and
- recommendation 6: Ensure that nurses engage in lifelong learning.

These recommendations fall under the Future of Nursing: Campaign for Action (the Campaign) pillar of "advancing education transformation" (CCNA, n.d.-a); each is discussed in turn in this chapter.

INCREASE THE PROPORTION OF NURSES WITH A
BACCALAUREATE DEGREE TO 80 PERCENT BY 2020

Nursing is a unique profession in that there are many different educational pathways to entry. A student may prepare for a career as a registered nurse (RN) in educational programs leading to a master's degree, a baccalaureate degree, an associate's degree, or a diploma in nursing. Some nurses who graduate with an associate's degree or diploma go on to enroll in baccalaureate completion programs, either before or after licensure. And increasingly, some nurses with baccalaureate degrees in other fields begin their nursing education in so-called direct entry master's degree programs, in which the first phase of their education prepares them for the licensure examination. Regardless of the pathway taken, students must pass the National Council Licensure Examination for Registered Nurses (NCLEX-RN) before entering the field. In 2010, when *The Future of Nursing* was released, only 36 percent of RNs entered the field with a baccalaureate degree (IOM, 2011). However, many nurses who enter the field with an associate's degree or diploma go on to obtain more education, and in 2010, half of the nursing workforce held a baccalaureate or higher degree. The report recommends that this proportion be increased, setting the ambitious goal of increasing the percentage of nurses holding a baccalaureate degree from 50 percent in 2010 to 80 percent by 2020 (see Box 3-1).

There are multiple reasons for this recommendation. *The Future of Nursing* states that more education would give nurses a wider range of competencies in such vital areas as leadership, systems thinking, evidence-based practice, health policy, and teamwork and collaboration (IOM, 2011). The report notes that the growing complexity of care requires that nurses be able to use advanced technology and to analyze and synthesize information in order to make critical decisions, and it posits that a more educated workforce would be better equipped to meet these demands. The report cites some evidence that higher education of nurses is associated with better patient outcomes.

Activity

Academic Progression in Nursing (APIN) is a program funded by the Robert Wood Johnson Foundation (RWJF) and led by the Tri-Council for Nursing (comprising the American Association of Colleges of Nursing [AACN], the American Nurses Association [ANA], the American Organization of Nurse Executives [AONE], and the National League for Nursing [NLN]). The APIN program office, located at AONE, has indicated that RWJF will have invested more than $9 million in this program by the end of 2016.[1] Nine states currently participate in APIN—California, Hawaii, Massachusetts, Montana, New Mexico, New York,

---

[1] Personal communication, B. Hoffman, Academic Progression in Nursing, July 21, 2015.

BOX 3-1

**Recommendation 4 from *The Future of Nursing*:
Increase the Proportion of Nurses with a
Baccalaureate Degree to 80 Percent by 2020**

Academic nurse leaders across all schools of nursing should work together to increase the proportion of nurses with a baccalaureate degree from 50 to 80 percent by 2020. These leaders should partner with education accrediting bodies, private and public funders, and employers to ensure funding, monitor progress, and increase the diversity of students to create a workforce prepared to meet the demands of diverse populations across the lifespan.

- The Commission on Collegiate Nursing Education, working in collaboration with the National League for Nursing Accrediting Commission, should require all nursing schools to offer defined academic pathways, beyond articulation agreements, that promote seamless access for nurses to higher levels of education.
- Health care organizations should encourage nurses with associate's and diploma degrees to enter baccalaureate nursing programs within 5 years of graduation by offering tuition reimbursement, creating a culture that fosters continuing education, and providing a salary differential and promotion.
- Private and public funders should collaborate, and when possible pool funds, to expand baccalaureate programs to enroll more students by offering scholarships and loan forgiveness, hiring more faculty, expanding clinical instruction through new clinical partnerships, and using technology to augment instruction. These efforts should take into consideration strategies to increase the diversity of the nursing workforce in terms of race/ethnicity, gender, and geographic distribution.
- The U.S. Secretary of Education, other federal agencies including the Health Resources and Services Administration, and state and private funders should expand loans and grants for second-degree nursing students.
- Schools of nursing, in collaboration with other health professional schools, should design and implement early and continuous interprofessional collaboration through joint classroom and clinical training opportunities.
- Academic nurse leaders should partner with health care organizations, leaders from primary and secondary school systems, and other community organizations to recruit and advance diverse nursing students.

SOURCE: IOM, 2011.

North Carolina, Texas, and Washington. States were selected to receive funding in the amount of $300,000 over 2 years from 2012 to 2014 and again from 2014 to 2016 because of their efforts to make progress at the state and/or regional level on increasing the proportion of baccalaureate-prepared nurses (RWJF, 2012, 2015b). The funding is intended to be used to advance strategies on academic progression and baccalaureate-prepared nurse employment (see Box 3-2).

The New Mexico Nursing Education Consortium (NMNEC), established in 2009-2010, has created a model whereby a common curriculum has been established and adopted by all state-funded nursing programs. The idea behind this model is that "a common nursing curriculum would provide the mechanism for seamless transfer between programs and build partnerships between universi-

---

BOX 3-2
Academic Progression in Nursing (APIN) Models

The following models for nurses' academic progression have been identified by the APIN program in collaboration with the Center to Champion Nursing in America (CCNA).

Baccalaureate Completion Programs at Community Colleges

This model enables registered nurses (RNs) to complete their baccalaureate degree in a community college setting. Nurses who have limited access to university options or are restricted by work or family commitments from moving out of the area can benefit in particular from this model. For community colleges to confer a baccalaureate degree, state legislative changes are often required, and the college's mission statement may have to be revised. Currently, 22 states allow community colleges to confer baccalaureate degrees, 7 of which can confer a baccalaureate in nursing. In only two of these seven states—Florida and Washington—is there a structured path to achieving baccalaureate completion at the community college level.

State or Regionally Shared Competency or Outcomes-Based Curriculum

In this model, a shared understanding and a common goal and framework are developed that extend across community college associate degree in nursing programs and includes baccalaureate completion at the university level. The curriculum is not standardized, but the model is intended to achieve standardized outcomes.

Accelerated Options: RN to Master of Science in Nursing (MSN)

This model often offers a shorter and more streamlined route for associate's degree–prepared nurses to obtain an advanced degree than is required for tradities and community colleges" (Landen, 2015; Liesveld et al., 2015, p. 16). The statewide curriculum received approval from the associate's and baccalaureate state-funded schools in 2012 (Landen, 2015). Students enroll at both the community college and the university. They complete their prerequisite courses at the community college level and receive their associate's degree from the community college and their baccalaureate degree from the university concurrently (Hoffman, 2015; Landen, 2015). This model allows students to remain in their rural communities rather than incur the time and expense of moving to a large university; while attending a local community college for the majority of required courses, they can complete all additional courses and the final semester for the baccalaureate program either online or in clinical settings (Landen, 2015). Both

---

tional MSN programs. The RN-to-MSN program is designed for RNs who do not hold a baccalaureate degree and who wish to move quickly into advanced practice. Some programs permit students to "step out" part way through the program with a baccalaureate, while others do not.

Shared Statewide or Regional Curriculum

In this model, universities and community colleges form partnerships to collaborate on a shared curriculum or shared components of a curriculum. This model permits students to transition seamlessly from an associate's to a baccalaureate program without repeating coursework or managing unfulfilled prerequisites. As part of the program, some schools also share faculty, which reduces faculty load and increases the availability of programs. Implementing a shared curriculum requires formal articulation agreements, changes to curricula, and buy-in from legislative bodies and institutions.

Shared Baccalaureate Curriculum

A fifth emerging model has community colleges and colleges/universities working together to establish a baccalaureate curriculum whereby the student is able to take some classes at both the community college and the university, obtaining RN licensure only upon completion of the baccalaureate degree. Such baccalaureate completion programs may shorten the time between nurses' attainment of associate's and baccalaureate degrees, facilitated by focused efforts such as those undertaken through APIN's shared curriculum models. In New York, for example, nearly 80 percent of participants in these programs progressed from an associate's to a baccalaureate degree within about 1 year.

SOURCES: CCNA, 2012, 2013a; Gerardi, 2015; Personal communication, B. Hoffman, Academic Progression in Nursing, July 21, 2015.

the New Mexico Board of Nursing and RWJF, through the APIN program, have provided funding to support this model (Liesveld et al., 2015).

Overall, several APIN states have reported that they have successfully increased the percentage of baccalaureate nurses in the workforce beyond the national average increase, although programs and outcomes have varied among states (Gerardi, 2015). The Campaign is coordinating and learning from these state-level efforts with the goal of standardizing and streamlining academic progression at the national level. The Campaign convened leaders in the area of academic progression in 2015 and is developing a strategy for advancing academic progression models. The impetus for these efforts is the belief that "standardizing prerequisites and general education requirements across the nation in all nursing programs is a fundamental step in advancing nursing education and removing barriers that make it difficult for nursing students to move from an associate degree in nursing to a [baccalaureate] program" (CCNA, 2015a, p. 4). The Campaign also has provided technical assistance on academic progression to 25 state Action Coalitions and State Implementation Program grantees.

In a survey conducted by TCC Group for the Campaign, the majority of state Action Coalitions indicated that education goals were their top priority, with 59 percent focusing on the goal of increasing the number of nurses with baccalaureates to 80 percent by 2020 (TCC Group, 2013). The Campaign's most recent biannual operations report showed that 45 percent of all state Action Coalition funding had supported efforts under the education pillar (CCNA, 2015a).

The 2013 TCC Group survey revealed that state Action Coalitions believed they were making progress on this recommendation. All of the states that responded to the survey believed that availability of educational pathways had improved; all believed that nursing schools, universities, and community colleges were working better together; and 74 percent believed that there had been improvements in workplace policies that promoted nurses' educational attainment (TCC Group, 2013).

Progress

The Campaign tracks the progress on recommendation 4 from *The Future of Nursing* (see Box 3-2) by looking at the percentage of employed nurses with a baccalaureate degree in nursing or a higher degree, using data provided by the American Community Survey (CCNA, 2015b).[2] According to this data source, the percentage of baccalaureate-educated nurses rose from 49 percent in 2010 to 51 percent in 2014.

Significant growth has occurred in the number of nursing programs over the

---

[2] The Campaign also uses several supplemental indicators, such as annual RN graduates by degree type, and the number of current RNs who return to school to receive a baccalaureate degree (CCNA, 2015b).

BOX 3-3
Educational Pathways to Achieving a
Baccalaureate Degree in Nursing

Entry-level baccalaureate programs prepare individuals who are not already licensed registered nurses (RNs) to enter the profession with a baccalaureate degree and become licensed to practice nursing upon completion. Many entry-level baccalaureate enrollees do not have another undergraduate degree in a non-nursing field. These programs also may be referred to as generic baccalaureate or entry-level or generic bachelor of science in nursing (BSN) programs.

Accelerated baccalaureate programs are prelicensure programs that allow individuals who hold an undergraduate degree in a non-nursing field to complete a baccalaureate in nursing in less time than would be required to complete an entry-level baccalaureate. These programs also may be referred to as second-degree bachelor's programs.

Baccalaureate completion programs are postlicensure programs that provide a pathway for individuals who already have a diploma or associate's degree in nursing and are already licensed RNs to complete their baccalaureate education in nursing. These programs also may be referred to as RN-to-baccalaureate, RN-to-BSN, or associate's degree in nursing (ADN)-to-BSN programs.

---

past decade. Between 2002 and 2012, more growth was observed among 4-year college programs (from 882 in 2002 to 1,413 in 2012, a 60 percent increase) than among 2-year college programs (from 729 to 857 programs, an 18 percent increase) (Buerhaus et al., 2014). The numbers of baccalaureate nursing programs, enrollees, and graduates—including both prelicensure (entry-level and accelerated baccalaureates) and postlicensure (baccalaureate completion) (see Box 3-3)—have increased over the past 15 years (see Figures 3-1, 3-2, and 3-3, respectively).

Prelicensure Baccalaureate

The number of entry-level baccalaureate programs increased from 641 in 2010 to 704 in 2014, and the number of accelerated baccalaureate programs increased from 233 to 299 (see Figure 3-1).[3] Enrollment in prelicensure baccalaureate programs, including entry-level and accelerated baccalaureate programs, increased by 17 percent, from 161,540 to 189,729 students, during this period.

---

[3] Data received from AACN, August 28, 2015.

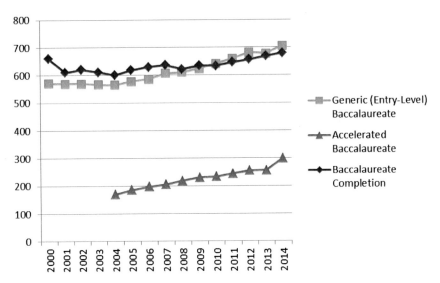

FIGURE 3-1 Number of baccalaureate nursing programs, 2000-2014.
SOURCE: Data received from the American Association of Colleges of Nursing (AACN), August 28, 2015.

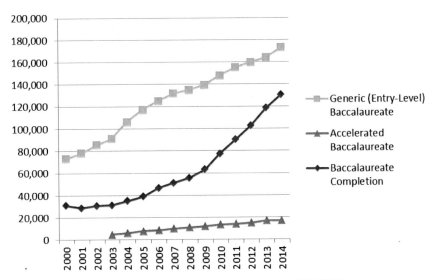

FIGURE 3-2 Enrollees in baccalaureate nursing programs 2000-2014.
NOTE: Number of enrollees is calculated from responses to American Association of Colleges of Nursing (AACN) surveying. Not all programs in the United States replied with enrollment data.
SOURCE: Data received from AACN, August 28, 2015.

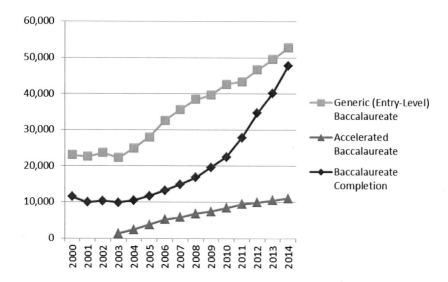

FIGURE 3-3 Graduates of baccalaureate nursing programs, 2000-2014.
NOTE: Number of graduates is calculated from responses to American Association of Colleges of Nursing (AACN) surveying. Not all programs in the United States replied with graduate data.
SOURCE: Data received from AACN, August 28, 2015.

AACN data show a consistent increase in enrollments in and graduations from entry-level baccalaureate programs over the past 10 years.

Postlicensure Baccalaureate

From 2010 to 2014, the number of baccalaureate completion programs increased steadily (see Figure 3-1), and enrollment in these programs increased by 69 percent, from 77,259 to 130,345 students (see Figure 3-2).[4] Schools have expanded capacity in baccalaureate completion programs accordingly. Given the tremendous increases in enrollment in and graduation from these programs (see Figure 3-3) and the modest increase in the number of programs in recent years, further exploration is warranted to determine how capacity has been increased, possibly through the use of innovative education delivery approaches, such as partially or fully online programs and programs offered at health care facilities (AACN, 2015a).

In addition to increased capacity in baccalaureate completion programs,

---

[4] Data received from AACN, August 28, 2015.

some state legislatures have undertaken efforts to require nurses to obtain a baccalaureate within 10 years of entry into practice (known colloquially as "BSN-in-10") (Larson, 2012). In 2008, ANA's House of Delegates passed a BSN-in-10 resolution that voices support for initiatives that require nurses to obtain a baccalaureate degree within 10 years after receiving their initial nursing license (Edwards, 2012; Larson, 2012; Trossman, 2008). Since 2005, legislation requiring a baccalaureate within 10 years of initial licensure has been introduced in three states—New Jersey,[5] New York,[6] and Rhode Island (ANA, 2013). In New York, for example, "North Shore–LIJ Health System has required all RNs hired after September 1, 2010, to either have a baccalaureate degree or enroll in an accredited baccalaureate program within 24 months of hire in order to earn the degree within five years" (Hendren, 2010; North Shore–LIJ, 2015).

Despite the increases in numbers of baccalaureate nursing programs, enrollees, and graduates, there were until 2012 more nurses graduating with associate's than baccalaureate degrees (Buerhaus et al., 2014). In 2012, however, the number of nurses with baccalaureate degrees (including those obtained through entry-level, accelerated, and baccalaureate completion programs) surpassed the number with associate's degrees, increasing to 53 percent of the nursing workforce (see Figure 3-4). The increase in first-time takers of the NCLEX-RN with a baccalaureate degree continues, while the growth of first-time takers with an associate's degree has slowed (Salsberg, 2015).

Funding for Nursing Education

The Future of Nursing calls on the Health Resources and Services Administration (HRSA) and other federal agencies to "expand loans and grants for second-degree nursing students." However, HRSA funding for nursing education programs has been relatively flat over the past decade, except for increased investments in the Nurse Corps Loan Repayment and Scholarship Program (formerly called the Nursing Education Loan Repayment Program) and the Nurse Faculty Loan Program, which saw increases in funding between 2008 and 2010. The Nurse Corps programs received an additional investment of $27 million from the American Recovery and Reinvestment Act (ARRA) in 2009, and since then has been funded at a higher level than before that increase occurred. Similarly, base appropriations for the Nurse Faculty Loan Program increased between 2008 and 2009 from $7,860,000 to $11,500,000, but in 2009, this program also received a further investment of $12,000,000 from the ARRA, and it has been funded at that higher level since then (HRSA, 2009, 2011, 2013, 2015) (see Figure 3-5).

---

[5] See http://www.njleg.state.nj.us/bills/BillView.asp?BillNumber=A3501 (accessed September 18, 2015); http://www.njleg.state.nj.us/bills/BillView.asp?BillNumber=S1182 (accessed September 18, 2015).

[6] See http://assembly.state.ny.us/leg/?bn=A03945 (accessed September 18, 2015).

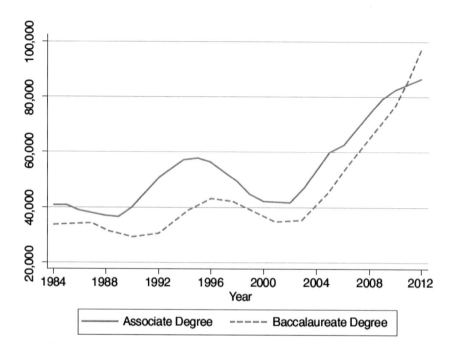

FIGURE 3-4 Number of nursing baccalaureate and associate's degree graduates, 1984-2012.
NOTE: Baccalaureate degrees encompass entry-level, accelerated, and baccalaureate completion programs. Data source: Integrated Postsecondary Education Data System (IPEDS).
SOURCE: Buerhaus et al., 2014. Reprinted from Nursing Economic$, 2014, Volume 32, Number 6, pp. 290-311. Reprinted with permission of the publisher, Jannetti Publications, Inc., East Holly Avenue/Box 56, Pitman, NJ 08071-0056; (856) 256-2300; FAX (856) 589-7463; www.nursingeconomics.net. For a sample copy of the journal, please contact the publisher.

Comprehensive information on sources of and recent trends in other funding for nursing education programs, including that provided by states and private sources, is lacking. AACN does provide a list of state loan forgiveness programs on its state policy resources page[7]; some of the listed programs are for practicing nurses, and many are for nurse educators and faculty.

---

[7] See http://www.aacn.nche.edu/government-affairs/state-advocacy/resources (accessed September 15, 2015).

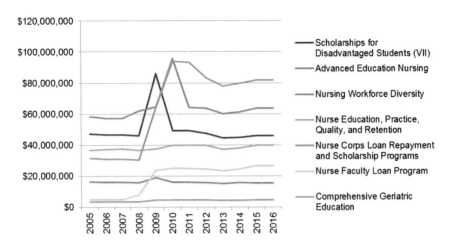

FIGURE 3-5 Health Resources and Services Administration (HRSA) Title VIII funding, fiscal years 2005-2016.
SOURCES: HRSA, 2009, 2011, 2013, 2015.

Employment

Employer preference for BSN AACN data indicate an increasing preference for hiring baccalaureate-educated nurses. However, a majority of employers do not require nurses to have a baccalaureate (see Table 3-1).

Other data likewise show that market forces tend to be favoring the baccalaureate over the associate's degree. At the committee's July workshop, the Accreditation Commission for Education in Nursing (ACEN) presented data showing that the mean job placement rate has decreased for nurses with associate's degrees and diplomas while remaining relatively steady for those with baccalaureate and master's degrees (Stoll, 2015) (see Figure 3-6).

An annual survey of California hospitals showed that in 2014, 9.8 percent of responding hospitals required nurses to have a baccalaureate as a condition

TABLE 3-1 Percentage of Employers Indicating a Requirement or Preference for Baccalaureate-Prepared Nurses, 2011-2014

	2011	2012	2013	2014
Require	30.1	39.1	43.7	45.1
Strong preference	76.6	77.4	78.6	79.6

SOURCES: AACN, 2011, 2012a, 2013, 2014.

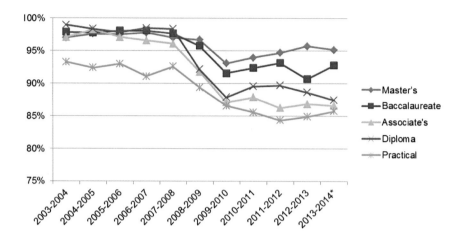

FIGURE 3-6 Mean job placement rate by degree type.
* Data for 2013-2014 are preliminary.
SOURCE: Stoll, 2015.

for employment, an increase from 8.2 percent in 2013, 7.3 percent in 2012, and 4.6 percent in 2011 (Bates et al., 2015). The percentage of responding hospitals preferring a baccalaureate degree also increased from 52.3 percent in 2011 to 60.5 percent in 2014. In 2014, 11.8 percent of hospitals said they required new hires to complete a baccalaureate within a certain amount of time, typically 2-3 years. While other studies have found that salary differentials between nurses with associate's and baccalaureate degrees are due to factors beyond just educational attainment (Duffy et al., 2014; Spetz, 2002), 69 hospitals in the California survey (32.9 percent of respondents) indicated that they do base salary on the type of degree held, and nearly half use advanced certification as a basis for salary differentials. Likewise, Auerbach and colleagues (2015) found that there has been a consistent $10,000 wage gap between nurses with an associate's degree in nursing (ADN) and those with a bachelor's degree in nursing (BSN) over the past decade, but this gap has not widened as might be expected with an increasing preference for BSN preparation.

In addition to the employment trends described above, as of 2013, ANCC Magnet® recognition required that organizations have a plan for how they will achieve an 80 percent baccalaureate-educated nursing workforce by 2020 (Lewis, 2015). However, ANCC is not prescriptive about how organizations should achieve this goal or what milestones should be reached in the interim. Currently, Magnet hospitals are more likely than other hospitals to employ baccalaureate-prepared nurses. According to ANCC, 55.6 percent of nurses working in Magnet hospitals have a BSN or higher degree (ANCC, 2014). As of January 1, 2013, Magnet recognition also required that nurse leaders have a minimum of a baccalaureate in nursing and that chief nursing officers (CNOs) have a master's or higher degree (ANCC, 2015).

Auerbach and colleagues (2015) report that the unemployment rate for nurses with a baccalaureate degree is lower than that for nurses with an associate's degree, and this gap has widened in recent years; a similar gap in hospital employment also appears to be growing. According to the authors, "the timing of the divergence in unemployment rates between ADN and BSN-prepared RNs, and to some extent, the increase in employment of BSNs in hospitals found in this analysis, appears to have occurred several years before the 2010 Institute of Medicine (IOM) report *The Future of Nursing: Leading Change, Advancing Health* was released. . . . The IOM emphasized the need for a more highly educated nursing workforce, and its wide dissemination more than likely provided 'tipping point' information that influenced employers' decisions to prefer the more highly educated BSN" (Auerbach et al., 2015, pp. 11-12). These authors also identify shifts in locations of practice for baccalaureate- and associate's-prepared nurses between 2003 and 2013. The percentage of nurses with baccalaureate degrees in office-based and ambulatory care settings fell from 9.1 percent in 2003 to 7.7 percent in 2013, while the percentage of nurses with associate's degrees in long-term care increased from 13.0 percent to 18.0 percent. Roughly 10 percent of nurses with associate's degrees "shifted from hospitals to long-term care settings over the period" (Auerbach et al., 2015, p. 10). Nurses with baccalaureate degrees bring skills and competencies, leadership capacity, and organizational skills that are needed in all practice settings, including, and perhaps increasingly, those outside of the hospital setting.

Discussion

The recommendation of *The Future of Nursing* calling for 80 percent of nurses to hold a baccalaureate degree by 2020 has been described as "aspirational" (McMenamin, 2015). With approximately half of the nation's 3 million nurses currently holding an associate's degree, it will be extraordinarily difficult to achieve this goal by 2020. The effort to build a baccalaureate-prepared nursing workforce is not new, but has been boosted by this recommendation of *The Future of Nursing*, as well as the efforts of the Campaign and other organizations. As far back as 1965, recognizing the increasing complexity of knowledge needed by nurses, ANA published a position paper recommending that "minimum preparation for beginning professional nursing practice . . . should be baccalaureate degree education in nursing" (ANA, 1965). This position paper was reaffirmed by an ANA House of Delegates resolution in 1978, calling for the baccalaureate degree to be the entry degree for nursing by 1985 (ANA, 1995).

The Future of Nursing cites evidence to support the association between higher proportions of nurses with a baccalaureate degree and better patient out-comes, but it characterizes this evidence as inconclusive. Since the report's publi-cation, however, the body of evidence on this association has strengthened (Aiken et al., 2011, 2014; Blegen et al., 2013; Cho et al., 2015; Kutney-Lee et al., 2013; Naylor et al., 2015; Yakusheva et al., 2014a,b; You et al., 2013). Studies show that hospitals with a higher percentage of nurses with baccalaureate degrees have bet-ter patient outcomes, and many of the outcomes associated with having a higher proportion of BSN-prepared nurses are associated with cost savings (Yakusheva et al., 2014a,b). With quality of care becoming increasingly important as a deter-minant of payment for health care services, this evidence suggests that providers may have a financial incentive to have a more highly educated nursing workforce.

Barriers to Nurses' Academic Progression

Despite the long history of the movement toward baccalaureate-prepared nurses and the apparent benefit of an increase in nurses with this level of educa-tion, barriers to meeting this recommendation of the Institute of Medicine (IOM) report remain. Schools of nursing report turning qualified applicants away from baccalaureate programs because of faculty shortages, a lack of clinical sites or classroom space, and budget constraints (AACN, 2015b). To advance achieve-ment of this recommendation, both entry-level baccalaureate and baccalaureate completion pathways need to be strengthened. Innovative models of academic progression such as those described earlier (see Box 3-3) need to be expanded upon and implemented more widely.

Nurses continue to perceive barriers and challenges to obtaining higher education both at the entry level and through academic progression programs. These barriers include financial concerns; a lack of time and competing priorities; logistical concerns; a lack of academic support; and a perceived lack of clinical, professional, or economic value in a higher degree (Altmann, 2011; Bates et al., 2014; Duffy et al., 2014; Orsolini-Hain, 2012; Rusin, 2015; Snyder, 2015).

Barriers identified by hospitals and health systems with regard to supporting academic progression for their nurse employees include insufficient funds for incentives (tuition reimbursement, promotions, pay differentials, bonuses) and a lack of baccalaureate programs in the community (Bates et al., 2014). There is evidence that some health care delivery systems do provide incentives and path-ways for their nurse employees to work toward higher degrees and certifications, including on-site training programs, partnerships with local colleges, tuition reimbursement, scheduling flexibility, and loan repayment (Bates et al., 2015; Pittman et al., 2013a). Some suggest, however, that these incentives and pathways are not widespread, particularly in nonhospital settings (Pittman et al., 2013a).

Issues of the cost and convenience to nurses of pursuing higher education—whether at the entry level or after entering the workforce—need to be addressed. Expanded use of online methods of delivering education may be one way to address barriers related to cost, scheduling, and convenience. A survey of ACEN-accredited nursing programs found that most now use some type of online delivery and have done so for the past 5 or more years, but that this approach is more common among master's and baccalaureate than among associate's degree programs (Stoll, 2015).

Requirements and preferences for BSN preparation appear to be widespread in hospitals, and incentives for nurses to attain a BSN and the promotion of academic progression are seen predominantly in hospitals and large health systems rather than in community settings. If incentives for an increasingly baccalaureate-prepared workforce and for baccalaureate completion—including tuition reimbursement, pay differentials, and greater opportunities for advancement—are offered mainly in acute care settings, nurses with associate's degrees may be channeled into other care settings, including long-term care, home health, and other community settings.

Quality of New Programs

Tremendous growth has been seen in the numbers of programs and enrollees in all types of nursing education programs over the last decade. This increase in quantity is commendable; however, corresponding attention to the quality of the education offered is essential. As discussed earlier, baccalaureate completion programs and enrollment in these programs, in particular, have increased dramatically in recent years. According to AACN, "Given the dramatic increase in the number of [baccalaureate completion] programs and enrolling students, the need to maintain academic rigor in these programs is growing in importance, including the need for quality practice experiences" (AACN, 2012b, p. 1). A 2014 study found that recent nursing literature and guidance from nursing accreditation bodies lacked information about the content and competencies that are or should be included in the curricula of baccalaureate completion programs (McEwen et al., 2014). Buerhaus and colleagues (2014) note that "worries about the quality of RN graduates extend across all program types, including doctor of nursing practice and traditional doctoral programs" (p. 295).

Implicit in the recommendation of *The Future of Nursing* to increase the percentage of nurses with baccalaureate degrees is an assumption that the added education would improve nurses' knowledge and skills. As educational institutions respond to the demand for baccalaureate-educated nurses, more attention will be needed to the quality of new programs and emerging models of education to ensure that nurses—and patients—are reaping the assumed benefits of additional education.

Educational Attainment and Diversity

Community colleges and associate's degree nursing programs are an important pathway into the profession for many people, in particular for economically and/or educationally disadvantaged and underrepresented populations (American Association of Community Colleges, 2010; Bell, 2012; Fulcher and Mullin, 2011; Mullin, 2012; Talamantes et al., 2014). Minority students are more likely than their white counterparts to enter the nursing field with an associate's degree rather than a baccalaureate: 40 percent of white new RN graduates held a baccalaureate in 2013, compared with just 36 percent of African American graduates and 26 percent of Hispanic/Latino graduates (CCNA, n.d.-b). However, minority nurses are slightly more likely than their white counterparts to obtain a baccalaureate or higher degree during their career (HRSA, 2010). These data indicate that minority nurses benefit from both associate's degree and baccalaureate completion programs.

Like minority students, students with lower incomes also benefit from associate's degree programs offered by community colleges. Students attending community colleges to earn an associate's degree generally have lower incomes and different economic backgrounds relative to their counterparts attending entry-level baccalaureate programs (Fulcher and Mullin, 2011), and 41 percent of all undergraduates living in poverty are enrolled in community colleges (Mullin, 2012; NCES, 2011).

Minority and disadvantaged students, then, utilize associate's degree programs, baccalaureate completion programs, and community colleges to enter and advance in the field of nursing. Even as the profession pursues the goal of an 80 percent baccalaureate-trained workforce, these pathways will remain important for maintaining or increasing the diversity of the nursing workforce.

Findings and Conclusions

Findings

This study yielded the following findings about baccalaureate education for nurses:

Finding 3-1. Between 2010 and 2014, the proportion of employed nurses with a baccalaureate degree or higher in nursing increased from 49 percent to 51 percent.

Finding 3-2. Baccalaureate nursing programs of various types (entry-level, accelerated, and baccalaureate completion) have increased in number, enrollees, and graduates. The number of such programs has been increasing at a faster rate than the number of associate's degree and diploma programs.

Since 2012, more nurses have graduated each year with baccalaureate degrees (including degrees from entry-level, accelerated, and baccalaureate completion programs) than with associate's degrees.

Finding 3-3. As baccalaureate programs have grown, some concerns have been raised about the quality of these new and expanded programs.

Finding 3-4. Some APIN states have reported greater increases in their BSN nursing workforce relative to the national average increase, although outcomes vary widely from state to state.

Finding 3-5. HRSA funding for nursing education and workforce programs (Title VIII) has remained relatively flat over the past decade, aside from the Nurse Corps Loan Repayment and Scholarship Program, which saw a boost in funding from the ARRA in 2009 and has received a sustained, higher level of funding since that time.

Finding 3-6. Increasing proportions of schools of nursing are recognizing and employers are showing a preference for BSN-prepared nurses over ADN-prepared nurses, especially in hospital and large health care systems.

Finding 3-7. Employer support for the academic progression of their associate's degree-prepared nurse employees varies, and it appears to be more common in hospitals than in other health care settings.

Finding 3-8. Associate's degree nursing programs and community colleges generally appear to provide entry into educational pathways and careers in nursing for disadvantaged and underrepresented populations.

Conclusions

The committee drew the following conclusions about progress toward a higher proportion of the nursing workforce with baccalaureate degrees:

Market forces are increasingly favoring baccalaureate-prepared nurses, particularly in hospital settings. As the RN population shifts to becoming increasingly baccalaureate-prepared, unintended consequences with respect to the employment, earning power, skills, and roles and responsibilities of those nurses who do not achieve higher education may occur.

New models of education, such as partnerships between community colleges and 4-year universities, show promise for increasing the percentage of baccalaureate-prepared nurses.

The increasing preference for baccalaureate-prepared nurses in hospital settings, as well as the provision of employee educational incentives in these settings, may result in associate's-degree RNs being shifted into nonhospital settings, especially long-term care.

IMPLEMENT NURSE RESIDENCY PROGRAMS

The Future of Nursing notes that there is a high turnover rate among newly graduated nurses: some nurses leave their first job to experience a different care setting, but some leave the profession entirely (IOM, 2011). In part to reduce this attrition, the report recommends that nurses be supported in their transition to practice through residency programs (see Box 3-4). These programs would

---

BOX 3-4
Recommendation 3 from *The Future of Nursing*:
Implement Nurse Residency Programs

State boards of nursing, accrediting bodies, the federal government, and health care organizations should take actions to support nurses' completion of a transition-to-practice program (nurse residency) after they have completed a prelicensure or advanced practice degree program or when they are transitioning into new clinical practice areas. The following actions should be taken to implement and support nurse residency programs:

- State boards of nursing, in collaboration with accrediting bodies such as the Joint Commission and the Community Health Accreditation Program, should support nurses' completion of a residency program after they have completed a prelicensure or advanced practice degree program or when they are transitioning into new clinical practice areas.
- The Secretary of Health and Human Services should redirect all graduate medical education funding from diploma nursing programs to support the implementation of nurse residency programs in rural and critical access areas.
- Health care organizations, the Health Resources and Services Administration and Centers for Medicare and Medicaid Services, and philanthropic organizations should fund the development and implementation of nurse residency programs across all practice settings.
- Health care organizations that offer nurse residency programs and foundations should evaluate the effectiveness of the residency programs in improving the retention of nurses, expanding competencies, and improving patient outcomes.

SOURCE: IOM, 2011.

---

help nurses develop such skills as organizing and prioritizing workflow and communicating with other members of the health care team. *The Future of Nursing* focuses largely on residencies for postlicensure RNs but acknowledges that going forward, residencies would be useful for nurses transitioning to new care settings or entering practice as advanced practice registered nurses (APRNs).

Activity

Residencies at various levels and in different settings have been developed or expanded in the years since the publication of *The Future of Nursing*. In general, these programs have been established and funded by the institutions that hire nurses, with the aim of enhancing on-the-job training and retention of new hires.

The University HealthSystem Consortium (UHC) and AACN have developed a program for postbaccalaureate residencies (McElroy, 2015; UHC/AACN, 2007). A UHC study conducted in 2000 showed that while many UHC hospitals had a program to prepare new graduates to become competent practitioners, there was little uniformity in the length, curriculum, or content of these programs. The UHC/AACN residency program, which started in 2002, is a year-long program built on an evidence-based curriculum, and it is designed for nurses providing direct care in a hospital acute care setting (Goode et al., 2013; McElroy, 2015; UHC/AACN, 2007). Evaluation of the program has shown that it improves retention; increases nurses' "confidence, competence, ability to organize and prioritize, communication, leadership"; and reduces stress levels (Goode et al., 2013; UHC/AACN, 2007, p. 1). More than 130 hospitals and health systems across the country are currently participating in the UHC/AACN program, and annual participation increased from 362 nurses in 2002 to 3,579 in 2010 to more than 9,000 in 2014 (McElroy, 2015). Overall, approximately 45,000 nurses have completed the program.

Transition-to-practice residency programs for nurse practitioners (NPs) operate in various health care settings, including retail clinics, federally qualified health centers (FQHCs), U.S. Department of Veterans Affairs (VA) primary care centers, and hospitals. CVS MinuteClinic has a 6-month program intended to better prepare new NP graduates for delivering care in the unique nontraditional context of a retail clinic (Gagliano, 2015). The program links new-graduate employees with preceptors who are available to support them and review their charts.

Community Health Center, Inc., an FQHC in Connecticut serving primarily low-income and uninsured populations, operates the nation's first NP transition-to-practice residency program, launched in 2007 (Flinter, 2015). At that time, the goals of the program included attracting and retaining NPs as primary care providers in the safety net setting, as well as preventing attrition by helping NPs attain the skills necessary to practice. The program has shown success in improving competence and clinical performance appraisals. The main challenge to maintaining the program is a lack of funding. Flinter (2011, 2015) notes that while the Patient Protection and Affordable Care Act (ACA) authorized funding for family NP residency programs[8] in FQHCs, that funding has never been appropriated. Some organizations have chosen to invest in these programs because of the potential return on investment, but many organizations have the will, need, and capability but not the funding to do so.

In addition to offering residencies for postbaccalaureate and mental health nurses, the Veterans Health Administration has 12-month residencies for NPs that are operated out of its VA Centers of Excellence in Primary Care Education (Gilman, 2015). This program, launched in 2011-2012 in part in response to recommendations of *The Future of Nursing* (see Box 3-4), involves formal instruction, clinical supervision and interprofessional precepting, and clinical electives. The objectives are to "advance clinical competency in team-based, patient-centered primary care," and to "advance [the] ability to work in, lead, and improve clinical teams" (Gilman, 2015). In its first 4 years, 42 residents completed the program.

Currently, 21 nurse residency programs are accredited by either the American Nurses Credentialing Center (ANCC) (accredits RN residencies, RN fellowships, and APRN fellowships) or the Commission on Collegiate Nursing Education (CCNE) (accredits postbaccalaureate nurse residencies).[9] An additional 11 programs have requested applicant status from CCNE, the first step in the accreditation review process.[10] CCNE's accreditation program grew out of recognition that the programs being implemented varied greatly, and it also was encouraged by the work of UHC and AACN to develop a curriculum that would create some commonality in year-long residency programs in acute care settings (although CCNE accreditation is not limited to programs subscribing to the UHC/AACN curriculum) (Butlin, 2015). Standards and procedures for nurse residencies are based largely on concepts of interprofessional education and collaboration. CCNE requires that residencies be built on an academic–practice partnership to bridge the transition between learning and entry into practice, and that programs be 1 year in length. Standards address faculty, institutional commitment and resources, curriculum, and program effectiveness (CCNE, 2008). To date, accreditation has been limited to acute care settings, but CCNE has heard from its communities of interest of the need to extend accreditation to all practice settings, including ambulatory care and home health (Murray, 2015).

---

[8] Section 5316 creates a "training demonstration program for family nurse practitioners to employ and provide one-year training for nurse practitioners who have graduated from a nurse practitioner program for careers as primary care providers in federally qualified health centers (FQHCs) and nurse-managed health clinics (NMHCs)."

[9] See http://directory.ccnecommunity.org/reports_residency/rptResAccreditedPrograms_New.asp? sort=institution&sProgramType= and http://www.nursecredentialing.org/Accreditation/Practice Transition/AccreditedPrograms (accessed November 22, 2015).

[10] See http://directory.ccnecommunity.org/reports_residency/rptResNewApplicants.asp?sort=residency &sProgramType= (accessed September 21, 2015).

The National Council of State Boards of Nursing (NCSBN) began work on transition-to-practice programs in 2007 (NCSBN, 2011, 2015b). In 2011, NCBSN began to study transition-to-practice models for new nurse graduates in hospitals (Phase I) and long-term care, home health, and other settings (Phase II) (NCSBN, 2015c). NCSBN's research shows that residencies in hospitals have better outcomes (in terms of competence, errors, work stress, job satisfaction, and retention) when they

- are formalized and integrated into the institution;
- last at least 6 months;
- include content on patient safety, clinical reasoning, communication and teamwork, patient-centered care, evidence-based practice, quality improvement, and informatics;
- are customized to specialty areas; and
- include time for graduates to apply the content and receive feedback (Spector et al., 2015a).

In 2012-2013, NCSBN studied the implementation of its transition-to-practice program in nonhospital settings, including nursing homes and public health and home health settings (Alexander, 2015; Spector et al., 2015b). NCSBN had difficulty finding health care delivery organizations to participate in the program (Alexander, 2015); 34 sites volunteered, but only 23 moved forward with the study and hired nurses during the study period (Spector et al., 2015b). Once settings had been separated into experimental (NCSBN transition-to-practice program) and control (existing transition-to-practice or similar programs), there was not enough statistical power to conduct quantitative analysis. The study did find, however, that NCSBN transition-to-practice sites had higher retention than the control programs, although retention was considerably lower than that seen in hospital settings (55 percent versus 83 percent) (Spector et al., 2015a,b). Qualitative analysis showed that site coordinators, preceptors, and participants held many positive views about the NCSBN program. New nurses indicated that their overall confidence and competence had improved. They did note that the curriculum of the program was too hospital-focused and should be tailored to include topics more related to long-term care and other nonhospital settings. Both participants and preceptors mentioned feeling overwhelmed at times by the added work. Some preceptors also felt that administrative support for the program was inadequate, and site coordinators noted a lack of resources as a barrier to the program's implementation.

Many of the Campaign's state Action Coalitions are working on transition-to-practice nurse residency programs. Nearly three-quarters of states responding to a 2013 survey indicated that they were working toward implementing this recommendation of *The Future of Nursing*, and 31 percent said it was a main area of focus.[11] The Campaign does not have a dashboard indicator for this recommendation, but "percent of hospitals that have new RN graduate residencies" is a supplemental indicator for the recommendation promoting baccalaureate-educated nurses (discussed in the previous section). This indicator uses data from surveys of hospitals conducted in 2011 (N = 214) and 2013 (N = 195) by Pittman and colleagues, which found an increase in the proportion of surveyed hospitals with RN graduate residency programs from 36.9 percent in 2011 to 45 percent in 2013 (CCNA, 2015b; Pittman et al., 2013b).

Several of the State Implementation Program (SIP) grants have residency programs as a primary focus (CCNA, 2013b). Examples include the following:

- Idaho has evaluated transition-to-practice nurse residency programs throughout the state to identify those that work best and are most appropriate for small, rural hospitals and critical access hospitals (CCNA, 2015c).
- The Nurse Residency Task Force in the Iowa Action Coalition has developed a competency-based curriculum for a nurse residency program that can be completed using online tools and learning modules (CCNA, 2014a; RWJF, 2014b).
- The New Jersey Action Coalition received $1.6 million from the Centers for Medicare & Medicaid Services (CMS) to develop an RN transition-to-practice program for long-term care (CCNA, 2013c). The first 1-year program started in spring 2014 and was recently completed (CCNA, 2014b), and a second iteration is currently under way (Boyd, 2015). The New Jersey Action Coalition also has created a curriculum outline for a 6-month APRN residency program in FQHCs (CCNA, 2014b).

In addition to activity at the state level, the Campaign has been working at the federal level to garner continued support for the Medicare Graduate Nursing Education (GNE) demonstration program (CCNA, 2015a). While not defined as a transition-to-practice nurse residency program, the GNE demonstration, which began in 2012, provides funds to hospitals to offset the cost of clinical training for APRNs (CMS, 2012). RWJF, AARP, and the Alliance for Health Reform hosted a briefing on Capitol Hill in 2015 to inform policy makers about the importance of graduate nursing education and training (Alliance for Health Reform, 2015).

Progress

Progress on recommendation 3 from *The Future of Nursing* is difficult to track for several reasons: the word "residency" is used for a variety of different programs, from simple workplace orientations to year-long intensive training and

---

[11] Personal communication, K. Locke, TCC Group, September 3, 2015.

education programs; there are residency programs offered to nurses at all levels of education (associate's, baccalaureate, and advanced practice); and residencies take place in all practice settings, from hospitals to home health care. The length of nurse residency programs varies greatly, ranging from 6 weeks to 1 year. Because of this variation and because comprehensive data on residencies are sparse, it is difficult to gauge growth in programs overall, within particular settings, and for nurses of different educational levels since *The Future of Nursing* was released in 2010. Pittman and colleagues (2013c) report that among the organizations they sampled, more were offering RN residencies in 2013 (41.6 percent) than in 2011 (31.7 percent). More than half of these residency programs were created between 2010 and 2013, suggesting that *The Future of Nursing* may have played a role in the increase. Among these residencies, 67 percent were required for new RN hires, up from 7.7 percent in 2011.

Discussion

While the educational programs available for nurses provide a solid foundation for the delivery of safe and effective care, rapid changes in the health care environment call for additional training to build on the fundamentals of nursing. Novice nurses need opportunities not only to practice their skills but also to learn how to apply those skills in the real world. Nurses today increasingly must care for multiple patients with complex needs, navigate new forms of technology, and manage the needs of the chronically ill in resource-constrained settings. Transition-to-practice residencies provide an opportunity for novice nurses to understand these complexities and learn how to use their nursing skills for optimal patient care.

While evidence regarding the impact of residency programs on patient outcomes is limited, the available evidence suggests that transition-to-practice residencies for nurses appear to have positive outcomes, including improving nurses' abilities to organize, manage, and communicate, as well as higher retention levels. For example, nurses who completed the UHC/AACN residency were more likely to be retained by their employers and reported improved abilities to organize, prioritize, communicate, and provider leadership (Goode et al., 2013; McElroy, 2015). Likewise, evaluations of APRN residency programs have found that graduates reported improved confidence and competence and strengthened role identity (Flinter, 2011, 2015).

Despite these benefits, information is lacking about whether these outcomes translate into better patient care. Moreover, barriers remain to implementing residencies for every nurse, including cost and a lack of data on the value of these programs. *The Future of Nursing* offers subrecommendations for addressing these barriers; however, few of these measures have been implemented.

Differing Needs of Residencies for APRNs and RNs

The word "residency" is used for programs for both APRNs and RNs; however, the needs of these nurses are different, necessitating differently designed residencies. RN residencies are generally a transition from student to first practice setting, so the focus tends to be fundamental and setting specific. The newly graduated nurse benefits from supervision and a graded increase in responsibility, and the institution benefits from greater retention. APRN residencies, on the other hand, are related more to professionalization and the establishment of independence for an already experienced clinician; the initial first year of practice provides the "critical foundation on which new professionals build their expertise" (Brown and Olshansky, 1997, p. 46; Bush, 2014). APRNs are expected to come to the work environment ready to care for patients independently, and residencies can give these nurses the opportunity for clinical support in this transition to practice (Flinter, 2005). The funding models for the two types of residencies may differ as well.

The Future of Nursing focuses primarily on the need for RN residencies, although it notes that "the benefit to APRNs of completing a residency is likely to grow," particularly as more students are progressing immediately from a baccalaureate to an advanced practice degree (IOM, 2011, p. 124). However, the need for NP residency programs is not universally accepted. At the committee's May 28, 2015, public workshop, Sheila Melander, president of the National Organization of Nurse Practitioner Faculties, stated that "the terminology 'transition to practice' has been picked up by challengers to NP authority and introduced in various state legislations in an attempt to implement more control over NPs. The proposed additional regulatory constraints for NPs are an unintended consequence of the [*Future of Nursing*] report's [residency] recommendation" (Melander, 2015). Others do not share this view, however. Carolinas Healthcare System's NP postgraduate fellowship program started in October 2013 and now offers fellowships in 16 different specialties. At the committee's July 27, 2015, public workshop, Britney Broyhill, NP fellowship director in the Center for Advanced Practice at Carolinas Healthcare System, supported the inclusion of NPs in the implementation of *The Future of Nursing* recommendation calling for nurse residency programs (Broyhill, 2015). She said, "we do not agree that these programs challenge the clinical ability of nurse practitioners, but can only enhance their performance."

Concentration in Hospital Settings

The Future of Nursing notes, and this committee heard in its public workshops and testimony, that residencies are based largely in hospital settings and larger health systems and tend to focus on acute care. A nonexhaustive list of hospital nurse residency and new-graduate programs is available from the Oregon

Health & Science University (OHSU) School of Nursing.[12] This list, last updated in August 2014, includes 138 programs. These programs vary in their titles (residency, internship, externship, fellowship) and in their length and composition. Some are open only to nurses who have completed a baccalaureate degree, while others are open to all new graduates with an RN license. The nurse residency programs on this list are offered predominantly in hospital settings.

Cost

Cost is a major barrier to the development of residency programs for nurses (Flinter, 2015; Wierzbinski-Cross et al., 2015). To lessen the financial burden on health care organizations, *The Future of Nursing* calls on HRSA, CMS, and philanthropic organizations to fund nurse residencies. Although CMS has not redirected graduate medical education funding from diploma nursing programs to the implementation of nurse residency programs, as called for in *The Future of Nursing*, it has funded APRN training through the GNE demonstration project. Under the ACA, $200 million was allocated over 4 years for this program, and CMS will use this funding to provide reimbursement for the reasonable cost of clinical training for APRN students (CMS, 2012). While the GNE demonstration is not a residency program, it fulfills a similar goal of providing incoming advanced practice nurses with clinical training. The ACA requires that GNE sites have agreements with a school of nursing and at least two community-based care settings, ensuring the expansion of clinical placement of students beyond hospitals. The GNE program is a current funding source for APRN training, and if shown to be successful, could be expanded to fund similar transition-to-practice residencies for nurses. A similar program, also authorized by the ACA,[13] would provide grants for family NP residencies in FQHCs and nurse-managed health clinics (Miyamoto, 2014; Redhead et al., 2014). However, no appropriations have been made for this demonstration project, and there is no requirement for sustained funding for the GNE program after the initial demonstration phase.

Many organizations self-fund their residency programs, and some have turned to outside funding; there remains no standard, sustainable funding mechanism for nurse residencies. In some APRN residencies, participants are licensed and credentialed providers who can bill and continue to generate revenue for the practice (Broyhill, 2015; Flinter, 2011); residents in other programs, however, are considered trainees (Broyhill, 2015). There are other challenges as well. For example, Gilman (2015) notes that electronic medical records have difficulty

---

[12] See http://www.ohsu.edu/xd/education/schools/school-of-nursing/students/resources/upload/Guide-to-Hospital-Nursing-Residency-and-New-Graduate-Programs-Updated-7-2014.pdf (accessed September 21, 2015).

[13] Section 5316 of the Patient Protection and Affordable Care Act of 2010, Public Law 111-148, 111th Cong., 2d sess. (March 23, 2010).

categorizing NP residents, which impacts supervision, ordering, and billing requirements. As payment systems shift, organizations may develop new business models for residency programs. Anderson and colleagues (2012) note that many administrators measure the success of their residency programs from a purely economic perspective, comparing the cost of the program with the financial savings from increased retention rates. Wierzbinski-Cross and colleagues (2015) assert that the advantages of residencies go beyond improved retention, noting that such benefits as improved job satisfaction, productivity, and competence can affect the quality of care and patient safety and ultimately have a positive impact on the bottom line.

Lack of Data

As called for by *The Future of Nursing*, organizations that are implementing residencies or promoting residency models are performing self-evaluations of their work. However, because residencies are largely operated by employers, these evaluations tend to focus more on retention and workplace skills than on quality of patient care or patient outcomes. For example, the national programs of UHC/AACN (postbaccalaureate) and Versant (RN) have both published outcome data based on 10 years of data collection (Goode et al., 2013; Ulrich et al., 2010), and NCSBN has published findings from the implementation of its transition-to-practice programs in hospital and nonhospital settings (Spector et al., 2015a,b; see also the Activity section on nurse residency programs earlier in this chapter).

Because of the wide variation in residency programs, it is difficult to gather data across programs. Multiple studies have noted difficulties with the lack of uniformity among nurse residency programs, and variations in content and strategies make comparisons and analysis of best practices difficult (Anderson et al., 2012; Barnett et al., 2014). A few organizations have developed systematic models or standards for residencies, including the UHC/AACN Nurse Residency Program, accreditation through CCNE or ANCC, and NCSBN's transition-to-practice program (discussed in the Activity section). The lack of uniformity among residency programs makes it difficult to determine whether and to what extent residencies affect nurse competencies and patient care. However, these existing models and accreditation standards can serve as a guide for developing more uniform residency programs in the future.

Findings and Conclusions

Findings

This study yielded the following findings about transition-to-practice programs:

Finding 3-9. Transition-to-practice residency programs have been shown to improve the efficiency of health care services and retention of new nurse graduates.

Finding 3-10. There are good models for RN residencies, including the UHC/ AACN program, ANCC and CCNE accreditation, and the NCSBN program. There are fewer models for APRN residencies.

Finding 3-11. Most transition-to-practice residency programs are hospital-based and focus on acute care.

Finding 3-12. Lack of funding has limited the growth of transition-to-practice residency programs. Some APRN residencies have addressed this issue by considering residents to be billable providers so that they can continue to generate revenue while participating in the residency program.

Finding 3-13. The Campaign does not have a major dashboard indicator for recommendation 3 of The Future of Nursing, *although a supplemental indicator under the recommendation related to increasing baccalaureate-prepared nurses is "percent of hospitals that have new RN graduate residencies." This indicator does not track APRN residencies or residencies in nonhospital settings. The data used for this indicator are surveys conducted in 2011 and 2013.*

Conclusions

The committee drew the following conclusions about progress toward establishing transition-to-practice residency programs:

Considerable variation among transition-to-practice residency programs makes their evaluation difficult.

Further evaluation of transition-to-practice residencies is needed to prove their value with measurable outcomes; in particular, more attention is needed to determine the effect of these programs on patient outcomes. Although robust evidence on the impact of nurse residencies on patient outcomes is lacking, the available evidence suggests that these programs have positive effects on retention and job satisfaction, both of which have implications for patient care.

Existing residency programs can be used as models for new transition-to-practice residencies for nurses. Use of these existing models could make the design, implementation, and evaluation of these new programs easier and more efficient.

Both RN and APRN transition-to-practice residencies appear to have increased over the past few years, but systematic efforts to track the growth of these opportunities accurately have been limited.

DOUBLE THE NUMBER OF NURSES WITH A DOCTORATE BY 2020

In 2010, fewer than 1 percent of nurses held a doctorate degree in nursing or a nursing-related field (IOM, 2011). According to *The Future of Nursing*, this number was insufficient to keep pace with the growing need for nurses with a doctorate to teach the next generation of nurses, to perform research, and to serve as leaders in clinical practice and health policy. Nursing doctoral degrees include the PhD—a research-oriented degree—and the doctor of nursing practice (DNP), which was first developed in 2002 and focuses more on clinical practice. *The Future of Nursing* recommends that the number of nurses with a doctorate be doubled by 2020, but it is not specific about growth in particular types of doctoral programs (DNP, PhD in nursing, PhD in another field) (see Box 3-5).

Activity

Several major initiatives, as well as a number of smaller funding programs, have been undertaken to support students in seeking doctoral degrees in nursing. Three private philanthropic organizations—the Jonas Center for Nursing and Veterans Healthcare, the Rita & Alex Hillman Foundation, and RWJF—have contributed significant funds to the effort to increase doctorally prepared nurses. These organizations' programs encourage nurses to pursue a doctorate earlier in their career and place emphasis, wholly or in part, on increasing the number of nurses with research-focused PhDs in nursing.

The Jonas Center has committed $25 million to doubling the number of nurses with doctorates, and the number of scholars it has funded increased from 6 in 2009 to 600 (400 PhD and 200 DNP) in 2015 (Curley, 2015). As the latter figures suggest, the Jonas Center supports PhD and DNP nurses in a 2:1 ratio. Scholars receive a $10,000 scholarship from the Jonas Center and $12,500 in matching funds from their school of nursing. The program focuses on diversity, with 38 percent of scholars coming from underrepresented groups, and on leadership, requiring scholars to complete a 40-hour leadership project.

The Rita & Alex Hillman Foundation's Hillman Scholars Program in Nursing Innovation was launched in 2011 to support PhD nursing students (Hillman Foundation, 2015). The program is now offered at the University of Michigan, University of North Carolina at Chapel Hill, and University of Pennsylvania, and it incorporates interdisciplinary coursework, clinical practice, research, and

---

BOX 3-5
Recommendation 5 from The *Future of Nursing*:
Double the Number of Nurses with a Doctorate by 2020

Schools of nursing, with support from private and public funders, academic administrators and university trustees, and accrediting bodies, should double the number of nurses with a doctorate by 2020 to add to the cadre of nurse faculty and researchers, with attention to increasing diversity.

- The Commission on Collegiate Nursing Education and the National League for Nursing Accrediting Commission should monitor the progress of each accredited nursing school to ensure that at least 10 percent of all baccalaureate graduates matriculate into a master's or doctoral program within 5 years of graduation.
- Private and public funders, including the Health Resources and Services Administration and the Department of Labor, should expand funding for programs offering accelerated graduate degrees for nurses to increase the production of master's and doctoral nurse graduates and to increase the diversity of nurse faculty and researchers.
- Academic administrators and university trustees should create salary and benefit packages that are market competitive to recruit and retain highly qualified academic and clinical nurse faculty.

SOURCE: IOM, 2011.

---

mentorship to advance innovation through nursing research and leadership. As with the RWJF and Jonas Center programs, the goal of the program is for nurses to achieve their doctorate early in their career so as to maximize opportunities and contribute to the improvement of health and health care.

RWJF has invested $20 million in the Future of Nursing Scholars program, whose mission is to create "a diverse cadre of PhD prepared nurses" (RWJF, 2013, 2015c). The program awards $75,000 to each scholar over the course of 3 years, and the scholar's school is required to provide $50,000 in support (RWJF, 2015d). Awards were provided to 14 schools to support 17 nurses in 2014, the program's inaugural cohort, and to 25 schools to support 48 nurses in 2015 (RWJF, 2014a, 2015a).

The American Cancer Society also supports nurses seeking graduate study in cancer nursing practice and research through two programs. The Graduate Scholarships in Cancer Nursing Practice program provides a stipend of $10,000 per year for graduate students pursuing a master's degree in cancer nursing or a DNP (American Cancer Society, 2015b). The Doctoral Degree Scholarships in Cancer Nursing program provides a stipend of $15,000 per year for 2 years for students pursuing a doctorate in nursing or a related area to prepare the graduate for a career as a cancer nurse scientist (American Cancer Society, 2015a).

CareFirst BlueCross BlueShield's (CareFirst) Project RN provides stipends to nursing students specifically pursuing advanced degrees to become nurse educators through the company's nurse education partnership program. Project RN was launched in 2007. Between 2007 and 2012, CareFirst invested more than $2 million in the program; it invested another $1 million in 2013 and $960,000 in 2014 (CareFirst BlueCross BlueShield, 2013, 2014, n.d.).

One Campaign state Action Coalition, Georgia, considered the doubling of doctorally prepared nurses to be its top priority (TCC Group, 2013; see Chapter 1, Figure 1-3). Of the states responding to a 2013 survey, 78 percent indicated that they were working toward implementing this recommendation, but only 25 percent said it was a main focus for them (see Chapter 1, Figure 1-2).[14]

The Campaign tracks progress on this recommendation by using data on the number of students enrolled in doctoral programs (CCNA, 2015b). The recommendation focuses on the number of nurses with doctorates in the workforce; however, progress in the workforce will take considerable time to become discernible because doctoral degrees typically take years to complete. The Campaign also has identified supplemental indicators with which to track progress on this recommendation, including the number of employed nurses with a doctoral degree, the number of doctoral program nurse graduates each year, and the diversity of nurse doctoral graduates.

Progress

Since *The Future of Nursing* was released, enrollment in doctoral programs has risen. Enrollment in DNP programs has grown rapidly over the past 5 years, while enrollment in PhD programs has grown at a slower rate. Since fall 2010, enrollment in DNP programs has more than doubled, from 7,034 to 18,352 students (a 161 percent increase).[15] Meanwhile, enrollment in PhD programs has increased by 15 percent over the past 5 years, with 5,290 students now pursuing the research-focused doctorate.

Doctoral programs that confer the DNP degree have grown rapidly over the past 10 years. In 2006, 20 such programs existed; by 2014, this number had grown more than 10-fold, to 262 programs.[16] PhD programs also have grown, from 103 programs in 2006 to 133 programs in 2014 (see Figure 3-7). DNP and PhD enrollments and graduations also have grown. Enrollments in and graduations from PhD programs have increased modestly over the past 15 years, while enrollments in and graduations from DNP programs have increased exponentially

---

[14] Personal communication, K. Locke, TCC Group, September 3, 2015.

[15] Data received from AACN, August 28, 2015.

[16] Ibid.

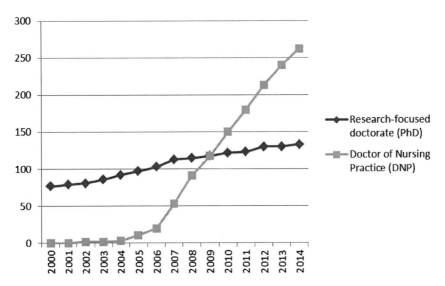

FIGURE 3-7 Numbers of nursing PhD and DNP programs, 2000-2014.
SOURCE: Data received from AACN, August 28, 2015.

(see Figures 3-8 and 3-9, respectively). Growth also appears to be occurring among baccalaureate-to-DNP and master's-to-DNP programs (Auerbach et al., 2014). Of 400 schools surveyed by AACN in 2013 that had APRN education programs, 25 percent had baccalaureate-to-DNP programs, and 57 percent had master's-to-DNP programs. A survey conducted in 2013 found that 11 to 14 percent of schools were providing baccalaureate-to-DNP programs without offering a terminal master's program, but more were planning to do so in the future. In 2010, by comparison, this was the case for only one school (Auerbach et al., 2014).

Discussion

As noted, both DNP and PhD nurses are critical to fill the need for faculty positions and for leadership roles in academics, health care delivery, health care planning and policy, and other arenas. In addition, nurses with doctoral degrees in fields outside of nursing, including public policy, business, health administration, public health, and other fields, will be especially well prepared for important leadership and educational roles in an evolving health care environment.

Although, as discussed above, there has been significant growth in enrollment in DNP programs in recent years, the relatively small increase in enrollment in PhD programs for nurses is concerning. According to testimony at the commit-

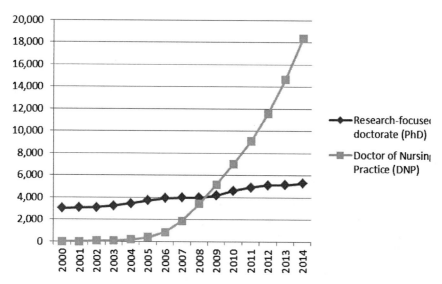

FIGURE 3-8 Enrollments in nursing PhD and DNP programs, 2000-2014.
SOURCE: Data received from AACN, August 28, 2015.

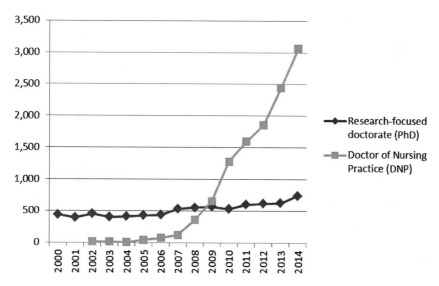

FIGURE 3-9 Numbers of nursing PhD and DNP graduates, 2000-2014.
SOURCE: Data received from AACN, August 28, 2015.

tee's July 2015 workshop from Darlene Curley, executive director, Jonas Center for Nursing and Veterans Healthcare, "PhD numbers are growing too slowly to fill the vacant faculty positions and impending baby boomer retirements." More emphasis is needed on increasing the number of PhD nurses through expansion of programs, incentives for nurses to return to school, and more scholarships for baccalaureate-to-PhD programs. Students also need to be encouraged to pursue a PhD early in their career so they can practice for a longer period of time in the research, faculty, and leadership roles that a doctorate enables.

Studies and stakeholders have noted that the progress seen in enrollments in and graduations from doctoral programs, primarily DNP programs, puts the field on track to achieve the goal in *The Future of Nursing* of doubling the number of nurses with doctorates by 2020 (Curley, 2015), despite some identified barriers. However, simply doubling the number of nurses with doctorates is not sufficient. An assessment of the mix of doctorally prepared nurses is needed. It should be noted that a DNP typically takes less time to complete than a PhD. A DNP usually takes 3-4 years to complete, while a PhD usually takes 4-6 years, including years spent on academic work and years spent conducting research and producing a dissertation (AACN, 2006; Ellenbecker, 2010; Johnson, 2014).

Role of the DNP

Despite rapid growth in DNP programs, enrollees, and graduates and schools' plans for continued expansion of BSN-to-DNP programs (Auerbach et al., 2014), some concern and confusion have been expressed regarding the role of the DNP-prepared nurse in certain settings. Understanding and awareness of and demand for the DNP varies considerably among nurses, students, nursing schools, and employers (Auerbach et al., 2014; Lee et al., 2013; Martsolf et al., 2015; Swanson and Stanton, 2013; Udlis and Mancuso, 2015). For example, Martsolf and colleagues (2015) heard from schools of nursing that "some employers were not familiar with the different capabilities of DNP-prepared APRNs and were unsure how to use them compared with MSN-prepared APRNs in a clinical setting" (p. 223). Cronenwett and colleagues (2011) state, "The confusion surrounding doctoral degrees is exacerbated if the meaning of master's education changes fundamentally" (p. 12). In August 2015, AACN acknowledged that "the national dialogue about the DNP has amplified the need to clarify" advanced nursing practice and the preparation and role of the DNP with regard to research and knowledge generation, leadership, and advanced practice (AACN, 2015c, p. 1). Despite recent rapid growth in DNPs, master's preparation remains the predominant entry into advanced practice (Auerbach et al., 2014), although AACN recommended in 2004 that the DNP become the terminal degree for advanced practice nursing by 2015 (AACN, 2004).

Faculty Considerations

Many schools need more faculty before they can enroll more qualified applicants at all levels, as evidenced by data showing that 40 percent of schools said they had no faculty vacancies but need additional faculty (Li and Fang, 2014; NCSBN, 2015a). Barriers to improving the faculty vacancy situation include insufficient funds, unwillingness to commit to hiring full-time employees, noncompetitive salaries, an inability to recruit qualified individuals or those with the right specialties or research or teaching interests, the limited number of doctorally prepared nurses, and a lack of qualified applicants in the school's area (Li and Fang, 2014; NCSBN, 2015a). The projected future faculty vacancy rate is of great concern (Berlin and Sechrist, 2002; Williamson et al., 2010). In 2009, NLN found that 30 percent of all full-time nurse educators were aged 60 or older (NLN, 2009), and state boards of nursing have highlighted as an emerging issue the expected high turnover due to faculty retirements (NCSBN, 2015a).

Nurses with doctorates are needed to fill these faculty positions. The educational attainment required for these positions varies among schools and program types (AACN, 2008; Bednash et al., 2014); however, 89.6 percent of the faculty vacancies at nursing schools are for positions for which a doctoral degree is required or preferred.[17] For nurses to be prepared to educate the next generation of nurses, AACN has called for nurses who plan to be educators to have "additional preparation in the science of pedagogy" (AACN, 2006, p. 7, 2010, p. 4). Instruction that prepares PhD and DNP nurses to teach about and in an evolving health care system that is less focused on acute care will be beneficial to these future faculty and their future students.

Findings and Conclusions

Findings

This study yielded the following findings on doctorally prepared nurses:

Finding 3-14. The recommendation of The Future of Nursing *calling for a doubling of the number of nurses with a doctorate by 2020 is not specific about growth in particular types of doctoral programs (DNP, PhD in nursing, PhD in another field).*

Finding 3-15. The number of DNP programs has increased more than 10-fold in the last decade, but expansion of PhD programs has been much more modest.

---

[17] Ibid.

Conclusions

The committee drew the following conclusions about progress toward in-creasing the number of nurses with doctorates:

The number of nursing students pursuing a PhD needs to be increased. There are barriers to meeting the demand for PhD programs for nurses, including issues of insufficient faculty.

Additional efforts are needed to clarify the roles of PhD and DNP nurses, especially with regard to teaching and research.

As nurses are increasingly looked to for leadership in health care, advanced education in clinical care, research, education, and other areas (including public policy and business), advanced degrees will be more useful than ever. Information exists and is readily available about the number of nurses with higher degrees in the workforce. However, the breakdown of nurses with these degrees (particularly those with non-nursing advanced degrees), the settings in which they practice, and the types of work they do is less accessible.

ENSURE THAT NURSES ENGAGE IN LIFELONG LEARNING

The Future of Nursing states that a single initial degree cannot "provide a nurse with all she or he will need to know over an entire career" (IOM, 2011, p. 202). It suggests an emphasis on "continuing competence" rather than "continu-ing education" and recommends that health care organizations, schools of nursing, and accrediting institutions do their part to ensure that lifelong learning—which "encompasses both continuing competence and advanced degrees" (IOM, 2011, p. 202)—gives nurses the skills necessary to provide quality care (see Box 3-6).

Activity

The Campaign has not focused a significant amount of activity on this rec-ommendation. There is no Campaign dashboard indicator in this area, and the Campaign noted that it has worked on this broad recommendation but has not worked toward the second or third subrecommendation.[18] A 2013 survey of state Action Coalitions conducted by the Campaign's external evaluators asked Action Coalitions to identify the level of focus and effort in 15 major topic areas relating to the recommendations of *The Future of Nursing* and Campaign goals, none of which concerned lifelong learning (TCC Group, 2013).

---

[18] Personal communication, D. Herrera, Robert Wood Johnson Foundation, May 14, 2015.

BOX 3-6
Recommendation 6 from *The Future of Nursing*: Ensure that Nurses Engage in Lifelong Learning

Accrediting bodies, schools of nursing, health care organizations, and continuing competency educators from multiple health professions should collaborate to ensure that nurses and nursing students and faculty continue their education and engage in lifelong learning to gain the competencies needed to provide care for diverse populations across the lifespan.

- Faculty should partner with health care organizations to develop and prioritize competencies so curricula can be updated regularly to ensure that graduates at all levels are prepared to meet the current and future health needs of the population.
- The Commission on Collegiate Nursing Education and the National League for Nursing Accrediting Commission should require that all nursing students demonstrate a comprehensive set of clinical performance competencies that encompass the knowledge and skills needed to provide care across settings and the lifespan.
- Academic administrators should require all faculty to participate in continuing professional development and to perform with cutting-edge competence in practice, teaching, and research.
- All health care organizations and schools of nursing should foster a culture of lifelong learning and provide resources for interprofessional continuing competency programs.
- Health care organizations and other organizations that offer continuing competency programs should regularly evaluate their programs for adaptability, flexibility, accessibility, and impact on clinical outcomes and update the programs accordingly.

SOURCE: IOM, 2011.

Beyond the Campaign, the Joint Accreditation for Interprofessional Continuing Education, established in 2009 as a collaboration among the Accreditation Council for Continuing Medical Education (ACCME), the Accreditation Council for Pharmacy Education (ACPE), and ANCC, provides a streamlined accreditation process and standards for interprofessional continuing education for these fields (Joint Accreditation for Interprofessional Continuing Education, 2013). Joint accreditation allows organizations to develop innovative programs to further build the competency of clinicians working in health care teams. "To be eligible for Joint Accreditation, an organization needs to demonstrate that for the previous 18 months its structure and processes to plan and present education by and for the healthcare team have been fully functional; and that at least 25% of its educational activities have been designed by and for healthcare teams" (Joint Accreditation for Interprofessional Continuing Education, 2013).

Progress

In the most recent NCSBN member board profile report, produced in 2014, 11 of the 49 responding jurisdictions (Colorado, Connecticut, Guam, Hawaii, Iowa, Maine, Maryland, Mississippi, Missouri, Oregon, Wisconsin) reported having no continuing competency requirements for licensure maintenance; 36 jurisdictions have such requirements (NCSBN, 2014).[19] Various methods can be used to meet these continuing competency requirements, including competency examinations or assessments, minimum practice hours, and continuing education. The content and quantity of continuing education requirements for RN licensure and NP credentialing also vary significantly across the United States (AACN and AAMC, 2010; NCSBN, 2014).

A few states have instituted continuing competency requirements for nurses since 2010:

- In Washington, continuing competency requirements were instituted for RNs and licensed practical nurses (LPNs) in 2011 (Washington State Department of Health, n.d.).
- In Georgia, Governor Nathan Deal signed a continuing competency bill into law on May 6, 2013, requiring that all RNs and LPNs meet continuing education competency requirements by January 1, 2016, and March 31, 2017, respectively (Georgia General Assembly, 2013).
- In Oklahoma, continuing competency requirements for RNs and LPNs were instituted effective January 1, 2014 (Oklahoma Board of Nursing, 2014).

Discussion

The Future of Nursing cites several contemporaneous reports covering continuing education (IOM, 2011). A 2010 IOM report, *Redesigning Continuing Education in the Health Professions*, states that there are "major flaws" in the way continuing education is "conducted, financed, regulated, and evaluated"; that the science behind continuing education is "fragmented and underdeveloped"; and that continuing education should bring health professionals together for interprofessional learning "with a common goal of improving patient outcomes" (IOM, 2010, pp. 2-3). The report notes that although some states have long required

---

[19] Ten jurisdictions did not respond to the survey: Alabama, American Samoa, California (vocational nursing), Indiana, Louisiana (practical nursing), Nebraska, Nebraska (advanced practice registered nursing), New York, Rhode Island, and South Carolina.

nurses to complete continuing education programs, these programs do not always increase competence. A 2010 report from the Association of American Medical Colleges (AAMC), AACN, and the Josiah Macy Jr. Foundation recommends that continuing education evolve away from classroom learning and toward action-oriented, site-of-care training; that education be focused on the development of key competencies rather than mere knowledge acquisition; and that health professionals be educated together in an interprofessional setting (AACN and AAMC, 2010).

Unfortunately, little progress has been made over the past 5 years on either the recommendation of *The Future of Nursing* or the findings of these other reports. While there have been some efforts toward interprofessional learning, such as the Joint Accreditation for Interprofessional Continuing Education, continuing education has not kept pace with the needs of the increasingly complex, team-based health care system.

One obstacle that stands in the way of achieving progress on the recommendation of *The Future of Nursing* related to lifelong learning is a lack of data on lifelong learning and continuing education for nurses. Information about requirements for licensure or accreditation is collected by individual organizations through member surveys, and thus there is no single, comprehensive source of such data. In addition, evidence is lacking with regard to whether nurse certification and credentialing lead to better patient outcomes (Hickey et al., 2014; IOM, 2015; Johantgen, 2013; Newhouse, 2014).

Recognizing this gap in knowledge, the IOM convened the Standing Committee on Credentialing Research in Nursing and held a public workshop in September 2014 to discuss priorities for research and knowledge in this area (IOM, 2015). Workshop speakers highlighted various barriers to understanding the impact of nurse credentialing, including the lack of common terms and data points, and limited and inconsistent data collection by multiple credentialing and certification organizations and through national datasets. Further, speakers noted the importance of connecting more comprehensive credentialing data with metrics on performance and outcomes. They also identified the need to align research in nurse credentialing with changes in health policy and health care systems, including greater emphasis on integrated and coordinated care, team-based care, and value-based payment. Specifically, participants noted that the shift toward global and quality-based payment schemes may make it more likely that organizations and nurses will obtain credentials, but only if strong evidence can show that credentials improve skills and outcomes. In talking about the maintenance of credentials, "[Jody] Frost [from the American Physical Therapy Association] added that ongoing assessment strategies have to consider that professions are changing, and individuals need to be measured against competencies relevant today, not when they graduated from their educational institution" (IOM, 2015, p. 62). Presenters Susan Hassmiller from RWJF and Robin Newhouse from the University of Maryland School of Nursing both noted that advances in nurse credentialing research could have implications not just for *The Future of Nursing* recommendation related to lifelong learning and continuing competencies but also for nurses being able to practice to the full extent of their education and training and nurses partnering with other health care professionals in the improvement and redesign of the health care system. Yet despite the potential for nurse credentialing to improve knowledge and practice competencies as suggested by the workshop participants, barriers exist for individuals and organizations, including the cost of initial and sustained certification and a lack of support for or perceived value of certification (Haskins et al., 2011; Perlstein et al., 2014).

AACN has said that it "would like to see more data collected about the full spectrum of educational experiences completed by RNs" and that it is "ready to work with the Health Resources and Services Administration, National Council of State Boards of Nursing, and other stakeholders to develop a plan to collect this data."[20]

A bullet under *The Future of Nursing* recommendation on lifelong learning calls for updating curricula to "ensure that graduates at all levels are prepared to meet the current and future health needs of the population" (see Box 3-6). In a changing health care environment, nurses and other providers will increasingly require skills necessary to be comfortable in providing care in both hospital and community-based settings. As Tanner (2010, p. 347) puts it, "As care continues to shift from hospitals to community-based settings, as the population ages and care management in the community becomes more complex, and as new health care needs emerge, a new kind of nurse will be needed. Educational programs must be redesigned to better prepare this nurse." Yet health professions education is still highly oriented toward acute care, despite some efforts to change this paradigm (Paterson et al., 2015; Spector, 2012; Thibault, 2013). Thibault (2013) acknowledges the important roles of competency-based educational models, technology, clinical education, and interprofessional education (see Chapter 5) and notes that "future needs will require more clinical experiences that are longitudinal, integrated, immersive, and community based" (p. 1930).

Findings and Conclusion

Findings

This study yielded the following findings on lifelong learning:

Finding 3-16. A single source of information about states' lifelong learning requirements for nurses is lacking, and health care settings impose varied requirements on their clinical staff for continuing competencies and education.

---

[20] Personal communication, R. Rosseter, AACN, August 13, 2015.

Finding 3-17. Efforts are being made to promote interprofessional continuing education.

Conclusion

The committee drew the following conclusion about progress toward ensuring that nurses engage in lifelong learning:

The current health care context makes interprofessional continuing education more important than ever. Current efforts by health care delivery organizations, accreditors, and state regulatory boards to promote these programs need to be expanded and promoted.

RECOMMENDATIONS

***Recommendation 2: Continue Pathways Toward Increasing the Percentage of Nurses with a Baccalaureate Degree.* The Campaign, the nursing education community, and state systems of higher education should continue efforts aimed at strengthening academic pathways for nurses toward the baccalaureate degree—both entry-level baccalaureate and baccalaureate completion programs.**

- **Efforts to expand and encourage partnerships between community colleges and 4-year universities, as well as other models for establishing these pathways, should continue to be promulgated. Employers play a critical role in promoting educational progression and should be encouraged to provide financial and logistical support for employees pursuing a baccalaureate degree.**
- **In addition, the quality of new programs should be monitored to ensure consistency in effective educational practices and to ensure the ability of nursing graduates to qualify to attend other accredited schools as they pursue advanced studies. This monitoring could be conducted through a national accrediting body such as the Commission on Collegiate Nursing Education or the American Commission for Education in Nursing.**

***Recommendation 3: Create and Fund Transition-to-Practice Residency Programs.* The Campaign, in coordination with health care providers, health care delivery organizations, and payers, should lead efforts to explore ways of creating and funding transition-to-practice residency programs at both the registered nurse and advanced practice registered nurse levels. Such programs are needed in all practice settings, including community-based practices and long-term care. These efforts should include determining the most appropriate program models; setting stan-**

dards for programs; exploring funding and business case models; and creating an overarching structure with which to track and evaluate the quality, effectiveness, and impact of transition-to-practice programs. With respect to funding models,

- government agencies, philanthropic organizations, and foundations should support these programs on a temporary basis to help better understand how the programs should be designed; and
- health care organizations should support these programs on a permanent basis as they can be beneficial in the evolving value-based payment system.

Recommendation 4: Promote Nurses' Pursuit of Doctoral Degrees. The Campaign should make efforts, through incentives and expansion of programs, to promote nurses' pursuit of both the doctor of nursing practice (DNP) and PhD degrees so as to have an adequate supply of nurses for clinical care, research, faculty, and leadership positions. More emphasis should be placed on increasing the number of PhD nurses in particular. To maximize the potential value of their additional education, nurses should be encouraged to pursue these degrees early in their careers. DNP and PhD programs should offer coursework that prepares students to serve as faculty, including preparing them to teach in an evolving health care system that is less focused on acute care than has previously been the case.

Recommendation 5: Promote Nurses' Interprofessional and Lifelong Learning. The Campaign should encourage nursing organizations, education programs, and professional societies, as well as individual nurses, to make lifelong learning a priority so that nurses are prepared to work in evolving health care environments. Lifelong learning should include continuing education that will enable nurses to gain, preserve, and measure the skills needed in the variety of environments and settings in which health care will be provided going forward, particularly community-based, outpatient, long-term care, primary care, and ambulatory settings. Nurses should work with other health care professionals to create opportunities for interprofessional collaboration and education. The Campaign could serve as a convener to bring together stakeholders from multiple areas of health care to discuss opportunities and strategies for interdisciplinary collaboration in this area.

REFERENCES

AACN (American Association of Colleges of Nursing). 2004. *AACN position statement on the practice doctorate in nursing.* http://www.aacn.nche.edu/publications/position/DNPposition statement.pdf (accessed September 19, 2015).

AACN. 2006. *The essentials of doctoral education for advanced practice.* http://www.aacn.nche.edu/dnp/Essentials.pdf (accessed September 20, 2015).

AACN. 2008. *Preferred vision of the professoriate in baccalaureate and graduate nursing programs.* http://www.aacn.nche.edu/publications/position/preferred-vision (accessed September 21, 2015).

AACN. 2010. *The research-focused doctoral program in nursing: Pathways to excellence.* http://www.aacn.nche.edu/education-resources/PhDPosition.pdf (accessed September 21, 2015).

AACN. 2011. *Employment of new nurse graduates and employer preferences for baccalaureate-prepared nurses.* http://www.aacn.nche.edu/leading_initiatives_news/news/2011/employment11 (accessed September 18, 2015).

AACN. 2012a. *Employment of new nurse graduates and employer preferences for baccalaureate-prepared nurses.* http://www.aacn.nche.edu/leading_initiatives_news/news/2012/employment12 (accessed September 18, 2015).

AACN. 2012b. *White paper: Expectations for practice experiences in the RN to baccalaureate curriculum.* http://www.aacn.nche.edu/aacn-publications/white-papers/RN-BSN-White-Paper.pdf (accessed September 28, 2015).

AACN. 2013. *Employment of new nurse graduates and employer preferences for baccalaureate-prepared nurses.* http://www.aacn.nche.edu/leading_initiatives_news/news/2013/employment13 (accessed September 18, 2015).

AACN. 2014. *Employment of new nurse graduates and employer preferences for baccalaureate-prepared nurses.* http://www.aacn.nche.edu/leading_initiatives_news/news/2014/employment14 (accessed September 18, 2015).

AACN. 2015a. *Degree completion programs for registered nurses: RN to master's degree and RN to baccalaureate programs.* http://www.aacn.nche.edu/media-relations/fact-sheets/degree-completion-programs (accessed November 7, 2015).

AACN. 2015b. *Nursing faculty shortage.* http://www.aacn.nche.edu/media-relations/fact-sheets/nursing-faculty-shortage (accessed September 18, 2015).

AACN. 2015c. *The doctor of nursing practice: Current issues and clarifying recommendations.* http://www.aacn.nche.edu/aacn-publications/white-papers/DNP-Implementation-TF-Report-8-15.pdf (accessed September 19, 2015).

AACN and AAMC (Association of American Medical Colleges). 2010. *Lifelong learning in medicine and nursing: Final conference report.* Washington, DC: AACN and AAMC.

Aiken, L. H., J. P. Cimiotti, D M. Sloan, H. L. Smith, L. Flynn, and D. F. Neff. 2011. The effects of nurse staffing and nurse education on patient deaths in hospitals with different nurse work environments. *Medical Care* 49(12):1047-1053.

Aiken, L. H., D. M. Sloane, L. Bruyneel, K. Van den Heede, P. Griffiths, R. Busse, M. Diomidous, J. Kinnunen, M. Kozka, E. Lesaffre, M. D. McHugh, M. T. Moreno-Casbas, A. M. Rafferty, R. Schwendimann, C. Tishelman, T. van Achterberg, and W. Sermeus. 2014. Nurse staffing and education and hospital mortality in 9 European countries: A retrospective observational study. *Lancet* 383(9931):1824-1830.

Alexander, M. 2015. Presentation to IOM Committee for Assessing Progress on Implementing the Recommendations of the Institute of Medicine Report *The Future of Nursing: Leading Change, Advancing Health.* Washington, DC, May 28, 2015.

Alliance for Health Reform. 2015. *Preparing the nursing workforce for a changing health system: The role of graduate nursing education.* http://www.allhealth.org/briefing_detail.asp?bi=346 (accessed September 20, 2015).

Altmann, T. K. 2011. Registered nurses returning to school for a bachelor's degree in nursing: Issues emerging from a meta-analysis of the research. *Contemporary Nurse* 39(2):256-272.

American Association of Community Colleges. 2010. *Community colleges issues brief prepared for the 2010 White House Summit on Community Colleges.* Washington, DC: American Association of Community Colleges. http://www.aacc.nche.edu/AboutCC/whsummit/Documents/whsummit_briefs.pdf (accessed September 18, 2015).

American Cancer Society. 2015a. *Doctoral degree scholarships in cancer nursing.* http://www.cancer.org/research/applyforaresearchgrant/granttypes/doctoral-degree-scholarship-nursing (accessed September 20, 2015).

American Cancer Society. 2015b. *Graduate scholarships in cancer nursing practice.* http://www.cancer.org/research/applyforaresearchgrant/granttypes/graduate-scholarships-cancer-nursing (accessed September 20, 2015).

ANA (American Nurses Association). 1965. American Nurses' Association's first position on education for nursing. *American Journal of Nursing* 65(12):106-111.

ANA. 1995. *Compendium of ANA education positions, position statements, and documents.* http://nursingworld.org/MainMenuCategories/Policy-Advocacy/State/Legislative-Agenda-Reports/NursingEducation/NursingEducationCompendium.pdf (accessed November 22, 2015).

ANA. 2013. *State legislative agenda: Nursing education.* http://www.nursingworld.org/MainMenuCategories/Policy-Advocacy/State/Legislative-Agenda-Reports/NursingEducation (accessed September 18, 2105).

ANCC (American Nurses Credentialing Center). 2014. *Average Magnet® organization characteristics.* http://nursecredentialing.org/CharacteristicsMagnetOrganizations.aspx (accessed September 21, 2015).

ANCC. 2015. *ANCC Magnet organization eligibility requirements.* http://www.nursecredentialing.org/OrgEligibilityRequirements (accessed September 18, 2015).

Anderson, G., C. Hair, and C. Todero. 2012. Nurse residency programs: An evidence-based review of theory, process, and outcomes. *Journal of Professional Nursing* 28(4):203-212.

Auerbach, D. I., G. Martsolf, M. L. Pearson, E. A. Taylor, M. Zaydman, A. Muchow, J. Spetz, and C. Dower. 2014. *The DNP by 2015: A study of the institutional, political, and professional issues that facilitate or impede establishing a post-baccalaureate doctor of nursing practice program.* Santa Monica, CA: RAND Corporation.

Auerbach, D. I., P. I. Buerhaus, and D. O. Staiger. 2015. Do associate degree registered nurses fare differently in the nurse labor market compared to baccalaureate-prepared RNs? *Nursing Economic$* 33(1):8-35.

Barnett, J. S., A. F. Minnick, and L. D. Norman. 2014. A description of U.S. post-graduation nurse residency programs. *Nursing Outlook* 62(3):174-184.

Bates, T., L. Chu, D. Keane, and J. Spetz. 2014. *Survey of nurse employers in California, fall 2013.* http://rnworkforce.ucsf.edu/sites/rnworkforce.ucsf.edu/files/CaliforniaEmployerSurvey2013_Report.pdf (accessed September 18, 2015).

Bates, T., L. Chu, and J. Spetz. 2015. *Survey of nurse employers in California, fall 2014.* http://rnworkforce.ucsf.edu/sites/rnworkforce.ucsf.edu/files/CaliforniaEmployerReport2014v1.1.pdf (accessed September 18, 2015).

Bednash, G., E. T. Breslin, J. M. Kirschling, and R. J. Rosseter. 2014. PhD or DNP: Planning for doctoral nursing education. *Nursing Science Quarterly* 27(4):296-301.

Bell, N. E. 2012. *Data sources: The role of community colleges on the pathway to graduate degree attainment.* http://www.cgsnet.org/data-sources-role-community-colleges-pathway-graduate-degree-attainment-0 (accessed September 18, 2015).

Berlin, L. E., and K. R. Sechrist. 2002. The shortage of doctorally prepared nursing faculty: A dire situation. *Nursing Outlook* 50(2):50-56.

Blegen, M. A., C. J. Goode, S. H. Park, T. Vaughn, and J. Spetz. 2013. Baccalaureate education in nursing and patient outcomes. *Journal of Nursing Administration* 43(2):89-94.

Boyd, T. 2015. *NJ's elderly receive support for nurse residency grads.* https://news.nurse. com/2015/07/01/njs-elderly-receive-support-from-nurse-residency-grads (accessed September 21, 2015).

Brown, M., and E. F. Olshansky. 1997. From limbo to legitimacy: A theoretical model of the transition to the primary care nurse practitioner role. *Nursing Research* 46(1):46-51.

Broyhill, B. 2015. Testimony provided to the IOM Committee for Assessing Progress on Implementing the Recommendations of the Institute of Medicine Report *The Future of Nursing: Leading Change, Advancing Health.* Washington, DC, July 27, 2015.

Buerhaus, P. I., D. I. Auerbach, and D. O. Staiger. 2014. The rapid growth of graduates from associate, baccalaureate, and graduate programs in nursing. *Nursing Economic$* 32(6):290-311.

Bush, C. T. 2014. Postgraduate nurse practitioner training. *Journal of Nursing Administration* 44(12):625-627.

Butlin, J. 2015. Presentation to IOM Committee for Assessing Progress on Implementing the Recommendations of the Institute of Medicine Report *The Future of Nursing: Leading Change, Advancing Health.* Washington, DC, May 28, 2015.

CareFirst BlueCross BlueShield. 2013. *CareFirst invests another $1 million in nursing shortage.* https://member.carefirst.com/individuals/news/media-news/2013/carefirst-invests-nursing-shortage.page (accessed September 20, 2015).

CareFirst BlueCross BlueShield. 2014. *CareFirst awards nearly $1 million through nurse-education partnership.* https://member.carefirst.com/individuals/news/media-news/2014/carefirst-awards-nearly-1-million-through-nurse-education-partnership.page? (accessed November 22, 2015).

CareFirst BlueCross BlueShield. n.d. *Closing the gap: CareFirst's Project RN program helps alleviate region's shortage of nurse educators.* http://www.carefirstcommitment.com/html/ProjectRN NursingStory_PopUp.html (accessed September 20, 2015).

CCNA (Center to Champion Nursing in America). 2012. *A resource guide based on the CCNA regional education meetings.* http://campaignforaction.org/sites/default/files/Education%20 Resource%20Guide%20%28Regional%20Meetings%29%20July%202012.pdf (accessed November 18, 2015).

CCNA. 2013a. *Advancing education transformation: Collaboration with community colleges.* Washington, DC: CCNA.

CCNA. 2013b (unpublished). *Focus areas: SIP I and II states.* Washington, DC: CCNA.

CCNA. 2013c. *NJAC receives $1.6 million to implement a long term care residency program.* http:// campaignforaction.org/community-post/njac-receives-16-million-implement-long-term-care-residency-program (accessed August 6, 2015).

CCNA. 2014a. *Iowa online nurse residency program.* http://campaignforaction.org/resource/iowa-online-nurse-residency-program (accessed September 21, 2015).

CCNA. 2014b. *NJ Action Coalition advances nurse residency program.* http://campaignforaction.org/ community-post/nj-action-coalition-advances-nurse-residency-programs-0 (accessed September 21, 2015).

CCNA. 2015a (unpublished). *Future of Nursing: Campaign for Action biannual operations report, August 1, 2014-May 31, 2015.* Washington, DC: The Center to Champion Nursing in America.

CCNA. 2015b. *Future of Nursing: Campaign for Action dashboard indicators.* http://campaignfor action.org/dashboard (accessed September 12, 2015).

CCNA. 2015c (unpublished). *State Implementation Program, January 1, 2015.* Washington, DC: CCNA.

CCNA. n.d.-a. *Campaign progress.* http://campaignforaction.org/campaign-progress (accessed September 23, 2015).

CCNA. n.d.-b. *Campaign progress: New RN graduates by degree type and race/ethnicity.* http:// campaignforaction.org/campaign-progress/new-rn-graduates-degree-type-and-raceethnicity (accessed November 18, 2015).

CCNE (Commission on Collegiate Nursing Education). 2008. *Standards for accreditation of post-baccalaureate nurse residency programs.* http://www.aacn.nche.edu/ccne-accreditation/resstandards08.pdf (accessed September 20, 2015).

Cho, E., D. M. Sloan, E. Kim, S. Kim, M. Choi, I. Y. Yoo, H. S. Lee, and L. H. Aiken. 2015. Effects of nurse staffing, work environments, and education on patient mortality: An observational study. *International Journal of Nursing Studies* 52(2):535-542.

CMS (Centers for Medicare & Medicaid Services). 2012. *Graduate nurse education demonstration.* http://innovation.cms.gov/Files/fact-sheet/GNE-Fact-Sheet.pdf (accessed September 20, 2015).

Cronenwett, L., K. Dracup, M. Grey, L. McCauley, A. Meleis, and M. Salmon. 2011. The doctor of nursing practice: A national workforce perspective. *Nursing Outlook* 59(1):9-17.

Curley, D. 2015. Presentation to IOM Committee for Assessing Progress on Implementing the Recommendations of the Institute of Medicine Report *The Future of Nursing: Leading Change, Advancing Health.* Washington, DC, July 27, 2015.

Duffy, M. T., M. A. Friesen, K. G. Speroni, D. Swengros, L. A. Shanks, P. A. Waiter, and M. J. Sheridan. 2014. BSN completion barriers, challenges, incentives, and strategies. *Journal of Nursing Administration* 44(4):232-236.

Edwards, D. S. 2012. An 80% BSN workforce by 2020? *Reflections on Nursing Leadership* 38(1). http://www.reflectionsonnursingleadership.org/Pages/Vol38_1_Edwards_IOM%20Report.aspx (accessed September 18, 2015).

Ellenbecker, C. H. 2010. Preparing the nursing workforce of the future. *Policy, Politics, & Nursing Practice* 11(2):115-125.

Flinter, M. 2005. Residency programs for primary care nurse practitioners in federal qualified health centers: A service perspective. *Online Journal of Issues in Nursing* 10(3).

Flinter, M. 2011. From new nurse practitioner to primary care provider: Bridging the transition through FQHC-based residency training. *Online Journal of Issues in Nursing* 17(1):6.

Flinter, M. 2015. Presentation to IOM Committee for Assessing Progress on Implementing the Recommendations of the Institute of Medicine Report *The Future of Nursing: Leading Change, Advancing Health.* Washington, DC, July 27, 2015.

Fulcher, R., and C. M. Mullin. 2011. *A data-driven examination of the impact of associate and bachelor's degree programs on the nation's nursing workforce.* AACC Policy Brief 2011-02PBL. Washington, DC: American Association of Community Colleges.

Gagliano, N. 2015. Presentation to IOM Committee for Assessing Progress on Implementing the Recommendations of the Institute of Medicine Report *The Future of Nursing: Leading Change, Advancing Health.* Washington, DC, July 28, 2015.

Georgia General Assembly. 2013. *2013-2014 regular session—H.B. 315.* http://www.legis.ga.gov/legislation/en-US/Display/20132014/HB/315 (accessed September 22, 2015).

Gerardi, T. 2015. Presentation to IOM Committee for Assessing Progress on Implementing the Recommendations of the Institute of Medicine Report *The Future of Nursing: Leading Change, Advancing Health.* Washington, DC, July 27, 2015.

Gilman, S. 2015. Presentation to IOM Committee for Assessing Progress on Implementing the Recommendations of the Institute of Medicine Report *The Future of Nursing: Leading Change, Advancing Health.* Washington, DC, July 27, 2015.

Goode, C. J., M. R. Lynn, D. McElroy, G. D. Bednash, and B. Murray. 2013. Lessons learned from 10 years of research on a post-baccalaureate nurse residency program. *Journal of Nursing Administration* 43(2):73-79.

Haskins, M., C. N. Hnatiuk, and L. H. Yoder. 2011. Medical-surgical nurses' perceived value of certification study. *MEDSURG Nursing* 20(2):71-93.

Hendren, R. 2010. NY health system's bold stance on nurse preparation. *HealthLeaders Media.* http://healthleadersmedia.com/page-2/NRS-254028/NY-Health-Systems-Bold-Stance-on-Nurse-Preparation (accessed September 18, 2015).

Hickey, J. V., L. Y. Unruh, R. P. Newhouse, M. Koithan, M. Johantegen, R. G. Hughes, K. B. Haller, and V. A. Lundmark. 2014. Credentialing: The need for a national research agenda. *Nursing Outlook* 62(2):119-127.

Hillman Foundation. 2015. *Our scholars program: Hillman Scholars in Nursing Innovation.* http://www.rahf.org/grant-programs/scholars (accessed November 7, 2015).

Hoffman, B. 2015. *Academic/practice partnership exemplars presented at conference.* http://www.aone.org/resources/APIN/PDF/July_2015_Voice_APIN.pdf (accessed September 18, 2015).

HRSA (Health Resources and Services Administration). 2009. *Health Resources and Services Administration fiscal year 2010 justification of estimates for appropriations committee.* http://www.hrsa.gov/about/budget/budgetjustification2010.pdf (accessed September 18, 2015).

HRSA. 2010. *The registered nurse population: Findings from the 2008 national sample survey of registered nurses.* http://bhpr.hrsa.gov/healthworkforce/rnsurveys/rnsurveyfinal.pdf (accessed November 5, 2015).

HRSA. 2011. *Health Resources and Services Administration fiscal year 2012 justification of estimates for appropriations committee.* http://www.hrsa.gov/about/budget/budgetjustification2012.pdf (accessed September 18, 2015).

HRSA. 2013. *Health Resources and Services Administration fiscal year 2014 justification of estimates for appropriations committee.* http://www.hrsa.gov/about/budget/budgetjustification2014.pdf (accessed November 22, 2015).

HRSA. 2015. *Health Resources and Services Administration fiscal year 2016 justification of estimates for appropriations committee.* http://www.hrsa.gov/about/budget/budgetjustification2016.pdf (accessed September 18, 2015).

IOM (Institute of Medicine). 2010. *Redesigning continuing education in the health professions.* Washington, DC: The National Academies Press.

IOM. 2011. *The future of nursing: Leading change, advancing health.* Washington, DC: The National Academies Press.

IOM. 2015. *Future directions of credentialing research in nursing: Workshop summary.* Washington, DC: The National Academies Press.

Johantgen, M. 2013. Overview of the state of the research: Individual credentialing. Presentation to the IOM Standing Committee on Credentialing Research in Nursing, Washington, DC, January 14. http://iom.nationalacademies.org/~/media/84A6BAA5E4734B84B2CFD37A7422161E.ashx (accessed November 5, 2015).

Johnson, M. 2014. *What's the difference between a DNP and PhD in nursing?* http://www.nursetogether.com/whats-difference-between-dnp-and-phd-nursing (accessed November 2, 2015).

Joint Accreditation for Interprofessional Continuing Education. 2013. *At a glance.* www.jointaccreditation.org/glance (accessed September 22, 2015).

Kutney-Lee, A., D. M. Sloane, and L. H. Aiken. 2013. An increase in the number of nurses with baccalaureate degrees is linked to lower rates of postsurgery mortality. *Health Affairs* 32(3):579-586.

Landen, J. 2015. Presentation to the IOM Committee for Assessing Progress on Implementing the Recommendations of the Institute of Medicine Report *The Future of Nursing: Leading Change, Advancing Health.* Washington, DC, July 27, 2015.

Larson, J. 2012. *"BSN in 10" bills could start a trend.* http://www.nursezone.com/Nursing-News-Events/more-news/%E2%80%98BSN-in-10%E2%80%99-Bills-Could-Start-a-Trend_38970.aspx (accessed September 18, 2015).

Lee, Y. M., K. Holm, E. Florez, M. Glauser, and E. Haswell. 2013. The DNP: Knowledge and perceptions of students in an accelerated master's program in nursing. *Open Journal of Nursing* 3:138-146.

Lewis, L. 2015. Presentation to IOM Committee for Assessing Progress on Implementing the Recommendations of the Institute of Medicine Report *The Future of Nursing: Leading Change, Advancing Health.* Washington, DC, July 27, 2015.

Li, Y., and D. Fang. 2014. *Special survey on vacant faculty positions for academic year 2014-2015.* http://www.aacn.nche.edu/leading-initiatives/research-data/vacancy14.pdf (accessed September 21, 2015).

Liesveld, J., J. Landen, and B. Dakin. 2015. *Nursing News & View.* http://www.nmnec.org/uploads/files/NMBN_ed_38.pdf (accessed September 16, 2015).

Martsolf, G. R., D. I. Auerbach, J. Spetz, M. L. Pearson, and A. N. Muchow. 2015. Doctor of nursing practice by 2015: An examination of nursing schools' decisions to offer a doctor of nursing practice degree. *Nursing Outlook* 63(2):219-226.

McElroy, D. 2015. Presentation to IOM Committee for Assessing Progress on Implementing the Recommendations of the Institute of Medicine Report *The Future of Nursing: Leading Change, Advancing Health.* Washington, DC, July 27, 2015.

McEwen, M., M. J. White, B. R. Pullis, and S. Krawtz. 2014. Essential content in RN-BSN programs. *Journal of Professional Nursing* 30(4):333-340.

McMenamin, P. 2015. *RN2BSN programs can change the game.* http://www.ananursespace.org/blogs/peter-mcmenamin/2015/06/30/rn2bsn-programs-can-change-the-game?ssopc=1 (accessed September 21, 2015).

Melander, S. 2015. Testimony provided to the IOM Committee for Assessing Progress on Implementing the Recommendations of the Institute of Medicine Report *The Future of Nursing: Leading Change, Advancing Health.* Washington, DC, May 28, 2015.

Miyamoto, S. 2014. Funding of advanced practice registered nurse education and residency programs. In *Health policy and advanced practice nursing: Impact and implications,* edited by K. A. Goudreau and M. C. Smolenski. New York: Springer Publishing Company. Pp. 145-161.

Mullin, C. M. 2012. *Why access matters: The community college student body.* AACC Policy Brief 2012-01PBL. Washington, DC: American Association of Community Colleges. http://www.aacc.nche.edu/Publications/Briefs/Documents/PB_AccessMatters.pdf (accessed September 18, 2015).

Murray, B. 2015. Presentation to IOM Committee for Assessing Progress on Implementing the Recommendations of the Institute of Medicine Report *The Future of Nursing: Leading Change, Advancing Health.* Washington, DC, July 27, 2015.

Naylor, M., L. Aiken, E. Fraher, J. Spetz, and O. Yakusheva. 2015 (unpublished). Progress in achieving the recommendations of the 2010 Institute of Medicine report on *The Future of Nursing: Leading Change, Advancing Health: A Review of the Evidence.* Princeton, NJ: Robert Wood Johnson Foundation.

NCES (National Center for Education Statistics). 2011. *2007-2008 national postsecondary student aid study* (NPSAS: 08) [Data file]. Washington, DC: U.S. Department of Education, Institute for Education Sciences.

NCSBN (National Council of State Boards of Nursing). 2011. *The National Council of State Boards of Nursing (NCSBN®) board of directors' (BOD) response to* The Future of Nursing: Leading Change, Advancing Health. http://campaignforaction.org/sites/default/files/NCSBN_BOD_Response_TheFutureofNursing_June2011_0.pdf (accessed August 6, 2015).

NCSBN. 2014. *NCSBN member board profiles, 2014, licensure.* https://www.ncsbn.org/Licensure_MBP_2014.pdf (accessed September 22, 2015).

NCSBN. 2015a. The 2015 Environmental Scan. *Journal of Nursing Regulation* 5(4):S3-S36.

NCSBN. 2015b. *Transition to practice.* https://www.ncsbn.org/transition-to-practice.htm (accessed August 6, 2015).

NCSBN. 2015c. *Transition to practice study results.* https://www.ncsbn.org/6889.htm (accessed August 6, 2015).

Newhouse, R. 2014. *Understanding the landscape and state of science in credentialing research in nursing.* Presentation at IOM Future Directions of Credentialing Research in Nursing: A Workshop, Washington, DC, September 3. http://iom.nationalacademies.org/~/media/Files/Activity%20Files/Workforce/FutureDirectionsCNRworkshop/NCR%20Workshop%20Presentations/Workshop_IOM_Newhouse.pdf (accessed November 5, 2015).

NLN (National League for Nursing). 2009. *Age of full-time nurse educators by rank, 2009.* http://www.nln.org/docs/default-source/newsroom/nursing-education-statistics/FC0809_F07.pdf-pdf.pdf (accessed September 18, 2015).

North Shore–LIJ (Long Island Jewish). 2015. *North Shore–LIJ Institute for Nursing: External nursing education.* https://www.northshorelij.com/research-and-education/continuing-and-professional-education/institute-nursing/external-nursing-education (accessed September 18, 2015).

Oklahoma Board of Nursing. 2014. *Meeting requirements for continuing qualifications for practice for license renewal guidelines.* ok.gov/nursing/cqlicenserenewal.pdf (accessed September 22, 2015).

Orsolini-Hain, L. 2012. Mixed messages: Hospital practices that serve as disincentives for associate degree-prepared nurses to return to school. *Nursing Outlook* 60(2):81-90.

Paterson, M. A., M. Fair, S. B. Cashman, C. Evans, and D. Garr. 2015. Achieving the triple aim: A curriculum, framework for health professions education. *American Journal of Preventive Medicine* 49(2):294-296.

Perlstein, L., R. L. Hoffmann, J. Lindberg, and D. Petras. 2014. Addressing barriers to achieving nursing certification. *Journal for Nurses in Professional Development* 30(6):309-315.

Pittman, P., C. S. Herrera, K. Horton, P. Thompson, and J. Ware. 2013a. Healthcare employers' policies on nurse education. *Journal of Healthcare Management* 58(6):399-410.

Pittman, P., C. Herrera, E. Bass, and P. Thompson. 2013b. Residency programs for new nurse graduates: How widespread are they and what are the primary obstacles to further adoption? *Journal of Nursing Administration* 43(11):597-602.

Pittman, P., E. Bass, J. Hargraves, C. Herrera, and P. Thompson. 2013c. The future of nursing: Monitoring the progress of recommended change in hospitals, nurse-led clinics, and home health and hospice agencies. *Journal of Nursing Administration* 45(2):93-99.

Redhead, C. S., K. J. Colello, E. J. Heisler, S. A. Lister, and A. K. Sarata. 2014. *Discretionary spending under the Affordable Care Act (ACA) (R41390).* Washington, DC: Congressional Research Service.

Rusin, M. 2015. Presentation to IOM Committee for Assessing Progress on Implementing the Recommendations of the Institute of Medicine Report *The Future of Nursing: Leading Change, Advancing Health.* Washington, DC, May 28, 2015.

RWJF (Robert Wood Johnson Foundation). 2012. *Robert Wood Johnson Foundation launches initiative to support academic progression in nursing.* http://www.rwjf.org/en/library/articles-and-news/2012/03/robert-wood-johnson-foundation-launches-initiative-to-support-ac.html (accessed September 18, 2015).

RWJF. 2013. *Robert Wood Johnson Foundation announces $20 million grant to support nurse PhD scientists.* http://www.rwjf.org/en/library/articles-and-news/2013/06/a-new-generation-of-nurse-scientists--educators--and-transformat.html; http://futureofnursingscholars.org (accessed September 21, 2015).

RWJF. 2014a. *Future of Nursing Scholars Program selects 14 schools of nursing to receive grants to prepare PhD nurses.* http://www.rwjf.org/en/library/articles-and-news/2014/07/future-of-nursing-scholars-program-selects-14-schools-of-nursing.html (accessed September 21, 2015).

RWJF. 2014b. *Iowa nurses build affordable, online nurse residency program.* http://www.rwjf.org/en/library/articles-and-news/2014/03/iowa-nurses-build-affordable--online-nurse-residency-program.html?cid=xsh_rwjf_em (accessed September 21, 2015).

RWJF. 2015a. *Future of Nursing Scholars Program selects 25 schools of nursing to receive grants to prepare PhD nurses.* http://www.rwjf.org/en/library/articles-and-news/2015/03/future-of-nursing-scholars-program-selects-25-schools.html (accessed September 21, 2015).

RWJF. 2015b. *Robert Wood Johnson Foundation academic progression in nursing.* http://www.rwjf.org/en/library/programs-and-initiatives/R/robert-wood-johnson-foundation-academic-progression-in-nursing-.html (accessed September 18, 2015).

RWJF. 2015c. *Robert Wood Johnson Foundation Future of Nursing Scholars.* http://futureofnursingscholars.org (accessed November 22, 2015).

RWJF. 2015d. *Robert Wood Johnson Foundation (RWJF) Future of Nursing Scholars Program frequently asked questions (FAQs).* http://futureofnursingscholars.org/wp-content/uploads/2015/06/FNS1_FAQs6-2-15.pdf (accessed September 21, 2015).

Salsberg, E. 2015. Recent trends in the nursing pipeline: US educated BSNs continue to increase. *Health Affairs Blog.* http://healthaffairs.org/blog/2015/04/09/recent-trends-in-the-nursing-pipeline-us-educated-bsns-continue-to-increase (accessed September 18, 2015).

Snyder, T. 2015. Presentation to IOM Committee for Assessing Progress on Implementing the Recommendations of the Institute of Medicine Report *The Future of Nursing: Leading Change, Advancing Health.* Washington, DC, May 28, 2015.

Spector, N. 2012. The initiative to advance innovations in nursing education: Three years later. *Journal of Nursing Regulation* 3(2):40-44.

Spector, N., M. A. Blegen, J. Silvestre, J. Barnsteiner, M. R. Lynn, B. Ulrich, L. Fogg, and M. Alexander. 2015a. Transition to practice study in hospital settings. *Journal of Nursing Regulation* 5(4):24-38.

Spector, N., M. A. Blegen, J. Silvestre, J. Barnsteiner, M. R. Lynn, and B. Ulrich. 2015b. Transition to practice in nonhospital settings. *Journal of Nursing Regulation* 6(1):4-13.

Spetz, J. 2002. The value of education in a licensed profession: The choice of associate or baccalaureate degree in nursing. *Economics of Education Review* 21(1):73-85.

Stoll, M. 2015. Presentation to IOM Committee for Assessing Progress on Implementing the Recommendations of the Institute of Medicine Report *The Future of Nursing: Leading Change, Advancing Health.* Washington, DC, July 27, 2015.

Swanson, M. L., and M. Stanton. 2013. Chief nursing officers' perceptions of the doctorate of nursing practice degree. *Nursing Forum* 48:35-44.

Talamantes, E., C. M. Mangione, K. Gonzalez, A. Jimenez, F. Gonzalez, and G. Moreno. 2014. Community college pathways: Improving the U.S. physician workforce pipeline. *Academic Medicine* 89(12):1649-1656.

Tanner, C. A. 2010. Transforming prelicensure nursing education: Preparing the new nurse to meet emerging health care needs. *Nursing Education Perspectives* 31(6):347-353.

TCC Group. 2013 (unpublished). *Future of Nursing: Campaign for Action: Action Coalition Survey.* Philadelphia: TCC Group.

Thibault, G. E. 2013. Reforming health professions education will require culture change and closer ties between classroom and practice. *Health Affairs* 32(11):1928-1932.

Trossman, S. 2008. *BSN in ten.* http://www.americannursetoday.com/bsn-in-ten (accessed September 18, 2015).

Udlis, K. A., and J. M. Mancuso. 2015. Perceptions of the role of doctor of nursing practice-prepared nurse: Clarity or confusion. *Journal of Professional Nursing* 31(4):274-283.

UHC/AACN (University HealthSystem Consortium/American Association of Colleges of Nursing). 2007. *Nurse Residency Program executive summary.* http://www.aacn.nche.edu/leading-initiatives/education-resources/NurseResidencyProgramExecSumm.pdf (accessed September 21, 2015).

Ulrich, B., C. Krozek, S. Early, C. H. Ashlock, L M. Africa, M. L. Carman. 2010. Improving retention, confidence, and competence of new graduate nurses: Results from a 10-year longitudinal database. *Nursing Economic$* 28(6):363-375.

Washington State Department of Health. n.d. *Continuing competency frequently asked questions.* http://www.doh.wa.gov/LicensesPermitsandCertificates/NursingCommission/Continuing Competency/FrequentlyAskedQuestionsFAQ (accessed September 22, 2015).

Wierzbinski-Cross, H., K. Ward, and P. Baumann. 2015. Nurses' perceptions of nurse residency: Identifying barriers to implementation. *Journal for Nurses in Professional Development* 31(1):15-20.

Williamson, M. K., L. Cook, L. Salmeron, and D. Burton. 2010. Retaining nursing faculty beyond retirement age. *Nurse Educator* 35(4):152-155.

Yakusheva, O., R. Lindrooth, and M. Weiss. 2014a. Economic evaluation of the 80% baccalaureate nurse workforce recommendation: A patient-level analysis. *Medical Care* 52(10):864-869.

Yakusheva, O., R. Lindrooth, and M. Weiss. 2014b. Nurse value-added and patient outcomes in acute care. *Health Services Research* 49(6):1767-1786.

You, L. M., L. H. Aiken, D. M. Sloane, K. Liu, G. He, Y. Hu, X. Jiang, X. Li, H. Liu, S. Shang, A. Kutney-Lee, and W. Sermeus. 2013. Hospital nursing, care quality, and patient satisfaction: Cross-sectional surveys of nurses and patients in hospitals in China and Europe. *International Journal of Nursing Studies* 50(2):154-161.

4

Promoting Diversity

Racial and ethnic minorities, notably African Americans and Hispanics/Latinos, are presently underrepresented in the nursing workforce, as well as in many health occupations. *The Future of Nursing* identifies this lack of diversity as a challenge for the nursing profession and states that a more diverse workforce will help better meet current and future health care needs and provide more culturally relevant care (IOM, 2011). The report notes that the most effective way to achieve workforce diversity is to increase diversity in the pipeline of students pursuing nursing education. The report does not offer any stand-alone recommendations addressing diversity, but it does include improving and increasing diversity in recommendations 4, 5, and 6 with reference to baccalaureate and doctoral education as well as lifelong learning (see Chapter 3). And one of the pillars of the Future of Nursing: Campaign for Action (the Campaign) is "promoting diversity" (CCNA, n.d.-a).[1]

INTRODUCTION

The lack of racial and ethnic diversity is a significant issue across the health care workforce that has been documented for decades. Present data show the current status of diversity in nursing and other health professions (HRSA, 2006, 2015a; IOM, 2004; NCSL, 2014; OMH, 2011; Sullivan Commission on Diversity in the Healthcare Workforce, 2004) (see Table 4-1).

As indicated in Table 4-1, the nursing workforce is more diverse than many

---

[1] Where possible, this chapter uses the racial and ethnic classifications (e.g., "Hispanic or Latino") used in the original data source.

TABLE 4-1 U.S. Health Occupations by Race, Ethnicity, and Sex, 2010-2012

	Race				Ethnicity	Sex	
	White (Non-Hispanic) (%)	African American (Non-Hispanic) (%)	Asian (Non-Hispanic) (%)		Hispanic or Latino (%)	Male (%)	Female (%)
U.S. Working-Age Population*	77.6	13.6	6.0		15.5	52.8	47.2
Advanced Practice Registered Nurses (APRNs)	89.5	5.2	4.0		4.4	15.0	85.0
Registered Nurses	78.6	10.7	8.8		5.4	9.2	90.8
Licensed Practical/Vocational Nurses	68.2	25.0	4.1		8.2	8.3	91.7
Nursing, Psychiatric, and Home Health Aides	54.0	37.5	5.1		13.4	13.0	87.0
Dental Assistants	81.1	8.8	6.9		22.5	4.6	95.4
Dental Hygienists	91.6	2.9	3.6		5.7	2.8	97.2
Dentists	80.5	3.3	14.5		6.1	74.5	25.5

Diagnostic-Related Technologists and Technicians	84.8	8.1	5.0	9.1	29.0	71.0
Dietitians and Nutritionists	76.0	15.4	6.6	9.1	10.3	89.7
Emergency Medical Technicians and Paramedics	89.3	6.7	1.3	10.9	69.3	30.7
Medical and Clinical Laboratory Technologists and Technicians	68.5	14.9	13.3	9.2	27.0	73.0
Medical Assistants and Other Health Support Occupations	72.6	18.4	5.3	19.0	12.4	87.6
Pharmacists	73.7	5.9	18.0	4.0	46.3	53.7
Physicians	72.2	5.3	20.0	6.0	65.1	34.9

* U.S. working-age population is defined as the population 16 years of age or older from the American Community Survey (ACS) Public Use Microdata Sample, 2010-2012.
SOURCE: HRSA, 2015a.

of the other health professions requiring advanced education. It also is worth noting that diversity is greatest among licensed practical nurses (LPNs)/licensed vocational nurses (LVNs); nursing, psychiatric, and home health aides; and medical assistants and other health support occupations. As the Sullivan Commission (2004) report notes, "minority students lag behind white students at every educational level, trailing in nearly all key scholastic indicators, such as . . . high school completion rates, college enrollment rates, and graduation rates. The gap between the primary and secondary educational experience of whites versus that of Hispanics, African Americans, Native Americans, and some Asian subgroups is wide, deep, and persistent" (p. 73). That report also observes that "underrepresented minority students come disproportionately from families with lower income and lower wealth than whites and are more likely to perceive the cost of an education as a deterrent or an unmanageable burden" (p. 92). A 2002 report by the Advisory Committee on Student Financial Assistance states that 48 percent of qualified low-income students forgo 4-year colleges and universities because of the financial burden (Advisory Committee on Student Financial Assistance, 2002). A 2013 presentation of the Advisory Committee noted that inequalities in access to college were worsening (Advisory Committee on Student Financial Assistance, 2013).

ACTIVITY

Nationwide, many stakeholder organizations in health care, education, and government have taken steps to increase the diversity of the nursing workforce and of the health professions more broadly. For example, the Sullivan Alliance to Transform the Health Professions was established in 2005 to advance the recommendations of two important reports released in 2004: the Sullivan Commission report cited above and the Institute of Medicine (IOM) report *In the Nation's Compelling Interest: Ensuring Diversity in the Health-Care Workforce* (IOM, 2004). The Sullivan Alliance became a 501(c)3 nonprofit organization in 2011. Six state alliances were established between 2004 and 2015. These alliances operate as "'pathfinders' to identify and test best practices to diversify the health workforce" by developing collaborations between educational institutions at both the community college and the university level and health centers (The Sullivan Alliance, 2015).

The Veterans Health Administration (VHA) has been committed to addressing workforce diversity, stating that "national and local strategic plans encompass required elements to attend to attracting, maintaining, and advancing personnel with diverse characteristics" (VA, 2015a, p. 22). The VHA has used workforce databases to track personnel characteristics and ensure the diversity of advisory groups and committees. The VHA's Nursing Innovation Award was launched in 2003. The following year, the theme of the award was "Enhancing the Diversity of the [U.S. Department of Veterans Affairs (VA)] Nursing Workforce and/or

Addressing Culturally Sensitive Patient Care," and 10 nurse-led interdisciplinary teams received awards for their contributions in these areas (VA, 2015a,b).

In the U.S. Department of Defense, the Tri-Service Nurse Corps has achieved greater success than the nation as a whole in recruiting and educating a nurse workforce that is more diverse in both gender and race/ethnicity than the civilian nurse workforce. Men represent 36.9 percent of nurses in the Army Nurse Corps, 36.0 percent in the Navy Nurse Corp, and 29.2 percent in the Air Force Nurse Corps.[2] Non-Hispanic whites make up 62 percent of nurses in the Army, 62.5 percent of nurses in the Navy, and 71.5 percent of nurses in the Air Force Nurse Corps.[3] The proportion of nurses in the military who are Hispanic or Latino is similar to that in the civilian workforce, but it is lower than the proportion in the U.S. population. A variety of financial incentive programs for the pursuit of nursing, including loan repayment programs for nurses already trained and financial support for ongoing nursing education, may help break down barriers to greater diversity in the military nursing workforce (Donelan et al., 2014; U.S. Army, n.d.). The workforce is recruited in part from enlisted personnel who already serve in health care roles and through new partnerships with colleges and universities that are located near major U.S. military bases. Recent research documenting factors driving career interest in these populations has helped to shape further recruitment efforts (Donelan et al., 2014).

As noted above, the Campaign has made promoting diversity one of its pillars (CCNA, n.d.-a), noting that "Action Coalitions should look at their state's demographics to determine what aspects of identity need to be addressed in regards to diversity and meeting the population's health care needs" (CCNA, n.d.-b). To support this pillar, the Campaign convenes a Diversity Steering Committee composed of representatives from the American Assembly for Men in Nursing, Asian American/Pacific Islander Nurses Association, National Alaska Native American Indian Nurses Association, National Association of Hispanic Nurses, National Black Nurses Association, National Coalition of Ethnic Minority Nurse Associations, and Philippine Nurses Association of America (CCNA, n.d.-d).

A 2013 survey of the Action Coalitions illustrates the degree of self-reported focus on racial/ethnic diversity in nursing. Among the survey respondents, 8 states and the District of Columbia said they considered this issue a high priority, while 18 states said they considered it a low priority (TCC Group, 2013) (see Figure 4-1). In the same survey, only 32 percent of respondents said they felt that the diversity of the nurse workforce had improved (TCC Group, 2013). Most state Action Coalitions said they did not consider diversity a "main focus" of their work (see Figure 4-2).

After this survey was conducted, the Campaign began requiring—not just

---

[2] Personal communications, C. Romano, Uniformed Services University, September 2, 2015, and September 13, 2015.
[3] Ibid.

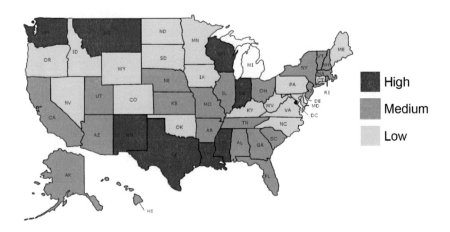

FIGURE 4-1 Level of focus on diversity among state Action Coalitions.
NOTE: This map is based on aggregated responses from states about their Action Coalition's focus on racial/ethnic and gender diversity in nursing. State scores were divided into high, medium, and low levels of focus. There were not enough respondents from Delaware or Michigan to calculate a score.
SOURCE: TCC Group, 2013.

recommending—that states receiving State Implementation Program (SIP) funding have a diversity action plan in place. This requirement evolved from a preference in the first SIP request for proposals (RFP), issued in 2011. At that time, the Campaign noted that "preference will be given to [Action Coalitions] that include a plan for advancing diversity as part of their recommendation implementation" (CCNA, 2011), whereas the most recent RFP states that "all proposals must address the goal of increasing the diversity of the nursing workforce, faculty, and leadership to meet the state population's health care needs. Preference will be given to [Action Coalition] applications that describe robust and achievable mechanisms to enhance diversity and inclusive practices" (CCNA, 2014). Grantees of the Robert Wood Johnson Foundation's (RWJF's) Academic Progression in Nursing program (see Chapter 3) also are required to have diversity action plans.[4]

According to the Campaign, as of May 2015, 41 state Action Coalitions were working on developing and/or implementing diversity action plans, while 21 Action Coalitions had an approved diversity action plan (CCNA, 2015a). The Campaign's Diversity Steering Committee has developed criteria for effective diversity action plans (Villarruel et al., 2015, p. 59):

---

[4] Personal communication, S. Hassmiller, Robert Wood Johnson Foundation, September 19, 2015.

- Strategies should be developed at the right "line of sight" (focusing not only on process but on outcomes), targeted to the state level, and grounded in the IOM recommendations. The committee encourages Action Coalitions to focus on their states' population and demographic needs.
- Efforts should be data based and data driven. The committee recommends that an Action Coalition's plans begin by determining baseline data regarding the state's population and workforce.
- Choice of focus, direction, and strategies should be evidence based. The committee encourages Action Coalitions to use lessons learned from other state-level coalitions, institutions, and minority organizations that implemented successful programs aimed at increasing diversity.
- The emphasis should be on sustainability and a credible infrastructure for continuous work. The committee wants to ensure that efforts can be sustained over time, and that plans can be replicated or adopted by other organizations or states.
- Diversity should be thoroughly embraced by each Action Coalition. The committee wants to ensure that the coalitions are addressing the diversity of their leadership as well as using diversity strategies with regard to education progression, removing barriers to practice and care, interprofessional collaboration, and data collection initiatives.

In addition, the Campaign sends diversity consultants to states to provide assistance, convenes an Increasing Diversity through Data Learning Collaborative for state Action Coalitions, and compiles resources relating to diversity on the Campaign website (CCNA, 2015a, n.d.-c).

Because *The Future of Nursing* does not include a stand-alone recommendation or key message relating to diversity, and because diversity is an issue that cuts across education, practice, and leadership, the Campaign does not have a primary dashboard indicator relating to diversity. However, it does track the following supplemental indicators that relate to the diversity of the nursing workforce and the workforce pipeline (CCNA, 2015b):

- racial and ethnic composition of the registered nurse (RN) workforce in the United States;
- new RN graduates by degree type, by race/ethnicity;
- new RN graduates by degree type, by gender;
- diversity of nursing doctoral graduates by race/ethnicity; and
- diversity of nursing doctoral graduates by gender.

The Campaign also tracks whether states are collecting race and ethnicity data on their nursing workforce. As noted in Chapter 6, the Campaign dashboard shows that as of 2013 most, but not all, states were collecting these data. Doing so

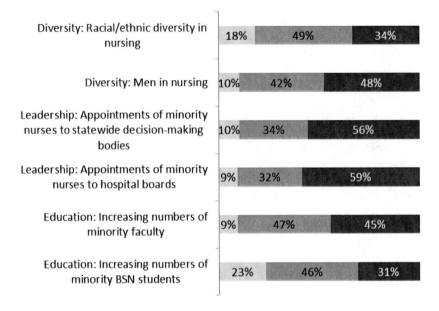

Diversity: Racial/ethnic diversity in nursing — 18% | 49% | 34%

Diversity: Men in nursing — 10% | 42% | 48%

Leadership: Appointments of minority nurses to statewide decision-making bodies — 10% | 34% | 56%

Leadership: Appointments of minority nurses to hospital boards — 9% | 32% | 59%

Education: Increasing numbers of minority faculty — 9% | 47% | 45%

Education: Increasing numbers of minority BSN students — 23% | 46% | 31%

▨ Main focus of our Action Coalition

▨ Some work done on this but not the main focus

■ We are not working on this issue

FIGURE 4-2 State Action Coalition members' focus on areas of diversity identified by *The Future of Nursing* and the Campaign.
NOTES: Data are based on responses of 1,100 survey respondents from 49 state Action Coalitions, including the District of Columbia. Scores were calculated for each state by aggregating and averaging all responses from that state. BSN = bachelor of science in nursing.
SOURCE: Personal communication, K. Locke, TCC Group, September 3, 2015.

could help states create benchmarks for workforce diversity and measure progress as diversity initiatives are implemented.

PROGRESS

Increasing the diversity of the overall nurse workforce is inevitably a slow process because only a small percentage of the workforce leaves and enters each year, whereas the pipeline can change more rapidly, as most degree programs cycle in 2 to 4 years. Thus, the pipeline will respond more quickly to efforts to increase diversity relative to the pool of all nurses; the pipeline also represents the future workforce. Changing the makeup of the pipeline depends, of course, on increasing diversity among those who apply to, are accepted to, enroll in, and graduate from nursing degree programs.

In the United States, according to the most recent data available to the committee, African Americans made up 13.6 percent of the general population aged 20 to 40 in 2011-2013,[5] but 10.7 percent of the RN workforce, 10.3 percent of 2011-2013 associate's degree graduates, and 9.3 percent of 2011-2013 baccalaureate graduates. The disparity is even wider for Hispanics/Latinos, who made up 20.3 percent of the general population aged 20 to 40 in 2011-2013,[6] but only 5.6 percent of the RN workforce, 8.8 percent of 2011-2013 associate's degree graduates, and 7.0 percent of 2011-2013 baccalaureate graduates. Men made up 9.2 percent of the RN workforce (see Table 4-1), 11.7 percent of baccalaureate nursing students, and 11.6 percent of baccalaureate nursing graduates in the 2013-2014 academic year.[7]

Trends in the Diversity of the Nursing Workforce

Only 5 years after the release of *The Future of Nursing*, it is still too soon to see significant changes in the diversity of the national nursing workforce that may be attributable to the recommendations of the report or the activities of the Campaign. To examine trends in the diversity of the nursing workforce, the present committee considered data over a period of time that includes but also predates the Campaign.

Gender Diversity

Changing career options for women and men have resulted in more gender diversity in many health care occupations in the United States. The proportion of nurses who are males remains below 10 percent of the nurse workforce, but it increased incrementally from 2.7 percent in 1970 to 9.6 percent in 2011 (U.S. Census Bureau, 2013). By contrast, in 1970, 7.6 percent of physicians were women, and by 2012 that proportion had risen to 35 percent (HRSA, 2015a; More and Greer, 2000). Gender diversity is greatest in advanced practice nursing. Nine percent of nurse practitioners (NPs) are male, compared with 41 percent of certified registered nurse anesthetists (CRNAs) (U.S. Census Bureau, 2013). Data from the 2011 American Community Survey (ACS) show that males nurses earn more than their female counterparts in several categories, including RNs, NPs, and CRNAs.

---

[5] Derived from 2011-2013 American Community Survey data.

[6] Ibid.

[7] Data received from the American Association of Colleges of Nursing (AACN), August 28, 2015.

TABLE 4-2 Number and Percentage of Active Registered Nurses (RNs) Who Are African American and Hispanic/Latino

| | African American | | Hispanic/Latino | | Total of All |
Year	Number	Percent	Number	Percent	Active RNs
2001	175,724	8.9	78,131	3.9	1,982,880
2002	185,171	9.0	70,397	3.4	2,059,804
2003	202,369	9.6	75,308	3.6	2,117,489
2004	187,468	8.8	87,311	4.1	2,128,411
2005	219,922	9.9	86,799	3.9	2,226,448
2006	237,044	10.0	101,895	4.3	2,361,841
2007	239,242	9.8	102,009	4.2	2,429,122
2008	261,662	10.4	115,261	4.6	2,513,494
2009	255,744	10.0	119,342	4.7	2,566,375
2010	260,196	10.0	136,760	5.2	2,611,598
2011	275,901	10.2	148,725	5.5	2,701,523
2012	289,747	10.4	163,391	5.8	2,797,828
2013	299,321	10.7	156,304	5.6	2,795,310

SOURCE: American Community Survey, U.S. Census Bureau, 2001-2013.

Racial and Ethnic Diversity

An analysis of the ACS from 2001 to 2013 indicates that racial and ethnic diversity in the nursing workforce has been increasing: over this period, the number of active Hispanic/Latino nurses doubled, and the number of African American nurses rose by 70 percent (see Table 4-2). Yet despite steady gains in the number of racial and ethnic minority nurses and advances in the proportion of nurses who are minorities, the diversity of the nursing workforce still is not representative of the diversity of the general U.S. population.

According to a 2015 report of the American Nurses Association (ANA) (McMenamin, 2015), the youngest generation of nurses is more diverse than the oldest: 80.7 percent of nurses over age 60 are white non-Hispanic, compared with 71.6 percent of nurses under 40. The report suggests that as older nurses retire, workforce diversity will improve; however, this analysis does not take into account the proportion of minority nurses in the pipeline.

Trends in the Diversity of the Pipeline

Associate's and Baccalaureate Degrees in Nursing

The number and proportion of enrollees in and graduates from baccalaureate nursing programs who are male increased between 2005 and 2014. Male enrollees in baccalaureate programs increased from 15,705 (9.7 percent) in 2005, to

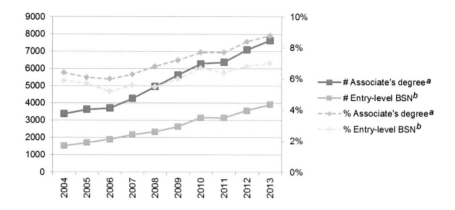

FIGURE 4-3 Number and percentage of Hispanic/Latino associate's degree and entry-level baccalaureate graduates, 2004-2014.

[a] SOURCE: The Integrated Postsecondary Education Data System (IPEDS), National Center for Education Statistics (NCES), U.S. Department of Education; 2004-2013.

[b] SOURCE: American Association of Colleges of Nursing (AACN), Annual Enrollment and Graduations in Baccalaureate and Graduate Programs in Nursing report 2004-2014, Table 9.

27,200 (11.4 percent) in 2010, to 37,410 (11.7 percent) in 2014.[8] Male graduates in baccalaureate nursing programs increased from 3,752 (9.1 percent) in 2005, to 8,046 (10.9 percent) in 2010, to 12,952 (11.6 percent) in 2014. These increases suggest that the number and proportion of males in the nursing workforce will likely continue to rise gradually. Likewise, the number of African American and Hispanic/Latino nursing graduates in both associate's and baccalaureate programs increased steadily from 2004 to 2014, consistent with the pace observed in the general nursing workforce.

The representation of minorities in the population of nursing students and graduates reveals some differences between Hispanics/Latinos and African Americans. The number of Hispanic/Latino nursing graduates rose steadily in both associate's and baccalaureate programs from 2004 to 2013, and the proportion of Hispanics/Latinos increased from 6.4 percent to 8.8 percent of associate's graduates and from 5.9 percent to 7.0 percent of baccalaureate graduates (see Figure 4-3). Despite these increases, however, the percentage of Hispanic/Latino graduates lags behind the percentage of Hispanics or Latinos in the general population aged 20 to 40 in 2013 (20.3 percent[9]). The number of African American graduates also increased over this period, but the proportion of African American

---

[8] Data received from AACN, August 28, 2015.

[9] Derived from 2011-2013 ACS data.

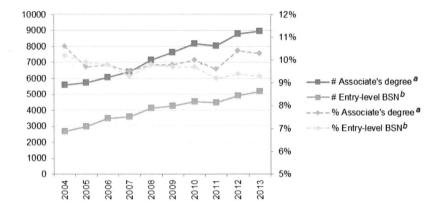

FIGURE 4-4 Number and percentage of African American associate's degree and entry-level baccalaureate graduates, 2004-2014.
[a] SOURCE: The Integrated Postsecondary Education Data System (IPEDS), National Center for Education Statistics (NCES), U.S. Department of Education, 2004-2013.
[b] SOURCE: American Association of Colleges of Nursing (AACN), Annual Enrollment and Graduations in Baccalaureate and Graduate Programs in Nursing report 2004-2014, Table 9.

nursing students and graduates remained essentially unchanged (see Figure 4-4). The percentages of African American graduates in 2013—10.3 percent for associate's degrees and 9.3 percent for baccalaureate degrees—are below the percentage of the general population aged 20 to 40 that is African American (13.6 percent[10]).

Baccalaureate Completion Programs

The past several years have seen a significant increase in the number of nurses with an associate's degree or diploma who have returned to school to obtain a baccalaureate degree. According to American Association of Colleges of Nursing (AACN) data, the number of Hispanic/Latino nurses graduating from baccalaureate completion programs also increased significantly, from 532 in 2004 to 2,220 in 2013. Hispanics/Latinos represent 6.3 percent of baccalaureate completion graduates in 2013, slightly lower than their proportion in entry-level baccalaureate programs (7 percent). The number of African Americans graduating from baccalaureate completion programs increased from 1,265 in 2004 to 5,151 in 2013. In 2013, African Americans represented 14.5 percent of baccalaureate completion graduates, compared with 9.3 percent of entry-level baccalaureate graduates, a striking difference that warrants further investigation (see Table 4-3).

---

[10] Ibid.

TABLE 4-3 Number and Percentage of African American and Hispanic/Latino Baccalaureate Completion Graduates, 2004-2013

Year	African American		Hispanic/Latino	
	Number	Percent of All Baccalaureate Completion Graduates	Number	Percent of All Baccalaureate Completion Graduates
2004	1,265	13.0	532	5.5
2005	1,403	13.7	521	5.1
2006	1,536	13.4	600	5.2
2007	1,844	14.1	652	5.0
2008	2,071	14.2	813	5.6
2009	2,408	14.3	945	5.6
2010	2,829	14.6	1,077	5.6
2011	3,099	14.4	1,127	5.2
2012	4,537	15.1	1,727	5.7
2013	5,151	14.5	2,220	6.3

SOURCE: American Association of Colleges of Nursing (AACN), Annual Enrollment and Graduations in Baccalaureate and Graduate Programs in Nursing report 2004-2014, Table 9.

Master's and Doctoral Programs

AACN data show that the numbers of African American and Hispanic/Latino enrollees in master's programs both more than tripled between 2005 and 2014. African American enrollees increased from 4,468 in 2005 to 14,911 in 2014, and Hispanic/Latino enrollees increased from 1,953 to 6,575 (see Figure 4-5). The proportion of all master's students that are African American increased from 10.7 percent to 14.7 percent, and that of Hispanic or Latino students increased from 4.7 percent to 6.5 percent (see Figure 4-5). The number of minority students enrolled in research-focused doctorate programs increased from 582 in 2005 to 1,339 in 2014 (see Figure 4-6).

State-by-State Variation in the Diversity of the RN Pipeline

While the percentage of minorities in nursing has been trending upward nationwide, there is a significant amount of variation at the state level with regard to the diversity of the nursing pipeline relative to the state population aged 20-40—the general age of nursing graduates (see Figures 4-7 through 4-10). It is important to compare the nursing pipeline and the general population at the

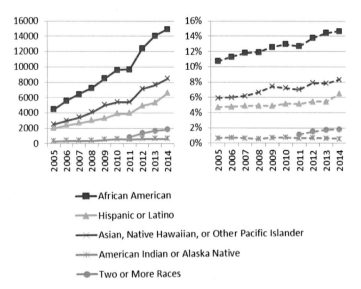

FIGURE 4-5 Numbers and percentages of racial and ethnic minority enrollees in nursing master's degree programs, 2005-2014.
SOURCE: Data received from AACN, August 28, 2015.

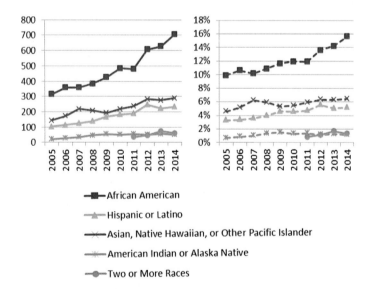

FIGURE 4-6 Numbers and percentages of racial and ethnic minority enrollees in research-focused nursing doctoral programs, 2005-2014.
SOURCE: Data received from AACN, August 28, 2015.

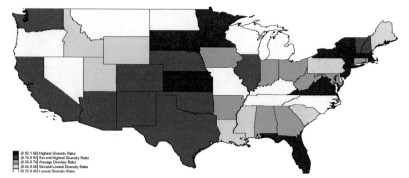

FIGURE 4-7 State-level diversity in African American graduates of associate's degree programs.

NOTE: An index showing the relative representation among nursing graduates is calculated by dividing the percentage of African American graduates by the percentage of African Americans in the population of the state aged 20-40, the general age of nursing graduates.

SOURCES: The Integrated Postsecondary Education Data System (IPEDS), National Center for Education Statistics (NCES), U.S. Department of Education, 2011-2013, for the percentage of graduates by race and ethnicity; American Community Survey, U.S. Census Bureau, for the percentage of the population aged 20 to 40 by race/ethnicity. Calculation of the state diversity index by the George Washington University Health Workforce Institute.

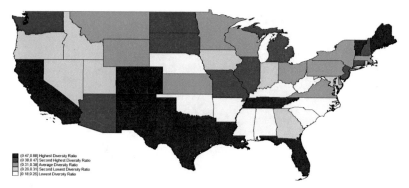

FIGURE 4-8 State-level diversity in Hispanic/Latino graduates of associate's degree programs.

NOTE: An index showing the relative representation among nursing graduates is calculated by dividing the percentage of Hispanic/Latino graduates by the percentage of Hispanics/Latinos in the population of the state aged 20-40, the general age of nursing graduates.

SOURCES: The Integrated Postsecondary Education Data System (IPEDS), National Center for Education Statistics (NCES), U.S. Department of Education, 2011-2013, for the percentage of graduates by race and ethnicity; American Community Survey, U.S. Census Bureau, for the percentage of the population aged 20 to 40 by race/ethnicity. Calculation of the state diversity index by the George Washington University Health Workforce Institute.

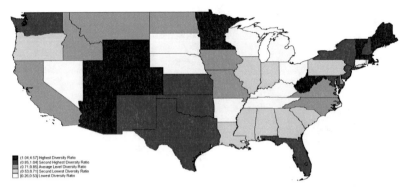

FIGURE 4-9 State-level diversity in African American graduates of baccalaureate nursing programs.

NOTE: An index showing the relative representation among nursing graduates is calculated by dividing the percentage of African American graduates by the percentage of African Americans in the population of the state aged 20-40, the general age of nursing graduates.

SOURCES: The Integrated Postsecondary Education Data System (IPEDS), National Center for Education Statistics (NCES), U.S. Department of Education, 2011-2013, for the percentage of graduates by race and ethnicity; American Community Survey, U.S. Census Bureau, for the percentage of the population aged 20 to 40 by race/ethnicity. Calculation of the state diversity index by the George Washington University Health Workforce Institute.

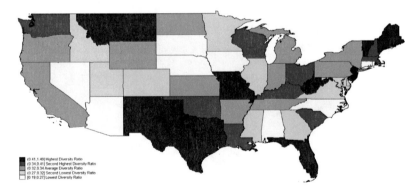

FIGURE 4-10 State-level diversity in Hispanic/Latino graduates of baccalaureate nursing programs.

NOTE: An index showing the relative representation among nursing graduates is calculated by dividing the percentage of Hispanic/Latino graduates by the percentage of Hispanics/Latinos in the population of the state aged 20-40, the general age of nursing graduates.

SOURCES: The Integrated Postsecondary Education Data System (IPEDS), National Center for Education Statistics (NCES), U.S. Department of Education, 2011-2013, for the percentage of graduates by race and ethnicity; American Community Survey, U.S. Census Bureau, for the percentage of the population aged 20 to 40 by race/ethnicity. Calculation of the state diversity index by the George Washington University Health Workforce Institute.

state level to inform state policy and planning around educational and practice diversity issues.

Faculty

In a 2015 fact sheet, AACN notes that "the need to attract diverse nursing students is paralleled by the need to recruit more faculty from minority populations. Few nurses from racial/ethnic minority groups with advanced nursing degrees pursue faculty careers" (AACN, 2015). Data from AACN's 2015 annual survey show that faculty in baccalaureate or higher-level programs are less diverse than both the nurse workforce overall and the enrollees and graduates of nursing degree programs (see Table 4-4). Among all full-time nursing school faculty, 7.1 percent are African American, and 2.3 percent are Hispanic/Latino; 5.7 percent are male.[11]

Funding

While initiatives to increase the diversity of the nursing workforce remain as important as ever, if not more so, critical funding sources for such initiatives have remained relatively flat. In fiscal year (FY) 2015, approximately $15 million was appropriated for the Health Resources and Services Administration (HRSA) Title VIII Nursing Workforce Diversity program, which promotes diversity by engaging and recruiting underrepresented individuals into nursing and providing them with resources that assist with their retention and advancement in educational programs. HRSA's FY2016 appropriations justification includes a request for $14 million for a new program, the Health Workforce Diversity Program, which would focus on education, training, and practice issues for individuals from disadvantaged backgrounds. HRSA's Health Careers Opportunity Program, although proposed twice for elimination, has remained funded at slightly below $15 million per year since FY2012, a sharp decline from FY2009 ($19.13 million + $2.51 million from the American Recovery and Reinvestment Act [ARRA]) (HRSA, 2012, 2015b).

DISCUSSION

A more diverse nursing workforce is needed to provide culturally relevant care to an increasingly diverse population. Evidence suggests that racially, ethnically, and socioeconomically diverse health care providers are likely to practice in communities with similar populations, improving access to and quality of health care in those communities (HRSA, 2006; IOM, 2004, 2011). To be successful, an effort to improve the diversity of the nursing workforce must focus on each

---

[11] Data received from AACN, August 28, 2015.

TABLE 4-4 Numbers and Percentages of Full-Time Nurse Faculty by Race/Ethnicity, 2005, 2010, and 2014

	2005		2010		2014	
	Number	Percentage	Number	Percentage	Number	Percentage
American Indian/Alaska Native	37	0.3	56	0.4	69	0.4
Asian	175	1.6	320	2.2	498	2.8
African American	631	5.8	954	6.5	1,279	7.1
Hispanic/Latino	189	1.7	298	2.0	416	2.3
Native Hawaiian/Other Pacific Islander	36	0.3	60	0.4	66	0.4
Two or More Races	Not collected	Not collected	Not collected	Not collected	195	1.1
White	9,867	90.2	12,797	87.7	15,120	84.5
Unknown/Not Reported/ Other	32	Not reported	110	0.8	257	1.4

SOURCE: Data received from AACN, August 28, 2015.

step along the professional pathway, from recruitment, to educational programs, to retention and success within those programs, to graduation and placement in a job, to retention and advancement within a nursing career. Recruitment of diverse populations, in particular, could help improve the diversity profile of the profession. As seen in Table 4-1, a significant proportion of non-RNs who are working in health care—LPNs/LVNs and nursing, psychiatric, and home health aides—are minorities. For example, African Americans represent 10.7 percent of RNs, but 25 percent of LPNs/LVNs and 37.5 percent of health aides. This diverse pool of health care professionals could, with proper incentives and training, move into RN positions and bolster the diversity of the profession. At the same time, a greater understanding of the reasons why racial and ethnic minorities are more likely to enter the workforce at the LPN/aide level than through educational programs leading to an RN could help elucidate mechanisms for recruiting and supporting these students in BSN, master's-level, and doctoral programs.

Associate's degree nursing programs and community colleges provide entry into the nursing profession for many nurses, but particularly for disadvantaged and underrepresented populations. Fulcher and Mullin (2011) note that "minority students in higher education are concentrated in community colleges" (p. 7), and studies have found that this holds true for both nursing and non-nursing students (American Association of Community Colleges, 2010; Bell, 2012; Mullin, 2012; Talamantes et al., 2014). African American and Hispanic/Latino graduates are more likely than their white counterparts to enter the nursing field with an associate's degree rather than a baccalaureate. Forty percent of new white RN graduates held a baccalaureate in 2013, compared with 36 percent of African American and 26 percent of Hispanic/Latino graduates (CCNA, n.d.-e). While white students may be more likely than minority students to enter the nursing profession with a baccalaureate degree, however, minority students may be slightly more likely to eventually hold a baccalaureate or higher degree. The 2008 National Sample Survey of RNs (HRSA, 2010) found that just under half (48.4 percent) of white non-Hispanic nurses held a baccalaureate or higher degree, compared with 52.5 percent of African Americans and 51.5 percent of Hispanics.

As these data indicate, both associate's degree programs and baccalaureate completion programs are important pathways for minority nurses. In addition, community college associate's degree programs make it easier for students with lower incomes to enter the profession. Because of the cost difference between community college and university programs, students attending community colleges to earn an associate's degree likely have lower incomes and different economic backgrounds relative to those attending entry-level baccalaureate programs (Fulcher and Mullin, 2011). Mullin (2012) highlights data (NCES, 2011) showing that community colleges enrolled 41 percent of all undergraduates living in poverty.

Community colleges, associate's degree programs, and baccalaureate completion programs all serve as pathways for minority and disadvantaged students to enter and succeed in nursing, and as the nursing profession moves toward the recommendation of *The Future of Nursing* for an 80 percent baccalaureate-trained workforce, these pathways—as well as the emerging models offering baccalaureate programs in community colleges—will remain important avenues to maintaining or increasing the diversity of the nursing workforce (see also Chapter 2). As noted by Jenny Landen, Leadership Council, New Mexico Nursing Education Consortium, at the committee's July 2015 workshop, "An important project goal [of the New Mexico Nursing Education Consortium] is to increase the diversity of the [baccalaureate]-prepared nursing workforce to better mirror our population. By placing the [baccalaureate] in the community colleges throughout the state with high minority populations, this opportunity will increase that diversity."

Initiatives to retain diverse and underrepresented students in nursing education programs include financial support, mentorship, social and academic support, and professional counseling (Bleich et al., 2015; Bond et al., 2012; Brooks Carthon et al., 2014; Carter et al., 2015). These programs address diversity at all stages of education, from admission, to support during school, to the transition to the workforce. For example, the University of Illinois at Chicago College of Nursing recently adopted a holistic admissions process, which attempts to shape a diverse class by taking multiple attributes into account, looking at such standard criteria as grade point average and standardized test scores but also such attributes as race/ethnicity, leadership skills, and physical abilities (Scott and Zerwic, 2015; Weaver, 2015). For support during school, the Clinical Leadership Collaborative for Diversity in Nursing provides leadership development to racially, ethnically, and economically diverse nursing students at the University of Massachusetts at Boston. The program offers a scholarship and also uses mentoring to support the students participating in the program, which has seen a 100 percent graduation rate among participants (Banister et al., 2014). Finally, to help transition diverse students into the workforce, the Hausman Program at Massachusetts General Hospital offers a 6-week paid fellowship program for rising senior nursing students. Participants gain hands-on clinical experience in inpatient and ambulatory care settings and benefit from mentoring from minority staff nurses and educators. Deborah Washington, Director of Diversity for Patient Care Services, Massachusetts General Hospital, noted that "mentoring has become fundamental to a programmatic approach to the retention of nursing students as well as the working nurse."[12] She went on to say, "What is unique about [the Hausman Program] is that we help students understand the importance of their cultural identity in the practice environment, not only to their benefit, but to the benefit of ethnic minority patients. These students are taught to use their culture-based knowledge to increase patient engagement and to educate staff with cultural information in a peer support environment."

---

[12] Personal communication, D. Washington, Massachusetts General Hospital, August 12, 2015.

FINDINGS AND CONCLUSIONS

Findings

This study yielded the following findings on diversity in the nursing profession:

Finding 4-1. Diversity continues to be a challenge in many health professions requiring postsecondary education, including nursing (see HRSA, 2015a).

Finding 4-2. Although the numbers and percentages of racial and ethnic minority nurses have generally increased in recent years, minority representation in the nursing workforce still is not representative of that in the general population. African American and Hispanic/Latino nurses in particular remain underrepresented in nursing.

Finding 4-3. There is significant variation from state to state in the diversity of both the nursing workforce and new nursing graduates compared with the diversity of the state population.

Finding 4-4. The Future of Nursing *does not offer a stand-alone recommendation pertaining to diversity, but instead makes it a crosscutting issue in recommendations relating to education and leadership.*

Finding 4-5. The Campaign established a Diversity Steering Committee and now requires all state Action Coalitions receiving funding through the Campaign's State Implementation Program or the RWJF-funded Academic Progression in Nursing program to develop diversity action plans.

Finding 4-6. As of May 2015, a total of 41 state Action Coalitions were working on developing or implementing diversity action plans, and 21 states had approved diversity action plans. Many state Action Coalitions are working on diversity issues even if this is not their main focus.

Finding 4-7. Most, but not all, states collect data on the racial/ethnic composition of their nursing workforce.

Finding 4-8. In addition to and outside of the work of the Campaign, many efforts have focused on increasing the diversity of the nursing workforce— especially programs designed to improve diversity in education—since the release of The Future of Nursing.

Conclusions

The committee drew the following conclusions about progress toward improving diversity in the nursing profession:

By making diversity one of its pillars, the Campaign has shone a spotlight on the issue of diversity in the nursing workforce. The requirement that states receiving funding through certain Campaign mechanisms (e.g., the State Implementation Program) focus on issues of diversity will help advance this issue at the state level. Further, work on diversity at the state level allows local coalitions to work toward creating a nursing workforce that is reflective of the diversity of the state's population.

Community colleges, associate's degree programs, and baccalaureate completion programs provide important pathways for diverse and disadvantaged students to enter the nursing profession; these educational pathways need to be maintained and strengthened.

The high proportions of underrepresented minorities among LPNs/LVNs and other health occupations requiring less education than RNs provides a potential pool of candidates for a more diverse nursing workforce.

RECOMMENDATION

Recommendation 6: Make Diversity in the Nursing Workforce a Priority. **The Campaign should continue to emphasize recruitment and retention of a diverse nursing workforce as a major priority for both its national efforts and the state Action Coalitions. In broadening its coalition to include more diverse stakeholders (see Recommendation 1), the Campaign should work with others to assess progress and exchange information about strategies that are effective in increasing the diversity of the health workforce. To that end, the Campaign should take the following actions:**

- **Develop a comprehensive, specific diversity plan with actionable steps that can be taken by state Action Coalitions and by nursing and other health professions stakeholders, including trade organizations and educational institutions.**
- **To assist planning and policy making at the state level, use the Campaign's dashboard infrastructure to develop and publish annual data reports on the diversity of nursing and other health professions graduates and enrollees by state, and compare the representation of minorities in each state with their representation in the state's general population.**

- Convene an advisory group to identify best practices from both within and outside of the Campaign that are improving the diversity of the nursing and other health professions workforce to reflect that of the general population. Areas for research and assessment might include barriers that prevent individuals from diverse backgrounds from entering the nursing profession and from achieving higher levels of education, modes of academic progression to promote diversity in nursing programs at all levels, and the use of holistic admissions policies and need-based aid to support students from underrepresented and economically challenged backgrounds in obtaining nursing degrees. Results of these studies could be disseminated to key relevant stakeholders, including schools of nursing and employers.
- Assist state Action Coalitions in obtaining funds available for the development of new, innovative, targeted programs and strategies aimed at increasing the diversity of nursing students and the nursing workforce and/or for the identification and tailoring of those programs that have been shown to be effective.
- Collect data to ensure that the call for higher educational attainment among nurses has positive implications for diversity (including economic, racial/ethnic, geographic, and gender diversity). The Campaign should research the opportunities for and barriers to utilization of baccalaureate completion programs by underrepresented minorities and economically and educationally disadvantaged individuals so that the Campaign and other stakeholders can more effectively implement programs to advance the educational attainment of African Americans, Hispanics/Latinos, and other underrepresented groups in nursing.
- Encourage state Action Coalitions to work with their state nursing workforce centers and state boards of nursing to collect and make available data on variables that can be used to assess progress toward increasing the diversity of the nurse workforce, the nursing student population, and nursing faculty.

REFERENCES

AACN (American Association of Colleges of Nursing). 2015. *Enhancing diversity in the workforce.* http://www.aacn.nche.edu/media-relations/fact-sheets/enhancing-diversity (accessed September 24, 2015).

Advisory Committee on Student Financial Assistance. 2002. *Empty promises: The myth of college access in America.* Washington, DC: Advisory Committee on Student Financial Assistance. http://files.eric.ed.gov/fulltext/ED466814.pdf (accessed November 21, 2015).

Advisory Committee on Student Financial Assistance. 2013. *Access matters: Meeting the nation's college completion goals requires large increases in need-based grant aid.* Washington, DC: Advisory Committee on Student Financial Assistance. http://files.eric.ed.gov/fulltext/ED553377. pdf (accessed November 21, 2015).

American Association of Community Colleges. 2010. *Community colleges issues brief prepared for the 2010 White House Summit on Community Colleges.* Washington, DC: American Association of Community Colleges. http://www.aacc.nche.edu/AboutCC/whsummit/Documents/whsummit_briefs.pdf (accessed September 18, 2015).

Banister, G., H. M. Bowen-Brady, and M. E. Winfrey. 2014. Using career mentors to support minority nursing students and facilitate their transition to practice. *Journal of Professional Nursing* 30(4):317-325.

Bell, N. E. 2012. *Data sources: The role of community colleges on the pathway to graduate degree attainment.* http://www.cgsnet.org/data-sources-role-community-colleges-pathway-graduate-degree-attainment-0 (accessed September 18, 2015).

Bleich, M. R., B. R. MacWilliams, and B. J. Schmidt. 2015. Advancing diversity through inclusive excellence in nursing education. *Journal of Professional Nursing* 31(2):89-94.

Bond, M. L., M. E. Jones, W. J. Barr, G. F. Carr, S. J. Williams, and S. Baxley. 2012. Hardiness, perceived social support, perceived institutional support, and progression of minority students in a masters of nursing program. *Hispanic Health Care International* 10(3):109-117.

Brooks Carthon, J. M., T. Nguyen, J. Chittams, E. Park, and J. Guevara. 2014. Measuring success: Results from a national survey of recruitment and retention initiatives in the nursing workforce. *Nursing Outlook* 62(4):259-267.

Carter, B. M., D. L. Powell, A. L. Derouin, and J. Cusatis. 2015. Beginning with the end in mind: Cultivating minority nurse leaders. *Journal of Professional Nursing* 31(2):95-103.

CCNA (Center to Champion Nursing in America). 2011. *Future of nursing: State Implementation Program 2012 request for proposals.* Washington, DC: CCNA.

CCNA. 2014. *Future of nursing: State Implementation Program 2014 request for proposals.* Washington, DC: CCNA.

CCNA. 2015a (unpublished). *Future of Nursing: Campaign for Action biannual operations report, August 1, 2014-May 31, 2015.* Washington, DC: CCNA.

CCNA. 2015b. *Future of Nursing: Campaign for Action dashboard indicators.* http://campaignfor action.org/dashboard (accessed September 12, 2015).

CCNA. n.d.-a. *Campaign progress.* http://campaignforaction.org/campaign-progress (accessed September 24, 2015).

CCNA. n.d.-b. *Campaign progress: Promoting diversity.* http://campaignforaction.org/campaign-progress/promoting-diversity (accessed September 24, 2015).

CCNA. n.d.-c. *Directory of resources: Increasing diversity.* http://campaignforaction.org/directory-of-resources/increasing-diversity (accessed September 24, 2015).

CCNA. n.d.-d. *Diversity steering committee.* http://campaignforaction.org/whos-involved/diversity-steering-committee (accessed September 24. 2015).

CCNA. n.d.-e. *New RN graduates by degree type and race/ethnicity.* http://campaignforaction.org/campaign-progress/new-rn-graduates-degree-type-and-raceethnicity (accessed November 5, 2015).

Donelan, K., C. Romano, C. DesRoches, S. Applebaum, J. R. Ward, B. A. Schoneboom, and A. S. Hinshaw. 2014. National surveys of military personnel, nursing students, and the public: Drivers of military nursing careers. *Military Medicine* 179(5):565-572.

Fulcher, R., and C. M. Mullin. 2011. *A data-driven examination of the impact of associate and bachelor's degree programs on the nation's nursing workforce.* AACC Policy Brief 2011-02PBL. Washington, DC: American Association of Community Colleges.

HRSA (Health Resources and Services Administration). 2006. *The rationale for diversity in the health professions: A review of the evidence.* Rockville, MD: U.S. Department of Health and Human Services.

HRSA. 2010. *The registered nurse population: Findings from the 2008 National Sample Survey of Registered Nurses.* http://bhpr.hrsa.gov/healthworkforce/rnsurveys/rnsurveyfinal.pdf (accessed November 5, 2015).

HRSA. 2012. *Health Resources and Services Administration fiscal year 2013 justification of estimates for Appropriations Committee.* http://www.hrsa.gov/about/budget/budgetjustification2013.pdf (accessed September 18, 2015).

HRSA. 2015a. *Sex, race, and ethnic diversity of U.S. health occupations (2010-2012).* Rockville, MD: U.S. Department of Health and Human Services, HRSA, National Center for Health Workforce Analysis.

HRSA. 2015b. *Health Resources and Services Administration fiscal year 2016 justification of estimates for Appropriations Committee.* http://www.hrsa.gov/about/budget/budget justification2016.pdf (accessed September 18, 2015).

IOM (Institute of Medicine). 2004. *In the nation's compelling interest: Ensuring diversity in the health-care workforce.* Washington, DC: The National Academies Press.

IOM. 2011. *The future of nursing: Leading change, advancing health.* Washington, DC: The National Academies Press.

Landen, J. 2015. Presentation to IOM Committee for Assessing Progress on Implementing the Recommendations of the Institute of Medicine Report *The Future of Nursing: Leading Change, Advancing Health.* Washington, DC, July 27, 2015.

McMenamin, P. 2015. *Diversity among registered nurses: Slow but steady progress.* http://www. ananurspace.org/blogs/peter-mcmenamin/2015/08/21/rn-diversity-note?ssopc=1 (accessed September 24, 2015).

More, M. S., and M. Greer. 2000. *American women physicians in 2000: A history in progress.* http:// escholarship.umassmed.edu/cgi/viewcontent.cgi?article=1050&context=lib_articles (accessed September 24, 2015).

Mullin, C. M. 2012. *Why access matters: The community college student body.* AACC Policy Brief 2012-01PBL. Washington, DC: American Association of Community Colleges. http://www. aacc.nche.edu/Publications/Briefs/Documents/PB_AccessMatters.pdf (accessed September 18, 2015).

NCES (National Center for Education Statistics). 2011. *2007-2008 National Postsecondary Student Aid Study (NPSAS: 08)* [Data file]. Washington, DC: U.S. Department of Education, Institute for Education Sciences.

NCSL (National Conference of State Legislatures). 2014. *Workforce diversity.* http://www.ncsl.org/ documents/health/workforcediversity814.pdf (accessed September 24, 2015).

OMH (Office of Minority Health). 2011. *Reflecting America's population: Diversifying a competent health care workforce for the 21st century.* http://minorityhealth.hhs.gov/Assets/pdf/Checked/1/ FinalACMHWorkforceReport.pdf (accessed September 24, 2015).

Scott, L. D., and J. Zerwic. 2015. Holistic review in admissions: A strategy to diversify the nursing workforce. *Nursing Outlook* 63(4):488-495.

The Sullivan Alliance. 2015. *Initiatives.* http://www.thesullivanalliance.org/cue/initiatives.html (accessed September 24, 2015).

Sullivan Commission on Diversity in the Healthcare Workforce. 2004. *Missing persons: Minorities in the health professions.* Washington, DC: The Sullivan Commission.

Talamantes, E., C. M. Mangione, K. Gonzalez, A. Jimenez, F. Gonzalez, and G. Moreno. 2014. Community college pathways: Improving the U.S. physician workforce pipeline. *Academic Medicine* 89(12):1649-1656.

TCC Group. 2013 (unpublished). *Future of Nursing: Campaign for Action: Action Coalition Survey.* Philadelphia, PA: TCC Group.

U.S. Army. n.d. *Army nursing career: Army nurse requirements & info*. http://www.goarmy.com/amedd/nurse.html (accessed September 24, 2015).

U.S. Census Bureau. 2013. *Men in nursing occupations: American Community Survey highlight report*. http://www.census.gov/people/io/files/Men_in_Nursing_Occupations.pdf (accessed September 24, 2015).

VA (U.S. Department of Veterans Affairs). 2015a. *Realizing the future of nursing: VA nurses tell their story*. Washington, DC: U.S. Department of Veterans Affairs, Veterans Health Administration.

VA. 2015b. *National nursing awards: Nursing innovation awards*. http://www.va.gov/NURSING/About/nationalawards.asp (accessed September 24, 2015).

Villarruel, A., D. Washington, W. T. Lecher, and N. A. Carver. 2015. A more diverse nursing workforce: Greater diversity is good for the country's health. *American Journal of Nursing* 115(5):57-62.

Weaver, T. 2015. Presentation to IOM Committee for Assessing Progress on Implementing the Recommendations of the Institute of Medicine Report *The Future of Nursing: Leading Change, Advancing Health*. Washington, DC, July 27, 2015.

5

Collaborating and Leading in Care Delivery and Redesign

According to *The Future of Nursing*, if nurses are to contribute fully to the transformation of the health care system, they must become leaders "from the bedside to the boardroom" (IOM, 2011). The report states that nurse leaders are needed to lead and participate in the ongoing reforms to the system, to direct research on evidence-based improvements in care, to translate research findings into the practice environment, to be full partners on the health care team, and to advocate for policy change. Rather than using a traditional top-down style of leadership, the report suggests that nurses should lead by engaging all members of the health care team in an environment of interprofessional collaboration and mutual respect. The report calls on health care organizations, nursing associations, nursing educators, and all nurses to create, support, and seek opportunities for collaboration and leadership at all levels and in every practice environment. The report offers two recommendations in this area:

- recommendation 2: Expand opportunities for nurses to lead and diffuse collaborative improvement efforts (see Box 5-1); and
- recommendation 7: Prepare and enable nurses to lead change to advance health (see Box 5-2).

These recommendations—and the Campaign's work in this area—fall into three broad categories: interprofessional collaboration, preparing nurses to serve as leaders, and opening up opportunities for nurses to lead.

BOX 5-1
Recommendation 2 from *The Future of Nursing*:
Expand Opportunities for Nurses to Lead and
Diffuse Collaborative Improvement Efforts

Private and public funders, health care organizations, nursing education programs, and nursing associations should expand opportunities for nurses to lead
and manage collaborative efforts with physicians and other members of the health
care team to conduct research and to redesign and improve practice environments
and health systems. These entities should also provide opportunities for nurses to
diffuse successful practices.

To this end:

- The Center for Medicare and Medicaid Innovation should support the
  development and evaluation of models of payment and care delivery that
  use nurses in an expanded and leadership capacity to improve health
  outcomes and reduce costs. Performance measures should be developed
  and implemented expeditiously where best practices are evident to reflect
  the contributions of nurses and ensure better-quality care.
- Private and public funders should collaborate, and when possible pool
  funds, to advance research on models of care and innovative solutions,
  including technology, that will enable nurses to contribute to improved
  health and health care.
- Health care organizations should support and help nurses in taking the
  lead in developing and adopting innovative, patient-centered care models.
- Health care organizations should engage nurses and other front-line staff
  to work with developers and manufacturers in the design, development,
  purchase, implementation, and evaluation of medical and health devices
  and health information technology products.
- Nursing education programs and nursing associations should provide
  entrepreneurial professional development that will enable nurses to initiate programs and businesses that will contribute to improved health and
  health care.

SOURCE: IOM, 2011.

INTERPROFESSIONAL COLLABORATION

Despite being rated highly by the public for ethical standards and honesty
and being considered "one of the most trusted sources of health information"
(Gallup, 2010, 2015), nurses often are excluded from decision making and rel-
egated to carrying out the instructions of others (IOM, 2011). *The Future of Nursing* notes that nurses often are the best source of knowledge and awareness of
patients, families, and communities, but "do not speak up as often as they should"

BOX 5-2
Recommendation 7 from *The Future of Nursing*:
Prepare and Enable Nurses to Lead
Change to Advance Health

Nurses, nursing education programs, and nursing associations should prepare the nursing workforce to assume leadership positions across all levels, while public, private, and governmental health care decision makers should ensure that leadership positions are available to and filled by nurses.

- Nurses should take responsibility for their personal and professional growth by continuing their education and seeking opportunities to develop and exercise their leadership skills.
- Nursing associations should provide leadership development, mentoring programs, and opportunities to lead for all their members.
- Nursing education programs should integrate leadership theory and business practices across the curriculum, including clinical practice.
- Public, private, and governmental health care decision makers at every level should include representation from nursing on boards, on executive management teams, and in other key leadership positions.

SOURCE: IOM, 2011.

(IOM, 2011, p. 224). The report calls on health care organizations, nursing educators, and nursing associations to train, support, and encourage nurses to lead and manage interprofessional collaboration efforts. The report cites evidence that collaboration and mutual respect among health care professionals have been associated with improved patient outcomes, cost savings, and increased job satisfaction.

The Future of Nursing therefore recommends that there be expanded "opportunities for nurses to lead and manage collaborative efforts with physicians and other members of the health care team" and "opportunities for nurses to diffuse successful practices" (IOM, 2011, p. 279). Specifically, the report calls for organizations, including the Center for Medicare & Medicaid Innovation (CMMI), to support the development of models of care that use nurses in a leadership capacity, and for health care organizations to support nurses in "taking the lead in developing and adopting innovative, patient-centered care models" (IOM, 2011, p. 280).

Activity

Interprofessional Education

Interprofessional education has received a great deal of attention in recent years, bolstered in part by numerous activities and reports around this issue, including

- the World Health Organization's *Framework for Action on Interprofessional Education and Collaborative Practice* (WHO, 2010);
- the report of the Lancet Commission on the Education of Health Professionals for the 21st Century titled *Health Professionals for a New Century: Transforming Education to Strengthen Health Systems in an Interdependent World* (Frenk et al., 2010);
- conferences and reports of the Josiah Macy Jr. Foundation, including the Conference on Interprofessional Education and Transforming Patient Care: Aligning Interprofessional Education with Clinical Practice Redesign (Josiah Macy Jr. Foundation, 2012, 2013b); and
- the Institute of Medicine (IOM) Global Forum on Innovation in Health Professional Education's workshop summary *Interprofessional Education for Collaboration: Learning How to Improve Health from Interprofessional Models Across the Continuum of Education to Practice* (IOM, 2013).

Yet, as Thibault (2011) notes,

Interprofessional education is one strategy to improve nursing education and enhance the role of nurses as collaborative leaders in the health care system. . . . Although we have good evidence that health care provided in teams of professionals is more efficient and is associated with better patient outcomes, we have not structured education to prepare students for team care or team leadership. (p. 313)

The American Association of Colleges of Nursing (AACN) considers "interprofessional collaboration for improving patient and population health outcomes" to be an essential part of baccalaureate, master's, and doctoral education, and has incorporated it into "Essentials" documents that outline necessary curriculum and expected competencies for each level of education (AACN, 2006, 2008, 2011). For a school to be accredited by the Commission on Collegiate Nursing Education (CCNE), it must comply with these Essentials documents (CCNE, 2013; Zorek and Raehl, 2012). For example, the Essentials document for baccalaureate programs in nursing states that the baccalaureate program prepares the graduate to, among other things, "use inter- and intraprofessional communication and collaborative skills to deliver evidence-based, patient-centered care"; "contribute the unique nursing perspective to interprofessional teams to optimize patient outcomes"; and "demonstrate appropriate teambuilding and collaborative strategies when working with interprofessional teams" (AACN, 2008, p. 22). A study of the effectiveness of these types of accreditation standards found that nursing graduates may be among the "most prepared" for interprofessional collaborative practice (Zorek and Raehl, 2012, p. 6). Another study, however, found that the interprofessional opportunities offered in nursing programs were narrow in scope and most commonly focused on acute care simulation and seminars rather than on interprofessional work in community settings (Hudson et al., 2013).

In December 2014, CCNE entered into an agreement with five other health professions accreditors (the Accreditation Council for Pharmacy Education, Commission on Dental Accreditation, Commission on Osteopathic College Accreditation, Council on Education for Public Health, and Liaison Committee for Medical Education) to form the Health Professions Accreditors Collaborative (HPAC) (CCNE, 2014). These organizations meet regularly to determine how they can work together on interprofessional education, showing that in addition to efforts within the nursing profession to expand interprofessional education, health professionals from many disciplines are partnering to develop competencies and curricula for such education. As emphasized by Steven Weinberger, Executive Vice President and CEO, American College of Physicians, at the committee's May 2015 workshop,

> What we really need is a cultural change. This is a good example of culture eats strategy for lunch. Getting a cultural change with the older physician population is going to be very difficult, and this is going to have to be something that occurs over time. The critical area is in the training environment. We need to have more and more effective interprofessional education so that there is this sense of mutual respect and trust that is built from day zero.

The Association of American Medical Colleges (AAMC) developed the MedEdPORTAL® in 2005 to enhance knowledge about medical education resources (AAMC, 2015). In the 10 years since, it has expanded this portal to promote interprofessional collaboration by including resources and materials from across the health professions. In 2012, AAMC expanded the portal to be a "clearinghouse of competency-linked IPE [interprofessional education] learning resources and educational materials" (AAMC, 2012). The IPE Portal is an initiative of AAMC and the Interprofessional Education Collaboration (IPEC). Since its creation, AAMC also has partnered with the American Psychological Association and the American Board of Medical Specialties to expand the portal (AAMC, 2015). In 2014, AAMC and AACN partnered to provide awards for the best materials and curricula for improving interprofessional education in support of the Lifelong Learning in Interprofessional Education initiative (AAMC, 2014).

IPEC was formed in 2009 as a joint effort of AACN, the American Association of Colleges of Pharmacy, the American Association of Colleges of Osteopathic Medicine, the American Dental Education Association, the Association of Schools of Public Health, and AAMC (IPEC, 2015). In 2011, IPEC published the report *Core Competencies for Interprofessional Collaborative Practice* (IPEC, 2011), which lays out a vision of interprofessional collaborative practice as "key to the safe, high quality, accessible, patient-centered care desired by all" (p. i) and specifies four core competencies that all health professionals need to develop. The report stresses that these competencies cannot be developed solely within the profession; rather, students of different professions must be engaged in interactive learning with each other. Within the competency domain relating to values and ethics for interprofessional practice are two specific competencies relating to cultural competency: "embrace the cultural diversity and individual differences that characterize patients, populations, and the health care team," and "respect the unique cultures, values, roles/responsibilities, and expertise of other health professions" (p. 19). Addressing issues around cultural competence during education, training, and practice may ensure that members of health care teams understand and embrace diversity of backgrounds, approaches, and values as interprofessional collaboration becomes increasingly emphasized.

Interprofessional Practice

The Future of Nursing calls on private and public funders to advance research on models of care and innovative solutions that can enable nurses to contribute to the improvement of health. The report specifically calls on CMMI to support the development and evaluation of models of care delivery that use nurses as leaders. CMMI has since created the Health Care Innovation Awards program, which provides up to $1 billion to organizations that are implementing innovative projects to improve health and lower costs (CMS, 2013, 2015). Several of the funded projects include nurses as leaders or members of interprofessional teams (CMS, 2013). For example,

- Cooper University Hospital in Camden, New Jersey, received funding to use nurse-led interdisciplinary outreach teams, with the goal of improving primary care access and reducing hospital readmissions; and
- Developmental Disabilities Health Services received funding to test a model in which teams of nurse practitioners and physicians work together to provide primary care and case management to persons with developmental disabilities.

Another government-led initiative is the Health Resources and Services Administration's (HRSA's) Nurse Education, Practice, Quality, and Retention Program, which has provided more than $67 million between 2012 and 2015 to 66 different grantees for interprofessional collaborative practice.[1] In its 2014 funding opportunity announcement, HRSA states that "the goals of the program and the purposes of the funding opportunity announcement are consistent with the statutory authority provided in Title VIII to provide coordinated care and for nurses to develop skills needed to practice in existing and emerging organized health care systems" (HRSA, 2014). One grantee, the Vanderbilt School of Nursing, has developed a model of interprofessional collaborative practice with an interprofessional team of providers comprising a family nurse practitioner, pharmacist, social worker, physician, community health advocate, part-time nurse, and medical assistant (Pilon et al., 2015a,b). The nurse practitioner is responsible for diagnosis, treatment, and referral and the overall care planning for the patient, and also has oversight of the care team and coordinates student clinical rotations. The team is based in a primary care clinic serving disadvantaged patients with complex health care needs. This clinic also serves as the clinical site for health professions students in the Vanderbilt Program in Interprofessional Learning (Pilon et al., 2015b).

In addition to government efforts, many organizations are working to expand interprofessional practice. The committee heard details about two such organizations:

- Community Health Center, Inc. (CHC) is a federally qualified health center that provides primary care and social services to primarily low-income persons in Connecticut (CHC, 2015). CHC uses innovative, team-based models of care and relies heavily on nurse practitioners as providers of primary care.
- The National Center for Interprofessional Practice and Education (NCIPE) was launched in 2012 through a cooperative agreement between HRSA and the University of Minnesota, and also is funded by the Robert Wood Johnson Foundation (RWJF), the Josiah Macy Jr. Foundation, and the Gordon and Betty Moore Foundation (NCIPE, 2013b,c). The center studies and advances collaborative, team-based care and health professions education (NCIPE, 2013a). Although NCIPE is a neutral convener that does not favor any one profession, many of the innovative models of care that are developed through the center are focused on nurses.

The Campaign addresses the recommendations of *The Future of Nursing* in the area of collaboration and leadership under the pillar of "fostering interprofessional collaboration" (CCNA, n.d.). As of December 2014, 25 state Action Coalitions were working to further interprofessional education and collaboration

---

[1] Information derived from the HRSA Data Portal, filtered by Grant Activity Code UD7, August 18, 2015.

(CCNA, 2014b). For example, Colorado has received a grant from HRSA to support the implementation of Interprofessional Collaborative Practice Teams at community health centers; Hawaii is building an interprofessional workforce database; and Virginia, in a partnership with the Medical Society of Virginia Foundation, is implementing a pilot clinical leadership program that encourages pairings between nurses and other providers.

Two states—Rhode Island and Utah—have implemented an interprofessional collaboration practice and/or education model, while 10 other Action Coalitions are working toward this goal (CCNA, 2015d). Rhode Island's collaborative practice is integrated into its residency model, while Utah's includes an interprofessional education program at the University of Utah, where all health science students are required to take an interprofessional course.

Progress

Since *The Future of Nursing* was released, interprofessional education has expanded rapidly at schools of nursing. The Campaign tracks progress in this area by looking at the number of required clinical courses and/or activities at the top 10 nursing schools that include both registered nurse (RN) students and other graduate health professional students. In 2011, only 6 such courses or activities were offered at the top 10 nursing schools; by 2013, there were 22 (see Figure 5-1). Eight of the 10 schools have added these courses or activities since 2011.

Discussion

Interprofessional education and team-based, collaborative practice are not new concepts in the health professions (Bodenheimer et al., 2002; Grumbach and Bodenheimer, 2004; IOM, 2003; Leape et al., 2009; Needleman and Hassmiller, 2009; Wagner, 2000). The 2003 IOM report *Health Professions Education: A Bridge to Quality* notes the importance of interprofessional education, stating that "all health professionals should be educated to deliver patient-centered care as members of an interdisciplinary team" (IOM, 2003, p. 3). This report further highlights work in interdisciplinary teams as one of five core competencies necessary for all clinicians to "cooperate, collaborate, communicate, and integrate care in teams to ensure that care is continuous and reliable" (p. 4). However, progress in advancing interprofessional education and collaboration has been particularly notable in recent years, both in the field of nursing and in other health care professions.

Since the release of *The Future of Nursing*, additional evidence has shown that when nurses collaborate with other health care professionals, outcomes are improved. For example, one study found that nurses' collaboration with other disciplines was essential to safe and effective care in hospitals, including avoiding

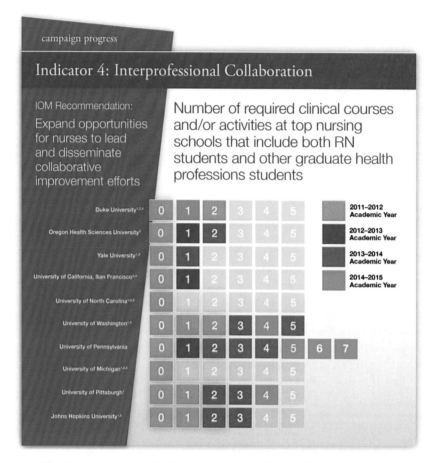

FIGURE 5-1 Number of required clinical courses and/or activities at the top 10 nursing schools that include both registered nurse (RN) students and other graduate health professional students.

NOTES:

[1] No change between the 2011-2012 and 2012-2013 academic years.

[2] No change between the 2012-2013 and 2013-2014 academic years.

[3] No change between the 2013-2014 and 2014-2015 academic years.

[4] This institution reduced the number of required courses and/or activities for the 2014-2015 academic year.

Data are from the top 10 nursing schools (as determined by *U.S. News & World Report* rankings) that also have graduate-level health professions schools at their academic institutions. Course offerings and requirements include clinical and/or simulation experiences.

SOURCE: CCNA, 2015e.

adverse drug events (Feldman et al., 2012). In another study, nurse leadership of teams was associated with improved safety and quality, including an 81 percent reduction in central line-associated bloodstream infections (Marstellar et al., 2012). The authors note that "this study was conceived as a nurse-led program and showed that nurses can effectively drive an interdisciplinary safety program in their units. Nurses did report during interviews, however, that greater physician engagement would have benefited them" (p. 2936). Thus, the study validated both the role of nurse leadership and the importance of interprofessional collaboration.

The trend toward interprofessional collaboration in all fields is consistent with recommendations 2 and 7 in *The Future of Nursing*, and progress has been made on many fronts, including some of the specific bullet points under these recommendations (see Boxes 5-1 and 5-2, respectively). Going forward, however, the scope of these recommendations will need to be broadened to acknowledge that nurses cannot expand interprofessional collaboration or education alone. Collaboration requires all members of a team working to their full potential on behalf of the patient and with respect for the contributions of other professions to the work. It will be important for health care teams to understand and navigate the professional and personal cultural backgrounds of individual team members. Nurses need to be prepared to serve as a part of the team and to lead or coordinate efforts as appropriate. To this end, it will be important to continue efforts to develop models of care that use nurses as team leaders. To achieve true interprofessional collaboration, however, all health care professionals will need to work together to plan how to attain this goal.

In 2013, the Campaign acknowledged that this shift was needed when it asked its Action Coalitions to "move beyond nursing and focus on improving health and healthcare for consumers and their families" and to "not ignore the diverse stakeholders critical to the [Action Coalitions'] success" (TCC Group, 2014, p. 1). In a survey conducted later that year, the vast majority of Action Coalitions (95 percent) stated that they did not ignore diverse stakeholders, but still only 27 percent of respondents agreed that their coalition "includes sufficient non-nursing-related organizations and representatives to make progress on [their] goals," despite reaching out to new and diverse members (TCC Group, 2013, p. 14). Further, only one-quarter of Action Coalitions said they had moved beyond nursing. The TCC Group evaluators concluded that "this may have a lot to do with states that used the first couple of years to coalesce their nursing groups, clear natural allies, and are now trying to figure out legitimate ways to bring in other stakeholders" (TCC Group, 2013, p. 10).

Findings and Conclusions

Findings

This study yielded the following findings on interprofessional collaboration:

Finding 5-1. Significant efforts are directed toward strengthening interprofessional education and practice in nursing as well as in other health care professions.

Finding 5-2. Health care is shifting toward a team-based, interprofessional approach.

Finding 5-3. Three-quarters of the Campaign's state Action Coalitions are not including non-nursing stakeholders in their coalitions.

Finding 5-4. The Campaign's measure of success on recommendations 2 and 7 of The Future of Nursing *is limited to counting interprofessional courses offered at the top 10 nursing schools.*

Conclusions

The committee drew the following conclusions about progress toward nurses engaging in collaborative activities:

True interprofessional collaboration can be accomplished only in concert with other health professionals, not within the nursing profession alone.

State Action Coalitions need assistance in reaching out to non-nursing stakeholders.

In the new context of health care, the Campaign itself needs to be a broader coalition of stakeholders from all health care professions if it is to make progress.

PREPARING NURSES TO LEAD

The Future of Nursing notes that nurses at all levels need strong leadership skills, but it observes that, historically, nurses have not held leadership positions that have enabled them to contribute fully (IOM, 2011). In recommendation 7 (see Box 5-2), *The Future of Nursing* calls on nurses and the organizations that train, support, and employ them to work on developing necessary leadership competencies and to provide opportunities for nurses to lead at every level. Specifically, the report recommends that nurses take responsibility by seeking opportunities to develop leadership skills, that nursing education programs include entrepreneurship and leadership skills in their curriculum, and that nursing associations provide leadership development opportunities for their members.

Activity

Leadership development opportunities have been established and expanded by nursing education programs, nursing associations, and private organizations since *The Future of Nursing* was released.

Nursing Education Programs

A number of nursing programs offer opportunities for students to learn leadership and entrepreneurship either at the nursing school or in combination with another school. For example,

- Columbia University School of Nursing has a combined (MS/MBA) program that includes classes at both the school of nursing and the school of business[2];
- Drexel University confers a master of science in nursing (MSN) degree in Innovation and Intra/Entrepreneurship in Advanced Nursing Practice[3];
- New York University College of Nursing offers an undergraduate honors elective in social entrepreneurship that incorporates content from business, the humanities, and service learning (Gilmartin, 2013); and
- the University of Pennsylvania offers a dual degree program whereby enrollees complete a bachelor of science in nursing (BSN) degree through the School of Nursing and a bachelor of science in economics degree through the Wharton School, with the Wharton curriculum focusing on health care management and policy (University of Pennsylvania, 2015a).

Nursing Associations

Nursing associations are among the most active sponsors of programs designed to develop leadership and entrepreneurial skills for nurse leaders in a variety of positions. The American Organization of Nurse Executives (AONE) offers a variety of programs and opportunities that prepare nurses for leadership roles, including the Emerging Nurse Leader Institute, the Nurse Manager Fellowship, a Certificate in Health Care Finance, and a program that prepares nurses to be leaders on hospital governance boards. AONE also has partnered with academic institutions and organizations to provide interprofessional leadership development for its members. For example, AONE and Arizona State University offer an Interprofessional Fellowship in Innovative Health Leadership in partnership

---

[2] See http://nursing.columbia.edu/academics/academic-programs/msmba-program-description-nursing-and-business-msmba (accessed September 11, 2015).

[3] See http://drexel.edu/cnhp/academics/graduate/MSN-Innovation-and-Intra-Entrepreneurship-Nursing-Practice (accessed September 11, 2015).

with the Mayo Clinic's Center for Innovation (Arizona State University, 2015). The fellowship is designed to help health professionals with executive leadership responsibilities develop the skills necessary to drive innovation at their organizations. AONE also has partnered with the Harvard Business School's Managing Health Care Delivery program, a leadership development program that explores "designing your organization from the ground up, managing performance, and improving and innovating over time" (AONE, 2015; Harvard Business School, 2015). This partnership allows AONE to offer reserved seats in the program specifically to nurses (AONE, 2015).

The AACN-Wharton Executive Leadership Program was launched in 2012, with the support of the Jonas Center for Nursing Excellence, with the goal of enhancing leadership for change in health care (AACN, 2015a). The program is open to deans and directors and associate deans and directors of AACN nursing schools who serve as chief or associate chief nursing academic officers. The program is aimed at helping participants develop skills needed to "manage and lead change at an enterprise level, strategically influence and negotiate, and skillfully strategize and innovate value with internal and external stakeholders" (AACN, 2015b). Together with AACN, the Wharton School also offers the Wharton Nursing Leaders Program to upper-level nurse managers (University of Pennsylvania, 2015b). This program, however, focuses on nursing leadership and support for nurse managers and executives in clinical settings.

The American Academy of Nursing's Jonas Policy Scholars Program was launched in 2014 to support 2-year fellowships for doctoral or postdoctoral nursing students to learn about health policy (AAN, 2014). According to Darlene Curley, executive director of the Jonas Center, "The Jonas Policy Scholars will serve at the highest levels of leadership in ensuring quality, cost-effective and accessible healthcare" (Jonas Center, 2015a).

Private Organizations

In addition to RWJF, other private, philanthropic organizations have been supporting the education and training of nurse leaders. For example, the Josiah Macy Jr. Foundation has a Faculty Scholars program, established in 2010, that provides support to faculty leaders at nursing and medical schools (Josiah Macy Jr. Foundation, 2013a). Five faculty leaders are chosen each year for the program, and they must commit to spending half of their time pursuing education reform projects at their institution; 40 percent of participants to date have been nursing faculty. Each scholar receives career advice from a committee of distinguished health care leaders.

The Jonas Center for Nursing and Veterans Healthcare has worked to improve nurse leadership by supporting the development of nursing doctoral students through its Jonas Nurse Leaders Scholar Program, which has grown dramatically since its launch in 2008 (Jonas Center, 2015b) (see Chapter 3). In addition to the scholars program, which requires each of its scholars to complete a 40-hour leadership project focusing on one of the recommendations of *The Future of Nursing* (Curley, 2015), the Jonas Center provides support for convening and recognizing nurse leaders. Support recently has been provided for the AACN Student Policy Summit, the Sigma Theta Tau International Foundation Convention, and the AACN-Wharton Executive Leadership Program (Jonas Center, 2015c).

The Campaign has created a national nursing leadership strategy under the pillar "leveraging nursing leadership" (CCNA, n.d.). This pillar encompasses efforts around preparing nurses to lead and ensuring that nurses have leadership roles in health care. At the state level, 41 Action Coalitions were in the process of developing or implementing at least one leadership program as of December 2014, and some states had already established leadership institutes, programs to identify emerging leaders, or mentorship programs (CCNA, 2014b).

The Campaign also recently established the Breakthrough Leadership in Nursing Awards program to recognize and advance 10 nurse leaders (CCNA, 2015b). The awardees receive scholarships for a Leadership Development Program at the Center for Creative Leadership, which is designed to build skills, knowledge, and confidence.

Progress

The Campaign has no indicator with which to track how and whether nurses are being prepared to lead. While the committee identified a number of leadership programs and courses offered at nursing and other schools, there is no single source of information about nurse training in leadership, entrepreneurship, or innovation.

Discussion, Findings, and Conclusion

The Future of Nursing recognizes that for nurses to contribute fully in leadership positions, they must first develop the skills and competencies needed to do so. The report's recommendations in this area are directed at the profession itself—a call for nurses to prepare themselves proactively for leadership roles. And as noted by Ann Kurth, Dean, Yale School of Nursing, at the committee's July 2015 workshop, "In addition to the clinical aspects, nurses must also understand the financial, IT [information technology], and operational components to effectively design a sustainable future state model."

Findings

This study yielded the following findings on nurse leadership:

Finding 5-5. A number of programs have been created or expanded to help nurses develop leadership, entrepreneurial, and managerial skills.

Finding 5-6. Data are lacking on how many nursing schools are offering courses in leadership, entrepreneurship, or management, or how many nursing students are taking these types of courses outside of their nursing school.

Conclusion

The committee drew the following conclusion about progress toward nurses becoming leaders:

To assess progress on leadership development, it is necessary to track programs and courses in leadership, entrepreneurship, and management in which nurses are participating.

NURSES IN LEADERSHIP POSITIONS

The Future of Nursing report's recommendation 7 includes as one of its bullet points that "public, private, and governmental health care decision makers at every level should include representation from nursing on boards, on executive management teams, and in other key leadership positions" (IOM, 2011, p. 283; see Box 5-2). This recommendation followed from the report's findings that nurses were greatly underrepresented in their own health care organizations' governance structures, as well as on institution and hospital boards. A 2011 survey found that physicians made up 20 percent of board membership and nurses accounted for 6 percent; in 2014, the percentage of physician board members remained the same, while the percentage of nurse board members decreased to 5 percent (AHA, 2014). The IOM report suggests that nurses are needed in these leadership positions in order to contribute their unique perspective and expertise on such issues as health care delivery, quality, and safety.

Activity

Much of the Campaign's focus has been on getting nurses appointed to health-related boards. The Nurses on Boards Coalition was launched in November 2014 as a "direct response" to the recommendation of *The Future of Nursing*, and in addition to RWJF and AARP, it includes as members 19 other nursing organizations (CCNA, 2015f). The goal of the effort is to place 10,000 nurses on corporate and nonprofit health-related boards of directors by 2020. The Nurses on Boards Coalition was born out of two national nursing leadership strategy meetings on April 21, 2014, and July 21, 2014, and a series of smaller meetings and webinars around nursing leadership (CCNA, 2014c,d, 2015d). The Campaign also has worked to increase the representation of nurses on the boards of the organizations that make up its Champion Nursing Coalition, whose members include Aetna, Johnson & Johnson, and Target.[4] At the state level, the Campaign assists Action Coalitions with collecting data on nursing leadership and increasing the numbers of nurse leaders on state and local boards. As of January 2015, 19 Action Coalitions were collecting data on nurses serving on boards, and 22 more planned to do so in the future (CCNA, 2015d).

Beyond the Campaign's efforts, the committee heard about other efforts to increase nurse leadership, including the American Nurses Credentialing Center's (ANCC's) Magnet® recognition program. Hospitals and other health care organizations designated as Magnet are required to have nurses integrated into their governance structure (ANCC, 2015). Specifically, organizations must have an individual serving as the chief nursing officer (CNO), who is responsible for the standards of nursing practice across the organization. The CNO must be a member of the organization's governing body, involved in decision making and strategic planning.

Progress

To assess progress on this recommendation, the Campaign tracks the percentage of hospital boards with RN members. In 2014, the Campaign reported a baseline of 5 percent, but it does not yet have updated numbers (CCNA, 2015e). The Campaign's efforts to increase nurse representation on the boards of its Champion Nursing Coalition has seen some success, with 45 nurses serving on boards in May 2015, up from 10 in July 2013 (CCNA, 2014a, 2015a,d). State Action Coalitions have seen an increase in nurses serving on state and local boards, with the number rising from 268 in July 2014 to 310 in May 2015 (CCNA, 2014a, 2015d). In addition to this progress, the American Nurses Association, which continually tracks calls for nominations for agencies and organizations, reported that 11 nurses were appointed to 13 positions at the U.S. Office of the National Coordinator for Health Information Technology (ONC) within the past year (Cipriano, 2015).

Discussion, Findings, and Conclusions

In this recommendation, *The Future of Nursing* calls on those outside of the nursing profession to appoint nurses to leadership positions in all types of organizations.

---

[4] See a full list of Champion Nursing Coalition members at http://campaignforaction.org/whos-involved/champion-nursing-coalition (accessed November 20, 2015).

Findings

This study yielded the following findings on nurses in leadership positions:

Finding 5-7. The Campaign has had some success in getting more nurses appointed to private boards—one part of recommendation 7 of The Future of Nursing—*but has been less active on the issue of nurses serving as leaders "on executive management teams, and in other key leadership positions" in "public, private, and governmental health care" organizations.*

Finding 5-8. Data on nurses serving as leaders are scarce; the data that are available are fragmented and incomplete.

Conclusions

The committee drew the following conclusions about progress toward having more nurses serve in leadership positions.

It is necessary to gather more data on nurses serving as leaders.

More focus is needed on nurses serving in leadership positions other than on private boards.

THE CAMPAIGN FOR ACTION'S COMMUNICATION EFFORTS TO SUPPORT COLLABORATION AND LEADERSHIP

As described in Chapter 1, the Campaign has made efforts to engage stakeholders in its activities. In addition to the nursing community, these stakeholders include business leaders, payers, philanthropic organizations, policy makers, consumers, and other health professionals. The ability to communicate effectively with these groups is critical to collaboration and leadership efforts. The Campaign has used a number of avenues for its communications through its state Action Coalitions, as well as at the national level (CCNA, 2015c; see also Chapter 1).

Activity and Progress

The Campaign acknowledges that the capacity and ability of the Action Coalitions to communicate about their efforts vary greatly, despite efforts by the Campaign's leaders to develop branding guidance, templates, and other communication tools (CCNA, 2015c). Many Action Coalition leaders lack expertise in and experience with traditional and social media, and they have little time to learn because of competing priorities and commitments. The Action Coalitions that have staff dedicated to communications have had successes, according to the Campaign (CCNA, 2015c). The Campaign thus believes that "decisions are needed about how important state-level communications are to the Campaign's success, and how to put resources toward efforts deemed most appropriate" (CCNA, 2015c, p. 7). In making these decisions, it may be important to consider that Action Coalitions indicate that communication support from the Campaign is useful. In 2013, 67 percent of survey respondents said they had used Campaign communication support services, and 85 percent of those that had done so found the services useful (TCC Group, 2013).

In addition to supporting the communications of the Action Coalitions, the Campaign has engaged in several other communication initiatives:

- The Campaign has engaged targeted audiences, primarily the nursing and higher education communities, through strategic communication initiatives that have leveraged both traditional media and new media platforms (CCNA, 2015c; see also Chapter 1).
- The Speakers Bureau has sent Campaign representatives and leaders to various conferences across the country to raise awareness of and inform key audiences about the recommendations of *The Future of Nursing*, and to gather relevant data and information to advance Campaign goals.
- Online communication tools provide Campaign volunteers with materials to use in engaging media, policy makers, and interested stakeholders.

By the Campaign's estimation, these communication efforts have "raised awareness [and] resulted in actions as well as policy and law changes. Consumers are more knowledgeable of efforts to advance nursing to create more affordable and accessible health care" (CCNA, 2015c, p. 5). However, a thorough evaluation of its many activities would be necessary to assess the actual impact of the Campaign's communication efforts.

The stated goal of the Campaign is to engage a wide range of stakeholders; however, the Campaign acknowledges that its efforts have been focused largely on engaging nurses and that it needs to use its extensive "communications channels and platforms to reach broader, strategically important audiences" (CCNA, 2015c, p. 5). In 2013, the Campaign developed new imperatives that reflect this gap, including to "move beyond nursing and focus on improving health and healthcare for consumers and their families" and to "not ignore the diverse stakeholders critical to success" (TCC Group, 2014; see also Chapter 1 and the Interprofessional Collaboration section of this chapter). As noted earlier, the majority of Action Coalitions have worked to engage diverse stakeholders but do not believe that they have adequate non-nursing representation to further their goals. They also overwhelmingly indicated that they have had difficulty moving beyond nursing to focus on health care more broadly. The Campaign's external evaluators concluded that the lack of progress in this area was due to the intense efforts of Action Coalitions in their formative years to gain the engagement of their allies

(TCC Group, 2013). The evaluators go on to suggest, "We would anticipate that groups will continue to benefit from communications support that helps them craft a message of broader health and healthcare, as well as new (and more visible existing) research demonstrating the health and healthcare benefits of each of the IOM recommendations" (p. 10). Indeed, a subsequent analysis by TCC Group (2014) showed that Action Coalitions that felt they were making progress in moving toward a more inclusive vision of health care had a clear understanding of the goals of the Campaign, were able to communicate effectively across their workgroups and stakeholders, and had used Campaign communication support.

Moving forward, the Campaign can, at both the national and the state level, expand the scope of its communication strategies to connect with a broader audience. For example, greater use of new media and other technology to inform health care consumers about *The Future of Nursing* could potentially help with the recruitment of volunteers from a cross-section of the community, including ethnic communities. The Campaign could engage physicians who support the recommendations of *The Future of Nursing*, particularly the recommendation on expanding nurses' scope of practice (see Chapter 2), as spokespersons to further demonstrate a collaborative approach involving other health professionals. The Campaign's social media engagement has been productive in disseminating messages in conjunction with National Nurses Week (CCNA, 2015c), but two-way engagement with key audiences has been limited by a lack of next steps for individuals to take to accomplish meaningful action. Development of an engagement ladder, including ways to work with the Action Coalitions on various tactics, would be a productive means of sustaining interest among a broader audience, including students, health care consumers, business leaders, philanthropic organizations, and payers. The Action Coalitions with little or no experience in working with traditional media and using social media tools could collaborate with those that have undertaken successful communication activities in order to learn best practices. In this way, Action Coalitions could learn from one another about which activities have had an impact on driving the recommendations of *The Future of Nursing* in specific states, and what resources are needed to increase public awareness of the recommendations that have been difficult to achieve.

Discussion

As the Campaign itself acknowledged, and the present report recommends, further progress on the implementation of the recommendations of *The Future of Nursing* will require diversifying the movement and going beyond nursing to engage other diverse stakeholders. It will be important for the Campaign to reassess its external messaging to determine whether the messages are broad enough or tailored to engage important allies outside of nursing, or outside of the health professional community entirely. The Jonas Center for Nursing and Veterans Healthcare has noted its own challenges with recruiting other stakeholders, such as philanthropic organizations, using messages that some considered to be focused too exclusively on the nursing profession (Curley, 2015). And the Jonas Center has revised Campaign messages to emphasize the goal of improving patient care and health care delivery.[5] As observed by Darlene Curley, executive director, Jonas Center for Nursing and Veterans Healthcare, at the committee's July 2015 workshop, "It has been difficult to develop funding partnerships with many of our external funders because they see the report as nursing-centric and very nursing professional focused, sort of inside baseball."

Strong relationships are needed with health policy and business reporters; editors and columnists at national, state, and local news outlets; and bloggers who cover issues related to the recommendations of *The Future of Nursing*. These relationships could enable members and stakeholders of the Campaign to promulgate stories, particularly patient and human interest stories, proactively and to become a credible resource on articles relevant to the nursing profession. Media outreach efforts and communication materials could be tailored for different target audiences. To increase engagement of frontline nurses, for example, communications could articulate how recent changes in the health care system, the recommendations of *The Future of Nursing*, and Campaign activities could affect their work, and encourage their involvement by describing specific ways they could be involved in the Campaign.

Spokesperson training courses, such as those conducted by the American Association of Nurse Anesthetists for its state association leaders (AANA, 2014), could confer a variety of skills that would be useful to nurses. For example, courses could teach nurses how to successfully handle media interviews, lead and manage collaborative efforts with physicians and other members of the health care team, lobby for legislative changes, negotiate contracts, and resolve workplace conflicts. The Campaign's development of these training courses could help nurses in their efforts to implement the recommendations of *The Future of Nursing*, as well as in their everyday practice. In regions that have had less success in advancing the IOM report's recommendations, multifaceted advertising and communication efforts could be beneficial (TCC Group, 2014). These advertising campaigns could include strategic use of traditional and new media and advertising methodologies to increase public awareness and to generate support among policy makers and those with influence.

For internal communications, the Campaign has sought to disseminate concise and timely information through the use of weekly email updates and quarterly newsletters. Continuing to disseminate this type of targeted communication, as well as identifying additional recipients within organizations and Action Coalitions, would help ensure that such information could be disseminated further and more effectively to a broader, more diverse audience of stakeholders.

---

[5] Personal communication, D. Curley, Jonas Center for Nursing and Veterans Healthcare, September 4, 2015.

Findings and Conclusions

Findings

This study yielded the following findings on communication strategies in support of collaboration:

Finding 5-9. The resources and ability to communicate effectively about their work vary among the Action Coalitions.

Finding 5-10. The Campaign's communication strategy has targeted, for the most part, the nursing community.

Conclusions

The committee drew the following conclusions about the Campaign's use of communication strategy and activities:

For the Campaign to progress further, its communication strategy needs to expand beyond the nursing profession to other diverse stakeholders, including consumers.

State Action Coalitions need assistance from the Campaign and from other successful Action Coalitions to develop messaging, utilize traditional and new media, and engage audiences.

Education in communication to enhance the skills of nursing spokespersons would help further collaborative efforts.

RECOMMENDATIONS

Recommendation 7: Expand Efforts and Opportunities for Interprofessional Collaboration and Leadership Development for Nurses. As the Campaign broadens its coalition (see Recommendation 1), it should expand its focus on supporting and promoting (1) interprofessional collaboration and opportunities for nurses to design, implement, and diffuse collaborative programs in care and delivery; and (2) interdisciplinary development programs that focus on leadership. Health care professionals from all disciplines should work together in the planning and implementation of strategies for improving health care, particularly in an interprofessional and collaborative environment. Interdisciplinary development programs and activities should:

- Feature content in leadership, management, entrepreneurship, innovation, and other skills that will enable nurses to help ensure that the public receives accessible and quality health care. Courses could be offered through or in partnership with other professional schools. The Campaign should monitor nursing programs that offer these types of courses and programs and track nurses' participation, if possible, in order to assess progress.
- Include interprofessional and collaborative development or continuing competence in leadership skills—for example, through the participation of nurses in spokesperson and communication programs designed to teach persuasive communication skills that will facilitate their leading and managing collaborative efforts.

Recommendation 8: Promote the Involvement of Nurses in the Redesign of Care Delivery and Payment Systems. The Campaign should work with payers, health care organizations, providers, employers, and regulators to involve nurses in the redesign of care delivery and payment systems. To this end, the Campaign should encourage nurses to serve in executive and leadership positions in government, for-profit and nonprofit organizations, health care delivery systems (e.g., as hospital chief executive officers or chief operations officers), and advisory committees. The Campaign should expand its metrics to measure the progress of nurses in these areas. Types of organizations targeted by this recommendation could include

- health care systems;
- insurance companies and for-profit health care delivery systems (e.g., Minute Clinic);
- not-for-profit organizations that work to improve health care (e.g., the National Quality Forum);
- the National Academy of Medicine and other professional membership groups; and
- federal, state, and local governmental bodies related to health (e.g., the Veterans Health Administration, U.S. Department of Defense, Centers for Medicare & Medicaid Services).

Recommendation 9: Communicate with a Wider and More Diverse Audience to Gain Broad Support for Campaign Objectives. The Campaign should expand the scope of its communication strategies to connect with a broader, more diverse, consumer-oriented audience and galvanize support at the grassroots level. The Campaign, including its state Action Coalitions, should bolster communication efforts geared toward the general public and consumers using messages that go beyond nursing and focus on improving health and health care for consumers and their families. **The Campaign should recruit more allies in the health care community (such as physicians, pharmacists, and other professionals, as well as those outside of health care, such as business leaders, employers, and policy makers) as health care stakeholders to further demonstrate a collaborative approach in advancing the recommendations of** *The Future of Nursing.*

REFERENCES

AACN (American Association of Colleges of Nursing). 2006. *The essentials of doctoral education for advanced nursing practice.* Washington, DC: AACN.

AACN. 2008. *The essentials of master's education in nursing.* Washington, DC: AACN.

AACN. 2011. *The essentials of baccalaureate education for professional nursing practice.* Washington, DC: AACN.

AACN. 2015a. *AACN-Wharton Executive Leadership Program.* http://www.aacn.nche.edu/leading-initiatives/aacn-wharton-executive-leadership-program (accessed September 11, 2015).

AACN. 2015b. *AACN/Wharton Executive Leadership Program, August 10-13, 2015, Philadelphia, PA.* http://www.aacn.nche.edu/leading-initiatives/2015-Wharton-Brochure.pdf (accessed September 11, 2015).

AAMC (Association of American Medical Colleges). 2012. *Changing delivery system increases focus on interprofessional education.* https://www.aamc.org/newsroom/reporter/sept2012/303656/ipe.html (accessed September 10, 2015).

AAMC. 2014. *Lifelong learning initiative: Call for interprofessional in quality improvement and patient safety curriculum.* https://www.staging.mededportal.org/icollaborative/about/initiatives/lifelonglearningcall (accessed September 11, 2015).

AAMC. 2015. *MedEdPORTAL: Ten years strong.* https://www.mededportal.org/about/10 (accessed September 10, 2015).

AAN (American Academy of Nursing). 2014. *American Academy of Nursing Jonas Policy Scholars Program.* http://www.aannet.org/academy-jonas-policy-scholars (accessed September 11, 2015).

AANA (American Association of Nurse Anesthetists). 2014. *Spokesperson training for state association leaders.* www.aana.com/meetings/aanaworkshops/Documents/SpokespersonTrainingforStateAssociationLeaders.pdf (accessed September 17, 2015).

AHA (American Hospital Association). 2014. *2014 National Health Care Governance Survey report.* Chicago, IL: AHA Center for Healthcare Governance.

ANCC (American Nurses Credentialing Center). 2015. *Magnet initial designation, organization eligibility requirements.* http://www.nursecredentialing.org/OrgEligibilityRequirements (accessed August 4, 2015).

AONE (American Organization of Nurse Executives). 2015. *Managing health care delivery.* http://www.aone.org/education/hbs.shtml (accessed September 11, 2015).

Arizona State University. 2015. *Interprofessional fellowship in innovative health leadership.* https://nursingandhealth.asu.edu/non-degree/continuing-education/innovative-health-leadership (accessed September 11, 2015).

Bodenheimer, T., E. H. Wagner, and K. Grumbach. 2002. Improving primary care for patients with chronic illness: The chronic care model, part 2. *Journal of the American Medical Association* 288(15):1909-1914.

CCNA (Center to Champion Nursing in America). 2014a (unpublished). *Future of Nursing: Campaign for Action biannual operations report, February 1, 2014-July 31, 2014.* Washington, DC: CCNA.

CCNA. 2014b (unpublished). *Future of Nursing: Campaign for Action presentation, December 19, 2014.* Washington, DC: CCNA.

CCNA. 2014c (unpublished). *National nursing leadership strategy meeting concept paper: A national strategy to increase the number of nurse leaders on boards, part II.* Washington, DC: CCNA.

CCNA. 2014d (unpublished). *National nursing leadership strategy meeting concept paper: One voice for nursing leadership: A national strategy meeting.* Washington, DC: CCNA.

CCNA. 2015a (unpublished). *CCNA 2014 workplan deliverables, November 2014-May 2015.* Washington, DC: CCNA.

CCNA. 2015b. *Culture of health: Breakthrough leaders in nursing.* http://campaignforaction.org/breakthrough2015 (accessed September 11, 2015).

CCNA. 2015c (unpublished). *Evaluation of the impact of the Institute of Medicine report "The Future of Nursing: Leading Change, Advancing Health" communications report, July 20, 2015.* Washington, DC: CCNA.

CCNA. 2015d (unpublished). *Future of Nursing: Campaign for Action biannual operations report, August 1, 2014-May 31, 2015.* Washington, DC: CCNA.

CCNA. 2015e. *Future of Nursing: Campaign for Action dashboard indicators.* http://campaignforaction.org/dashboard (accessed October 29, 2015).

CCNA. 2015f. *National coalition launches effort to place 10,000 nurses on governing boards by 2020.* http://campaignforaction.org/news/national-coalition-launches-effort-place-10000-nurses-governing-boards-2020 (accessed September 12, 2015).

CCNA. n.d. Campaign progress. http://campaignforaction.org/campaign-progress (accessed September 23, 2015).

CCNE (Commission on Collegiate Nursing Education). 2013. *Standards for accreditation of baccalaureate and graduate nursing programs.* Washington, DC: CCNE.

CCNE. 2014. New health professions accreditors collaborative forms to stimulate interprofessional engagement. Washington, DC: CCNE. http://www.aacn.nche.edu/ccne-accreditation/HPAC-Forms-Engagement.pdf (accessed November 20, 2015).

CHC (Community Health Center, Inc.). 2015. *About us.* http://chc1.com/About/AboutUS.html (accessed September 11, 2015).

Cipriano, P. 2015. Presentation to IOM Committee for Assessing Progress on Implementing the Recommendations of the Institute of Medicine Report *The Future of Nursing: Leading Change, Advancing Health.* Washington, DC, May 28, 2015.

CMS (Centers for Medicare & Medicaid Services). 2013. *Health care innovation awards round one project profiles.* http://innovation.cms.gov/files/x/hcia-project-profiles.pdf (accessed September 11, 2015).

CMS. 2015. *Health care innovation awards.* http://innovation.cms.gov/initiatives/Health-Care-Innovation-Awards (accessed September 11, 2015).

Curley, D. 2015. Presentation to IOM Committee for Assessing Progress on Implementing the Recommendations of the Institute of Medicine Report *The Future of Nursing: Leading Change, Advancing Health.* Washington, DC, July 27, 2015.

Feldman, L. S., L. L. Costa, E. R. Feroli, T. Nelson, S. S. Poe, K. D. Frick, L. E. Efird, and R. G. Miller. 2012. Nurse-pharmacist collaboration on medication reconciliation prevents potential harm. *Journal of Hospital Medicine* 7(5):396-401.

Frenk, J., L. Chen, Z. A. Bhutta, J. Cohen, N. Crisp, T. Evans, H. Fineberg, P. Garcia, Y. Ke, P. Kelley, B. Kistnasamy, A. Meleis, D. Naylor, A. Pablos-Mendez, S. Reddy, S. Scrimshaw, J. Sepulveda, D. Serwadda, and H. Zurayk. 2010. Health professionals for a new century: Transforming education to strengthen health systems in an interdependent world. *Lancet* 376(9756):1923-1958.

Gallup. 2010. *Nursing leadership from bedside to boardroom: Opinion leaders' perceptions.* http://www.rwjf.org/content/dam/web-assets/2010/01/nursing-leadership-from-bedside-to-boardroom (accessed September 10, 2015).

Gallup. 2015. *Honesty/ethics in professions.* http://www.gallup.com/poll/1654/honesty-ethics-professions.aspx (accessed September 10, 2015).

Gilmartin, M. J. 2013. Principles and practices of social entrepreneurship for nursing. *Journal of Nursing Education* 52(11):641-644.

Grumbach, K., and T. Bodenheimer. 2004. Can health care teams improve primary care practice? *Journal of the American Medical Association* 291(10):1246-1251.

Harvard Business School. 2015. *Managing health care delivery.* http://www.exed.hbs.edu/programs/mhcd/pages/default.aspx (accessed September 11, 2015).

HRSA (Health Resources and Services Administration). 2014. *HRSA-14-070 Nurse Education, Practice, Quality and Retention (NEPQR) program—interprofessional collaborative practice.* http://www.grants.gov/view-opportunity.html?oppId=248734 (accessed September 11, 2015).

Hudson, C. E., M. K. Sanders, and C. Pepper. 2013. Interprofessional education and prelicensure baccalaureate nursing students. *Nurse Educator* 38(2):76-80.

IOM (Institute of Medicine). 2003. *Health professions education: A bridge to quality.* Washington, DC: The National Academies Press.

IOM. 2011. *The future of nursing: Leading change, advancing health.* Washington, DC: The National Academies Press.

IOM. 2013. *Interprofessional education for collaboration: Learning how to improve health from interprofessional models across the continuum of education to practice: Workshop summary.* Washington, DC: The National Academies Press.

IPEC (Interprofessional Education Collaborative). 2011. *Core competencies for interprofessional collaborative practice: Report of an expert panel.* Washington, DC: IPEC.

IPEC. 2015. *About IPEC.* https://ipecollaborative.org/About_IPEC.html (accessed September 11, 2015).

Jonas Center (Jonas Center for Nursing and Veterans Healthcare). 2015a. *American Academy of Nursing announces second cohort of students in program connecting nurse leaders with emerging scholars.* http://www.jonascenter.org/news/post/american-academy-of-nursing-announces-second-cohort-of-students-in-program-connecting-nurse-leaders-with-emerging-scholars (accessed September 11, 2015).

Jonas Center. 2015b. *Jonas Nurse Leaders Scholars.* http://www.jonascenter.org/program-areas/jonas-nurse-leaders-scholars (accessed September 11, 2015).

Jonas Center. 2015c. *Leadership grantees.* http://www.jonascenter.org/program-areas/leadership/grantees (accessed September 11, 2015).

Josiah Macy Jr. Foundation. 2012. *Conference on interprofessional education, April 1-3, 2012.* New York: Josiah Macy Jr. Foundation.

Josiah Macy Jr. Foundation. 2013a. *Macy Faculty Scholars.* http://macyfoundation.org/macy-scholars (accessed September 11, 2015).

Josiah Macy Jr. Foundation. 2013b. *Transforming patient care: Aligning interprofessional education with clinical practice redesign.* New York: Josiah Macy Jr. Foundation.

Leape, L., D. Berwick, C. Clancy, J. Conway, P. Gluck, J. Guest, D. Lawrence, J. Morath, D. O'Leary, P. O'Neill, D. Pinakiewicz, and T. Isaac. 2009. Transforming healthcare: A safety imperative. *Quality and Safety in Health Care* 18(6):424-428.

Marsteller, J. A., J. B. Sexton, Y. J. Hsu, C. J. Hsiao, C. G. Holzmueller, P. J. Pronovost, and D. A. Thompson. 2012. A multicenter, phased, cluster-randomized controlled trial to reduce central line-associated bloodstream infections in intensive care units. *Critical Care Medicine* 40(11):2933-2939.

NCIPE (National Center for Interprofessional Practice and Education). 2013a. *About us.* https://nexusipe.org/about (accessed September 11, 2015).

NCIPE. 2013b. *Funding.* https://nexusipe.org/funding (accessed September 11, 2015).

NCIPE. 2013c. *Vision and goals.* https://nexusipe.org/vision (accessed September 11, 2015).

Needleman, J., and S. Hassmiller. 2009. The role of nurses in improving hospital quality and efficiency: Real-world results. *Health Affairs* 28(4):w625-w633.

Pilon, B. A., C. Ketel, and H. Davidson. 2015a. Evidence-based development in nurse-led interprofessional teams. *Nursing Management* 22(3):35-40.

Pilon, B. A., C. Ketel, H. A. Davidson, C. K. Gentry, T. D. Crutcher, A. W. Scott, R. M. Moore, and S. T. Rosenbloom. 2015b. Evidence-guided integration of interprofessional collaborative practice into nurse managed health centers. *Journal of Professional Nursing* 31(4):340-350.

TCC Group. 2013 (unpublished). *Future of Nursing: Campaign for Action: Action Coalition Survey.* Philadelphia, PA: TCC Group.

TCC Group. 2014 (unpublished). *Robert Wood Johnson Foundation Future of Nursing Campaign imperative analysis.* Philadelphia, PA: TCC Group.

Thibault, G. E. 2011. Interprofessional education: An essential strategy to accomplish *The Future of Nursing* goals. *Journal of Nursing Education* 50(6):313-317.

University of Pennsylvania. 2015a. *Dual degree in nursing and Wharton.* https://hcmg.wharton.upenn.edu/programs/undergraduate/program-information/dual-degree-nursing-wharton (accessed October 29, 2015).

University of Pennsylvania. 2015b. *Wharton Nursing Leaders Program.* http://executiveeducation.wharton.upenn.edu/for-individuals/all-programs/wharton-nursing-leaders-program (accessed October 29, 2015).

Wagner, E. H. 2000. The role of patient care teams in chronic disease management. *British Medical Journal* 320(7234):569-572.

WHO (World Health Organization). 2010. *Framework for action on interprofessional education and collaborative practice.* Geneva, Switzerland: WHO.

Zorek, J., and C. Raehl. 2012. Interprofessional education accreditation standards in the USA: A comparative analysis. *Journal of Interprofessional Care* 27(2):123-130.

6

Improving Workforce Data Infrastructure

According to *The Future of Nursing*, there are major gaps in the available data on the health care workforce, and closing these gaps is critical to achieving a fundamental transformation of the health care system (IOM, 2011). Data are needed to understand the numbers and types of health professionals, where they are employed, and in what roles. To support the ongoing transformation of the health care system and the Triple Aim, data are essential to help answer such questions as how many providers the nation needs, what types of providers can be used to meet that need, and whether educational capacity is sufficient to prepare them. Accordingly, *The Future of Nursing* recommends that an infrastructure be built to improve the collection and analysis of data on the health care workforce (see Box 6-1). The Future of Nursing: Campaign for Action (the Campaign) has focused on this recommendation under the pillar "bolstering workforce data" (CCNA, n.d.-b).

The recommendation on workforce data in *The Future of Nursing* assumes the existence of the National Health Care Workforce Commission, and each of the recommendation's bullet points calls on the Commission and the Health Resources and Services Administration (HRSA) to take steps to improve the infrastructure for collecting and analyzing these data. Although the Commission was authorized by the Patient Protection and Affordable Care Act (ACA), and commissioners were appointed in September 2010 (one nurse among them), it has yet to be funded by Congress and thus is not operational (Buerhaus and Retchin, 2013; GAO, 2015; IOM, 2011). While progress on a single, coordinated national data infrastructure has been limited, progress has been made by many different organizations over the past 5 years on the collection and analysis of health workforce data generally and nursing workforce data specifically. The

BOX 6-1
Recommendation 8 from *The Future of Nursing*:
Build an Infrastructure for the Collection and Analysis
of Interprofessional Health Care Workforce Data

The National Health Care Workforce Commission, with oversight from the Government Accountability Office and the Health Resources and Services Administration, should lead a collaborative effort to improve research and the collection and analysis of data on health care workforce requirements. The Workforce Commission and the Health Resources and Services Administration should collaborate with state licensing boards, state nursing workforce centers, and the Department of Labor in this effort to ensure that the data are timely and publicly accessible.

- The Workforce Commission and the Health Resources and Services Administration should coordinate with state licensing boards, including those for nursing, medicine, dentistry, and pharmacy, to develop and promulgate a standardized minimum data set across states and professions that can be used to assess health care workforce needs by demographics, numbers, skill mix, and geographic distribution.
- The Workforce Commission and the Health Resources and Services Administration should set standards for the collection of the minimum data set by state licensing boards; oversee, coordinate, and house the data; and make the data publicly accessible.
- The Workforce Commission and the Health Resources and Services Administration should retain, but bolster, the Health Resources and Services Administration's registered nurse sample survey by increasing the sample size, fielding the survey every other year, expanding the data collected on advanced practice registered nurses, and releasing survey results more quickly.
- The Workforce Commission and the Health Resources and Services Administration should establish a monitoring system that uses the most current analytic approaches and data from the minimum data set to systematically measure and project nursing workforce requirements by role, skill mix, region, and demographics.
- The Workforce Commission and the Health Resources and Services Administration should coordinate workforce research efforts with the Department of Labor, state and regional educators, employers, and state nursing workforce centers to identify regional health care workforce needs, and establish regional targets and plans for appropriately increasing the supply of health professionals.
- The Government Accountability Office should ensure that the Workforce Commission membership includes adequate nursing expertise.

SOURCE: IOM, 2011.

challenge going forward is to find a way to build on this progress by developing a national infrastructure that can synthesize, link, and support the multiple currently uncoordinated efforts. With an increasing emphasis on interprofessional collaboration and team-based care (see Chapters 2 and 5) in a health care system that is being redesigned, establishing a national infrastructure for collecting and analyzing robust and multidisciplinary data on the health care workforce is more important than ever.

ACTIVITY AND PROGRESS

Because the National Health Care Workforce Commission is nonoperational, recommendation 8 from *The Future of Nursing* cannot be implemented as it was written. As noted above, however, despite the absence of a formal national infrastructure and despite some setbacks, significant progress has been made in the past 5 years toward improving the collection and analysis of data on the nursing workforce for use in health workforce planning and policy relating to education, training, and practice.

HRSA has not administered the National Sample Survey of Registered Nurses (NSSRN) since 2008, a gap that runs counter to the recommendation of the Institute of Medicine (IOM) report and represents the loss of an important source of data on the nursing workforce. Still, HRSA's National Center for Workforce Analysis continues to provide important data relating to the nursing workforce. In 2012, HRSA administered the first National Sample Survey of Nurse Practitioners (NSSNP), and in 2014, it issued a summary report on the survey findings and made a public use data file available to researchers (HRSA, 2014a). In October 2013, HRSA produced *The U.S. Nursing Workforce: Trends in the Supply and Education* (HRSA, 2013). In December 2014, HRSA published *The Future of the Nursing Workforce: National- and State-Level Projections, 2012-2025*, providing supply and demand projections for registered nurses (RNs) and licensed practical nurses/licensed vocational nurses (LPNs/LVNs) using data from HRSA's Health Workforce Simulation Model (HRSA, 2014b). New projections of supply and demand at the national level and a Web-based platform are available that states can use to generate supply and demand models by entering their state-based data and other assumptions about attrition from or entrance into the profession (Zangaro, 2015a,b). These state-level data can inform workforce policy at the state level. Nursing workforce projections will be made again in 2016 and will be reported at the national, regional, and state levels. This type of resource and the information provided thereby directly address the IOM recommendation that efforts be made to "identify regional health care workforce needs, and establish regional targets and plans for appropriately increasing the supply of health professionals" (IOM, 2011, p. 284).

Progress has been made on other existing federal instruments for collecting health care workforce data. The National Ambulatory Medical Care Survey

(NAMCS), a comprehensive national survey of ambulatory care services administered annually by the National Center for Health Statistics, was expanded to include data on nurse practitioners (NPs) and other nonphysician clinicians in physician practices. This expansion occurred in part to determine "how advanced practice registered nurses (APRNs) and physician assistants (PAs) are utilized and whether they are used to the full extent of their licenses and training" (CDC, 2015b). Further, the Centers for Disease Control and Prevention (CDC) noted with regard to the NAMCS that "fueled in part by changes in the delivery system, there is strong interest in understanding the dynamics of practice redesign and how team-based medical care is actually delivered" (CDC, 2015b). The collection of data on more members of the health care team will help achieve that understanding. The National Health Interview Survey (NHIS) question "Did you see a general doctor, specialist, nurse practitioner/physician assistant or someone else?" was modified in 2012 to include NPs/PAs (CDC, 2015a; State Health Access Data Assistance Center, 2013). With the inclusion of NPs, certified nurse midwives (CNMs), and certified registered nurse anesthetists (CRNAs) in the Standard Occupational Classification (SOC) system in 2010 (OMB, 2009), data on these nursing professions are now available from the American Community Survey (ACS) and the Bureau of Labor Statistics (BLS, 2010; Watson, 2013). Prior to that update, NPs, CNMs, and CRNAs were classified in the SOC as RNs. The National Council of State Boards of Nursing (NCSBN) has developed the Nursys database, containing data on licensure, discipline, and practice privileges of licensed nurses, both RNs and LPNs/LVNs, in participating states (NCSBN, 2015a). Using licensure data from the 54 boards of nursing that provide this information through Nursys, NCSBN is developing a comprehensive census of nursing licensure statistics (currently, Alabama, Hawaii, and Oklahoma do not provide these data) (NCSBN, 2015b).

To fill the gap in national data on RNs left when the NSSRN was discontinued, NCSBN and the Forum of State Nursing Workforce Centers conducted the National Workforce Survey of more than 42,000 RNs in 2013 (Budden et al., 2013). The 2015 survey collected data from RNs and LPNs/LVNs through September 2015, and these data are expected to be published in spring 2016 (Alexander, 2015a,b).

In 2008, the National Forum of State Nursing Workforce Centers (National Forum) began efforts to develop national nursing datasets on supply, demand, and education, with the support of the Center to Champion Nursing (Moulton, 2015; Moulton et al., 2012; National Forum of State Nursing Workforce Centers, 2015b; Nooney et al., 2010). NCSBN, the National Forum, and HRSA have agreed on the data elements of the Minimum Data Set (MDS) (HRSA, n.d.). There are now 34 State Nursing Workforce Centers; 30 collect supply data, 20 demand data, and 31 education data (National Forum of State Nursing Workforce Centers, 2015a). Sixteen states do not have State Nursing Workforce Centers: Alabama, Alaska, Arkansas, Delaware, Kansas, Maine, Maryland, Massachusetts,

Nevada, New Hampshire, North Carolina, Pennsylvania, Tennessee, Virginia, West Virginia, and Wyoming (National Forum of State Nursing Workforce Centers, 2015b).

The Campaign measures progress on this recommendation of *The Future of Nursing* by tracking the number of recommended nursing workforce data items collected by states. The Campaign tracked states' collection of 14 items about the nursing workforce identified as important by the National Forum (CCNA, 2015b, n.d.-a). The Campaign found that between 2010 and 2014, 23 states were making progress toward collecting all or most of these data items; 16 states were already collecting all or most of the items; and 11 still were collecting only between 1 and 11 of the items (CCNA, 2015b). Two supplemental indicators also show progress on this recommendation: state boards of nursing that participate in the NCSBN Nursys data system and states that collect race/ethnicity data on their nursing workforce. Not all state boards of nursing participate in NCSBN's Nursys data system, but the number of participating states has increased in recent years (NCSBN, 2015c,d,e). Connecticut, Georgia, and Pennsylvania began providing licensure data to the system in 2013-2014 (NCSBN, 2014). The Campaign's dashboard indicators reveal that progress also has been made on the number of states that collect race/ethnicity data on their nursing workforce. In 2013, 44 states collected such data, compared with 34 states in 2011 (information on Connecticut was not available) (CCNA, 2015b).

In the external evaluation conducted by TCC Group (2013), only Maine and New Hampshire indicated that improving data on the nursing workforce was the greatest priority for their state; nevertheless, 46 percent of state Action Coalitions noted that workforce data was a main focus of their work, and another 44 percent said they were doing some work to advance this recommendation. The National Forum reports significant involvement of data stakeholders, particularly State Nursing Workforce Centers, in the state Action Coalitions, stating that more than "70% of workforce centers are co-leads for their state's Action Coalition" (National Forum of State Nursing Workforce Centers, 2015a, p. 2). And 76 percent of Action Coalitions indicated that they thought the availability of data on the nursing workforce was improving (TCC Group, 2013). Still, the Campaign indicated that just 2 percent of state Action Coalition funding was spent on advancing data collection (CCNA, 2015a).

The Campaign's external evaluators made the following observation about state Action Coalitions' perceived progress on issues around workforce data:

> Those [Action Coalitions] using more national [Campaign] resources showed better availability of workforce data. . . . The finding on availability of workforce data may reflect a couple of things. One, it may reflect the work of Joanne Spetz and others helping to make data available at the national level and increase availability of state level breakdowns from national data. Two, it may be a correlation that those groups that have workforce data are better poised to use national resources. We heard through several of our site visits that having good data was

an important starting point for organizations and if they didn't have that, it was the primary focus. (TCC Group, 2013, p. 5)

DISCUSSION

Barriers remain to the robust data collection and analysis needed to understand the nursing workforce and, especially, the health workforce more broadly. The Campaign has recognized limitations in the data available for measuring progress toward implementation of this IOM recommendation. These include the lack of national indicators providing consistent information across states, lag time in the collection and reporting of data, the lack of standardized databases with which to track ideal indicators of progress, and the need to use proxy measures to assess progress within such a short time frame (e.g., using student enrollment rather than graduations or changes in the nursing workforce) (CCNA, n.d.-a; Spetz, 2013b; Spetz et al., 2013).

Barriers to Data Collection and Analysis

Some nursing workforce demand models incorporate changing demographics and population characteristics (HRSA, 2014b; Spetz, 2013a), but they cannot include consideration of changes in the health care delivery system. As David Auerbach, Deputy Director for Research and Cost Trends at the Massachusetts Health Policy Commission, noted at the committee's July 2015 workshop: "Some [nursing workforce demand] models match workforce with utilization today, projecting how the population is going to change, and then outputting what the implication of that is. And that gets us far down the road, but it doesn't answer as well, and can't, the question about what happens if the delivery system changes? How does that change the equation?" One method of addressing this gap is to look at how some of the leading organizations are using workforce data (Peikes et al., 2014; Pittman and Forrest, 2015).

New and greater opportunities for data collection exist now than was the case even 5 years ago, yet barriers still need to be addressed. As mentioned in Chapter 2, as more APRNs begin obtaining and using their own National Provider Identifier (NPI), opportunities may increase for collecting and analyzing data on the services these clinicians provide and the settings in which they work; however, because many NPs—particularly those that provide care in hospitals and those that work under the supervision of or under collaborative agreements with physicians—do not use their own NPIs, limitations remain to the use of this information to determine comprehensively the types of services provided by APRNs (Buerhaus et al., 2015; HRSA, 2014a).

The discontinuation of HRSA's NSSRN left a gap in the collection of data from a national sample of nurses. As Spetz (2013b) points out, "Research on the employment decisions of RNs, their educational trajectories, specific subpopulations, job satisfaction, future employment intentions, and migration across state lines will be severely limited by the lack of the NSSRN" (p. 6). Yet he notes that changes in the nation's health care environment make this information more critical than ever. In addition to the National Workforce Survey of RNs in 2013 and of RNs and LPNs/LVNs in 2015, HRSA is considering reinstituting a national sample survey of nurses, although in modified form (Zangaro, 2015a,b). At the committee's May 2015 workshop, George Zangaro, Director of the National Center for Health Workforce Analysis at HRSA, noted that he is working with the administration on this. The current thinking is to survey a sample of all licensed nurses and include a question asking respondents to identify their specialty (e.g., CRNA, NP), if applicable (Zangaro, 2015a). The survey is expected to continue to collect demographic and educational information, and also is expected to include questions on health care reform and on the roles of nurses and how they contribute within a team-based care environment (Zangaro, 2015a,b). By collecting this information, Zangaro said, HRSA hopes to go beyond describing the demographics of the nursing workforce to inform health policy. HRSA plans on convening leaders in 2016 to assist with the development of the new survey and provide feedback on the survey instrument, the sampling plan, and the implementation plan.

In addition to the lack of an overall infrastructure for the collection and analysis of data on the nursing or interprofessional health workforce, the existing sources of nursing workforce data have many gaps. For example, the American Association of Colleges of Nursing has extensive data on its members, but less on nonmembers. The American Association of Nurse Practitioners has invested considerable resources in building its databases, but the data are proprietary and are not readily shared with other organizations or researchers. Data on demand are limited. The U.S. Census Bureau collects valuable data through the ACS, but an important missing data element is whether the individual has or had a license or certification in a profession, data that would help identify nurses working in related but non-nursing positions, such as administration or research. The National Center for Health Statistics collects systematic data on physician practices and services to patients on the physician's panel through the NAMCS, and it recently added collection of data on the role of nonphysicians in the practices. However, the survey does not sample records of patients on panels of NPs and PAs even in the physician offices that are surveyed, nor does it survey NPs not working in physician practices. The collection of these data would provide important information on the roles of and services provided by NPs and others. Actions are needed both to build the infrastructure for collecting the data and to fill the most serious gaps.

In addition to the ACS, robust data sources for assessing how the nursing workforce is changing include the NSSRN, which has not been conducted since 2008, and the U.S. Census Bureau's Current Population Survey (CPS). Table 6-1 compares the characteristics of these sources. Compared with the ACS and the

TABLE 6-1 Comparison of Sources of Data on the Nursing Workforce

	NSSRN (was quadrennial)	ACS (annual)	CPS (annual)
Lag Time	~2 years in former survey	2014 data available in November 2015	2014 data available in February 2015
Number of RN respondents	~35,000	~35,000	~4,200
Representative of	Licensed RNs	People claiming RN as their occupation	
Demographics	Yes	Yes+	Yes+
Earnings	Yes, annual	Yes, annual	Yes (hourly wages)
Work setting	Yes+	Yes	Yes
Education	Nursing-specific; includes foreign	General, by degree type	General, by degree type
Time spent/roles	Yes	No	No
APRN status	Yes	NP/CNM, CRNA (2010-)	
Other pluses	Certifications, specialties, residence from previous year	Geography, immigration, health status and insurance; other occupations for comparison	

NOTE: ACS = American Community Survey; APRN = advanced practice registered nurse; CNM = certified nurse midwife; CPS = Current Population Survey; CRNA = certified registered nurse anesthetist; NP = nurse practitioner; NSSRN = National Sample Survey of Registered Nurses; RN = registered nurse.
SOURCE: Auerbach, 2015.

CPS, the NSSRN required a great deal of time to process and was conducted only every 4 years. It was, on the other hand, a nursing-specific survey, which allowed for more data collection on nurses' work settings and education and more detail on APRNs. One challenge with both the ACS and the CPS data is that respondents need to indicate that their occupation is RN, which most, but not all, will do—particularly those who are not currently working or are working in non-nursing positions.

As noted above, the National Forum, in collaboration with NCSBN and HRSA, has developed and expanded the use of the MDS. Spetz (2013b) notes that legislation "may be required in some states to authorize such data collection, appropriate funds, and guarantee public reporting" (p. 6). In addition to legislative changes to allow the collection of data on license renewal, other barriers to state implementation of the MDS exist, including leadership's unwillingness to contribute to national datasets and technological misalignment of the state and NCSBN data systems (Alexander, 2015b). A closer examination of these barriers could elucidate the most effective means for removing them. Speakers at the committee's July 2015 workshop noted barriers to expanding the data infrastructure at the state level, including high fixed costs that prohibit small states from conducting surveys or adding the MDS to the license renewal process and also inhibit the collection of data from smaller ambulatory practices as opposed to large hospitals and health systems (Auerbach, 2015; Moulton, 2015).

These logistical and methodological shortcomings in the collection and use of nursing workforce data at the national level pose an issue for national workforce policy and planning. The National Forum (2015b) emphasizes this point and expands the call for support for comprehensive workforce data collection to legislators and planners at the state level: "Without current and accurate national data, best policy approaches for resolving the national shortage may not be implemented at the federal level. . . . Without consistently collected state-level data and reliable national benchmarks, legislators and workforce planners at the state level have fewer resources to guide their use of scarce state funding" (p. 2).

Yet little progress has been made on building a national infrastructure that could integrate the diverse sources of health workforce data; identify gaps; and improve and expand usable data not just on the nursing workforce but also on the entire health care workforce. Health professionals have worked to bolster data collection efforts within their professions and also have united around the need for comprehensive and interprofessional workforce data. For example, dozens of health professions associations have urged Congress to appropriate funds to allow the Commission recommended in *The Future of Nursing* to be operational.[1,2]

Data Needs for Assessing Progress

In assessing the landscape of the nursing and broader health care professions workforce, the committee identified a number of areas that require improved data collection, analysis, and availability to help in assessing progress toward implementing the recommendations of *The Future of Nursing*:

- National surveys of nurses need to continue to have sample frames that include licensed RNs with an associate's degree in nursing (ADN), a bachelor of science in nursing (BSN), and a master of science in nursing (MSN) instead of conducting separate surveys for these populations (see above).

---

[1] A November 29, 2012, letter to Senate and House leaders was signed by 33 health professions associations and organizations (https://www.aamc.org/download/343168/data/groupletterurgingfunding forthenationalhealthcareworkforcecommis.pdf [accessed September 24, 2015]).

[2] A May 21, 2013, letter to leadership of Senate and House Appropriation Committees was signed by 36 health professions associations and organizations (https://www.aamc.org/download/322424/ data/groupletterregardingthenationalhealthcareworkforcecommission.pdf [accessed September 24, 2015]).

- Better data are needed on the settings where nurses are working (e.g., hospitals, ambulatory care, nursing homes, nurse-led practices, retail clinics) and what services they are providing in those settings (see Chapter 2).
- Better data are needed on the range and cost of services provided by APRNs and PAs in hospitals and other care settings (see Chapter 2 and the Barriers to Data Collection and Analysis section of this chapter).
- Better data are needed with which to assess whether there is a shift of baccalaureate-prepared RNs and NPs out of primary care and a subsequent shift of LPNs and associate's degree–prepared RNs into outpatient and community care settings, including long-term care (see Chapter 2).
- A consistent way of measuring outcomes of RN and APRN transition-to-practice residencies, including retention, satisfaction, and support, as well as patient outcomes, is needed (see Chapter 3).
- Better data are needed on the diversity of the pipeline (see Chapter 4).
- The number of degrees obtained by nurses (bachelor's, master's, and doctorates) that are outside of nursing (e.g., business, public policy, public health, sociology, health care administration) needs to be quantified (see Chapter 3). The MDS may be one opportunity to collect these data. Particularly if these data were collected upon license renewal, it would be possible to take a longitudinal look at educational attainment and in what fields.
- The efforts of colleges and universities to develop interdisciplinary activities for students in the health professions need to be tracked (see Chapters 3 and 5).
- Expanded and more robust data need to be collected on leadership positions held by nurses (see Chapter 5).
- Nurse-related measures need to be included in demand-side surveys (e.g., surveys of employers, hospitals, government agencies, and trade associations) (see Chapters 2, 3, and 5).

FINDINGS AND CONCLUSIONS

The nursing community and other stakeholders, including nursing associations, state nursing workforce centers, and federal agencies, have made strides toward collecting more and more consistent and robust data on the nursing workforce. However, a broad, interprofessional infrastructure for the collection of these data is lacking and is more important now than ever.

Findings

This study yielded the following findings on improving the infrastructure for the collection of workforce data:

Finding 6-1. Many of the recommendations of The Future of Nursing *call for the National Health Care Workforce Commission to work with HRSA on implementation. Established under the ACA, the Commission has yet to be funded and thus has not met.*

Finding 6-2. HRSA conducted the first ever National Sample Survey of Nurse Practitioners in 2012.

Finding 6-3. HRSA has discontinued its National Sample Survey of Registered Nurses but is in talks to reinstate a modified version.

Finding 6-4. Other existing federal data collection instruments (National Health Interview Survey, Standard Occupational Classification, National Ambulatory Medical Care Survey) have been updated to provide opportunities for assessing the services and characteristics of nurses in the health care workforce.

Finding 6-5. More APRNs have obtained NPIs, but not all bill for all their services under their own NPI.

Finding 6-6. Nursing and other health professions associations and organizations, including state boards of nursing, collect vast amounts of data on the nursing workforce. There has been a significant increase in the number of State Nursing Workforce Centers collecting data on the supply, demand, and education of nurses, and in those collecting all or most of the data items suggested by the National Forum of State Nursing Workforce Centers. NCSBN also has put great effort into developing and populating its Nursys data system and building a workforce database using the MDS through the participation of state boards of nursing.

Conclusions

The committee drew the following conclusions about progress toward improving the collection and analysis of data on the nursing workforce and the health care workforce more broadly:

Numerous health professional organizations have urged funding of the National Health Care Workforce Commission and have been active in bolstering workforce data collection with their own professions. These efforts suggest that common ground and interprofessional collaboration may be achieved to advance this recommendation of The Future of Nursing.

The greatest progress has been made on expanding data collected within, but not across, the health professions. The intended purpose of the National Health Care Workforce Commission was to assess the existing and future needs for all health professionals in order to establish national goals and priorities for the health workforce, and thus for health care delivery. Absent the convening of the Commission, alternative sources of data and alternative means of assessing the data are needed.

Opportunities will increase for the use of data from the Centers for Medicare & Medicaid Services to assess the services provided by APRNs, but only if APRNs bill for the services they provide under their NPIs.

Significant progress has been made on accelerating uptake of the MDS for the collection of data on the supply, demand, and education of nurses among State Nursing Workforce Centers, thanks to efforts by the National Forum of State Nursing Workforce Centers, NCSBN, and HRSA.

RECOMMENDATION

Recommendation 10: Improve Workforce Data Collection. **The Campaign should promote collaboration among organizations that collect workforce-related data. Given the absence of the National Health Care Workforce Commission, the Campaign can use its strong brand and partnerships to help improve the collection of data on the nursing workforce.**

- **The Campaign should play a role in convening, supporting, and promoting collaboration among organizations and associations to consider how they might create more robust datasets and how various datasets can be organized and made available to researchers, policy makers, and planners. Specifically, the Campaign should encourage**
  - **organizations and agencies to build national databases that could be shared and accessed by the Health Resources and Services Administration (HRSA) and researchers;**
  - **states to implement the Minimum Data Set (MDS) and to share their data with the National Council of State Boards of Nursing (NCSBN) so they can build a national dataset on practicing nurses; and**
  - **nursing organizations that currently engage in independent data collection efforts (such as American Association of Colleges of Nursing, the National League for Nursing, NCSBN, and the American Association of Nurse Practitioners) to collaborate and share their data to build more comprehensive datasets. Other or-**

ganizations representing providers that employ nurses and other health professionals, such as the American Heart Association, should be invited to participate in this collaboration.

- The federal government and states should expand existing data collection activities to better measure and monitor the roles of registered nurses and advanced practice registered nurses. This expansion should include the collection of data on current and former licensees in the American Community Survey and a sampling of services provided by nurse practitioners and physician assistants for their own patient panels and outside of physician offices in the National Ambulatory Medical Care Survey.
- HRSA should undertake a combined National Sample Survey of Registered Nurses and National Sample Survey of Nurse Practitioners that can be administered more frequently than once every 4 years. This effort should include the involvement of national and state nursing organizations. HRSA should continue to promote the use of the MDS and assist in and support its implementation.

REFERENCES

Alexander, M. 2015a. Presentation to IOM Committee for Assessing Progress on Implementing the Recommendations of the Institute of Medicine Report *The Future of Nursing: Leading Change, Advancing Health*. Washington, DC, May 28, 2015.

Alexander, M. 2015b. Presentation to IOM Committee for Assessing Progress on Implementing the Recommendations of the Institute of Medicine Report *The Future of Nursing: Leading Change, Advancing Health*. Washington, DC, July 27, 2015.

Auerbach, D. 2015. Presentation to IOM Committee for Assessing Progress on Implementing the Recommendations of the Institute of Medicine Report *The Future of Nursing: Leading Change, Advancing Health*. Washington, DC, July 27, 2015.

BLS (U.S. Bureau of Labor Statistics). 2010. *2010 SOC user guide*. http://www.bls.gov/soc/soc_2010_user_guide.pdf (accessed September 24, 2015).

Budden, J. S., E. H. Zhong, P. Moulton, and J. P. Cimiotti. 2013. Highlights of the National Workforce Survey of Registered Nurses. *Journal of Nursing Regulation* 4(2):5-14.

Buerhaus, P. I., and S. M. Retchin. 2013. The dormant National Health Care Workforce Commission needs congressional funding to fulfill its promise. *Health Affairs* 32(11):2021-2024.

Buerhaus, P. I., C. M. DesRoches, R. Dittus, and K. Donelan. 2015. Practice characteristics of primary care nurse practitioners and physicians. *Nursing Outlook* 63(2):144-153.

CCNA (Center to Champion Nursing in America). 2015a (unpublished). *Future of Nursing: Campaign for Action biannual operations report, August 1, 2014-May 31, 2015*. Washington, DC: The Center to Champion Nursing in America.

CCNA. 2015b. *Future of nursing: Campaign for action dashboard indicators*. http://campaignforaction.org/dashboard (accessed September 12, 2015).

CCNA. n.d.-a. *Frequently asked questions about the campaign for Action dashboard*. http://campaignforaction.org/sites/default/files/CFA%20Dashboard%20FAQ%20FINAL.docx (accessed September 24, 2015).

CCNA. n.d.-b. *Campaign progress*. http://campaignforaction.org/campaign-progress (accessed September 23, 2015).

CDC (Centers for Disease Control and Prevention). 2015a. *National Health Interview Survey, sample adult, document version date: 22-Jun-15*. ftp://ftp.cdc.gov/pub/Health_Statistics/NCHS/Dataset_Documentation/NHIS/2014/samadult_layout.pdf (accessed September 24, 2015).

CDC. 2015b. *Welcome NAMCS participants*. http://www.cdc.gov/nchs/ahcd/namcs_participant.htm (accessed September 24, 2015).

GAO (U.S. Government Accountability Office). 2015. *National Health Care Workforce Commission*. http://www.gao.gov/about/hcac/nat_hcwc.html (accessed September 24, 2015).

HRSA (Health Resources and Services Administration). 2013. *The U.S. nursing workforce: Trends in supply and education*. Rockville, MD: U.S. Department of Health and Human Services.

HRSA. 2014a. *Highlights from the 2012 national sample survey of nurse practitioners*. Rockville, MD: U.S. Department of Health and Human Services. http://bhpr.hrsa.gov/healthworkforce/supplydemand/nursing/nursepractitionersurvey/npsurveyhighlights.pdf (accessed September 23, 2015).

HRSA. 2014b. *The future of the nursing workforce: National- and state-level projections, 2012-2025*. Rockville, MD: U.S. Department of Health and Human Services.

HRSA. n.d. *Health professions minimum data set*. http://bhpr.hrsa.gov/healthworkforce/data/minimumdataset/index.html (accessed September 24, 2015).

IOM (Institute of Medicine). 2011. *The future of nursing: Leading change, advancing health*. Washington, DC: The National Academies Press.

Moulton, P. 2015. Presentation to IOM Committee for Assessing Progress on Implementing the Recommendations of the Institute of Medicine Report *The Future of Nursing: Leading Change, Advancing Health*. Washington, DC, July 27, 2015.

Moulton, P., P. L. Wiebusch, B. L. Cleary, M. L. Brunell, D. F. Fapier, C. Bienemy, S. A. LeVasseur, and J. P. Cimiotti. 2012. Towards standardization (part 2): Status of implementation of national nursing workforce minimum data sets. *Policy, Politics and Nursing Practice* 13(3):162-169.

National Forum of State Nursing Workforce Centers. 2015a. *National Forum member data collection*. http://www.nursingworkforcecenters.org/minimumdatasets.aspx (accessed August 25, 2015).

National Forum of State Nursing Workforce Centers. 2015b. *Report to the Committee for the Evaluation of the Impact of the Institute of Medicine report "The Future of Nursing: Leading Change, Advancing Health."* http://www.nursingworkforcecenters.org/Resources/files/Final_IOM_Future_of_Nursing_Evaluation_Committee_Report.pdf (accessed September 24, 2015).

NCSBN (National Council of State Boards of Nursing). 2014. 2013 *Environmental scan: Annual review of emerging issues and trends that impact nursing regulation*. https://www.ncsbn.org/NCSBN_2013-14_Environmental_Scan.pdf (accessed September 24, 2015).

NCSBN. 2015a. *About Nursys*. https://www.nursys.com/About.aspx (accessed September 24, 2015).

NCSBN. 2015b. *The national nursing database*. https://www.ncsbn.org/national-nursing-database.htm (accessed September 24, 2015).

NCSBN. 2015c. *48 nurse license verification boards of nursing*. https://www.nursys.com/NLV/NLVJurisdictions.aspx (accessed August 28, 2015).

NCSBN. 2015d. *54 licensure QuickConfirm boards of nursing*. https://www.nursys.com/LQC/LQCJurisdictions.aspx (accessed August 28, 2015).

NCSBN. 2015e. *53 Nursys e-Notify boards of nursing*. https://www.nursys.com/EN/ENJurisdictions.aspx (accessed August 28, 2015).

Nooney, J., B. Cleary, P. Moulton, P. Wiebusch, J. Murray, M. Yore, and M. Brunell. 2010. Towards standardization (part 1): Assessment of state and national nursing workforce data sources. *Policy, Politics and Nursing Practice* 11(3):173-183.

OMB (Office of Management and Budget). 2009. 2010 Standard occupational classification (SOC)—OMB's final decisions. *Federal Register* 74(12):3920-3936.

Peikes, D. N., R. J. Reid, T. J. Day, D. D. Cornwell, S. B. Dale, R. J. Baron, R. S. Brown, and R. J. Shapiro. 2014. Staffing patterns of primary care practices in the comprehensive primary care initiative. *The Annals of Family Medicine* 12(2):142-149.

Pittman, P., and E. Forrest. 2015. The changing roles of registered nurses in Pioneer Accountable Care Organizations. *Nursing Outlook* 63(5):554-565.

Spetz, J. 2013a. *Forecasts of the registered nurse workforce in California.* http://rn.ca.gov/pdfs/forms/forecasts2013.pdf (accessed September 24, 2015).

Spetz, J. 2013b. The research and policy important of nursing sample surveys and minimum data sets. *Policy, Politics and Nursing Practice* 14(1):33-40.

Spetz, J., T. Bates, L. Chu, J. Lin, N. W. Fishman, and L. Melichar. 2013. Creating a dashboard to track progress toward IOM recommendations for the Future of Nursing. *Policy, Politics and Nursing Practice* 14(3-4):117-124.

State Health Access Data Assistance Center. 2013. *NHIS questionnaire changes addressing the Patient Protection and Affordable Care Act.* http://www.shadac.org/files/shadac/publications/NHIS_ACA_Brief34.pdf (accessed September 24, 2015).

TCC Group. 2013. *Future of Nursing: Campaign for Action: Action coalition survey.* Philadelphia, PA: TCC Group.

Watson, A. L. 2013. Implementing the 2010 Standard Occupational Classification in the Occupational Employment Statistics program. *Monthly Labor Review* (May):36-49. http://www.bls.gov/opub/mlr/2013/05/art3full.pdf (accessed September 24, 2015).

Zangaro, G. 2015a. Presentation to IOM Committee for Assessing Progress on Implementing the Recommendations of the Institute of Medicine Report *The Future of Nursing: Leading Change, Advancing Health.* Washington, DC, May 28, 2015.

Zangaro, G. 2015b. Presentation to IOM Committee for Assessing Progress on Implementing the Recommendations of the Institute of Medicine Report *The Future of Nursing: Leading Change, Advancing Health.* Washington, DC, July 27, 2015.

Appendix A

Data Sources and Methods

The Committee for Assessing Progress on Implementing the Recommendations of the Institute of Medicine (IOM) Report *The Future of Nursing: Leading Change, Advancing Health* was asked to assess the changes in the field of nursing and peripheral areas over the past 5 years resulting from that report. The role of AARP and Robert Wood Johnson Foundation (RWJF) Future of Nursing: Campaign for Action (the Campaign) was considered in assessing these field changes. The committee also was asked to assess the Campaign's progress in meeting its stated goals and to identify areas that should be emphasized over the next 5 years to help the Campaign fulfill the recommendations of *The Future of Nursing*.

To respond to its charge, the committee examined data from a variety of sources. These sources included a literature review on actions taken and progress made toward implementing the recommendations of *The Future of Nursing*, reports and information provided by the Campaign documenting its activities and progress, public input obtained through a series of workshops and meetings, and written public comments on aspects of the study charge. The study was conducted over a 12-month period.

DESCRIPTION OF THE STUDY COMMITTEE

The study committee comprised 12 individuals with expertise in nursing and health professions education and practice, health services research, health policy, workforce data, health systems, economics, and communications. See Appendix C for biographical sketches of the committee members. The committee convened for four 2-day meetings in April, May, July, and August 2015.

LITERATURE REVIEW

Several strategies were used to identify literature relevant to the committee's charge. First, a reference search for *The Future of Nursing: Leading Change, Advancing Health* conducted in SCOPUS and Web of Science yielded more than 1,600 journal articles and books that cite the report. A LexisNexis news search for the report's title resulted in more than 900 articles. A LexisNexis search for the report's title within the *Congressional Record*, the *Federal Register*, law reviews, federal and state cases, and legislative history also was conducted. A separate LexisNexis search of congressional records, committee reports, statutes, state administrative codes, bills, and registers was carried out using keywords from each of the eight recommendations of *The Future of Nursing*. A more extensive search of bibliographic databases, including MEDLINE and SCOPUS, was conducted to identify additional articles on relevant topics from peer-reviewed journals. The keywords used in searches included *nurse, registered nurse, advanced practice registered nurse, APRN, nurse practitioner, nurse anesthetist, nurse midwife, nonphysician practitioners, nonphysician provider, federal funding, Centers for Medicare & Medicaid Services, Medicare, Medicaid, Center for Medicare & Medicaid Innovation, reimbursement, payment model, care delivery model, health information technology, primary care, ambulatory care, National Council of State Boards of Nursing, third party payer, insurer, scope of practice, practice authority, clinical privileges, admitting privileges, conditions of participation, medical staff, Federal Employee Health Benefits, Federal Trade Commission, regulations, state regulations, entrepreneurship, business, Health Resources and Services Administration, Community Health Accreditation Program, transition to practice, nurse residency, nurse fellowship, graduate medical education, accreditation, evaluation, competencies, baccalaureate, BSN, associate degree, ADN, master's, MSN, doctorate, PhD, DNP, academic pathway, academic progression, RN-to-BSN, ADN-to-BSN, higher education, articulation agreement, tuition reimbursement, scholarship, loan forgiveness, financial support, second-degree, returning student, interprofessional education, interprofessional collaboration, interprofessional training, health professions education, faculty, recruitment, enrollment, vacancy, education funding, diversity, lifelong learning, continuing education, continuing competency, clinical competency, performance competency, professional development, faculty development, leadership, leadership development, leadership positions, leadership education, management position, National Health Care Workforce Commission, health workforce data, health workforce statistics, minimum data set, data collection, data standards, workforce projections, nursing supply,* and *nursing demand.*

Staff sorted through approximately 2,100 articles, reports, issue briefs, and other documents and pieces of information to identify those relevant to the committee's charge and created an EndNote database. In addition, committee members, Campaign staff, meeting participants, and members of the public submitted articles and reports on these topics.

PUBLIC MEETINGS

The committee hosted three public workshops to obtain additional information on specific aspects of the study charge. These meetings were held on May 28, July 27, and July 28, 2015. Subject-matter experts were invited to present information and recommendations for the committee's consideration. The workshops brought together stakeholders and leaders from the areas of health professions education and training, policy and regulation in care delivery, provider and organizational efforts in care delivery, and health workforce data to discuss the efforts, successes, and barriers related to implementing the recommendations of *The Future of Nursing*. Specific topics included

- working toward and achieving a more highly educated nursing workforce, including the development and implementation of models of academic progression, and implications for education and health care delivery;
- development and evaluation of nurse residency programs for registered nurses (RNs) and advanced practice registered nurses (APRNs);
- recruitment and retention of a diverse nursing workforce;
- impacts of health care system changes and culture change on health care delivery; and
- information and data available for assessing health professions education, training, and demand to inform workforce policy.

Speakers included leaders from health professions associations, health delivery organizations, health insurance organizations, higher education, academia and research, government agencies, health professions education and training accrediting agencies, and more.

The committee also held open forums at each workshop at which members of the public were encouraged to provide testimony on topics related to the study charge. Agendas for the three public meetings are presented in Boxes A-1 through A-3.

BOX A-1
PUBLIC SESSION AGENDA

20 F Street NW Conference Center
20 F Street NW
Washington, DC 20001

Thursday, May 28, 2015

9:00 a.m.   **Welcome and Introductions**

Stuart Altman, Ph.D., Chair, Committee for Assessing Progress on Implementing the Recommendations of the Institute of Medicine Report *The Future of Nursing: Leading Change, Advancing Health*; and Sol C. Chaikin Professor of National Health Policy, The Heller School for Social Policy and Management, Brandeis University

9:15 a.m.   **The Future of Nursing: Campaign for Action Research, Data, and Evaluation**

The goal of this session is for the committee to gain a better understanding of the data and information that have been identified by the Future of Nursing: Campaign for Action relating to progress on implementing *The Future of Nursing* report's recommendations and on the Campaign activities.

Moderator: *Karen Donelan, Sc.D., Ed.M.,* Senior Scientist in Health Policy, Mongan Institute for Health Policy, Massachusetts General Hospital Institute for Technology Assessment, Massachusetts General Hospital
Panelists:
Kate Locke, M.P.H., Associate Director of Evaluation, TCC Group
Mary D. Naylor, Ph.D., R.N., FAAN, Marian S. Ware Professor in Gerontology, and Director of the NewCourtland Center for Transitions and Health, University of Pennsylvania School of Nursing
Jared Raynor, M.S., Director of Evaluation, TCC Group
Joanne Spetz, Ph.D., Director, Health Workforce Research Center, and Associate Director for Research Strategy, Center for the Health Professions, University of California, San Francisco

10:15 a.m. **Health Professions Education and Training Stakeholders**

Moderator: *George Thibault, M.D.,* President, Josiah Macy Jr. Foundation

Panelists:

Marsha Howell Adams, Ph.D., R.N., CNE, FAAN, ANEF, President, National League for Nursing, and Dean and Professor, University of Alabama in Huntsville College of Nursing

Mary Beth Bigley, Dr.P.H., M.S.N., APRN, Director, Division of Nursing and Public Health, Bureau of Health Workforce, Health Resources and Services Administration

Eileen T. Breslin, Ph.D., R.N., FAAN, Dean and Professor, University of Texas Health Science Center at San Antonio, School of Nursing, and President, American Association of Colleges of Nursing

Jennifer Butlin, Ed.D., Executive Director, Commission on Collegiate Nursing Education

Donna Meyer, M.S.N., R.N., Chief Executive Officer, Organization for Associate Degree Nursing

Mary Lou Rusin, Ed.D., R.N., ANEF, Chair, Accreditation Commission for Education in Nursing

Thomas J. Snyder, M.B.A., President, Ivy Tech Community College, representing the American Association of Community Colleges

11:30 a.m. BREAK FOR LUNCH

12:30 p.m. Delivery of Care Stakeholders: Policy and Regulation

Moderator: *Bob Phillips, M.D., M.S.P.H.,* Vice President for Research and Policy, American Board of Family Medicine

Panelists:

Maryann Alexander, Ph.D., R.N., FAAN, Chief Officer, Nursing Regulation, National Council of State Boards of Nursing

Humayun J. Chaudhry, D.O., MACP, President and Chief Executive Officer, Federation of State Medical Boards

Janet Heinrich, Dr.P.H., R.N., Senior Advisor, Center for Medicare & Medicaid Innovation, Centers for Medicare & Medicaid Services

Mary E. Picerno, R.N., Chief Nursing Officer, Cigna

George Zangaro, Ph.D., R.N., FAAN, Director, National Center for Health Workforce Analysis, Health Resources and Services Administration

1:45 p.m. Delivery of Care Stakeholders: Health Care Organizations and Providers

Moderator: *Cynthia Barginere, D.N.P., R.N., FACHE,* Vice President, Chief Nursing Officer, Rush University Medical Center

continued

BOX A-1 Continued

Panelists:

Linda Burnes Bolton, Dr.P.H., R.N., FAAN, Vice President, Nursing; Chief Nursing Officer; and Director of Nursing Research, Cedars-Sinai Medical Center, and President, American Organization of Nurse Executives *(by phone)*

Pamela F. Cipriano, Ph.D., R.N., NEA-BC, FAAN, President, American Nurses Association

Catherine M. Dower, J.D., Director, National Nursing Research and Policy, Kaiser Permanente

Kenneth P. Miller, Ph.D., F.N.P.-C, FAAN, FAANP, President, American Association of Nurse Practitioners

Steven E. Weinberger, M.D., FACP, Executive Vice President and Chief Executive Officer, American College of Physicians

Robert L. Wergin, M.D., FAAFP, President, American Academy of Family Physicians

3:00 p.m.   BREAK

3:15 p.m.   Public Testimony

Members of the public who register in advance will have 3 minutes to provide public comment on progress toward implementation of *The Future of Nursing* report's recommendations, and successes and barriers to moving the recommendations to reality.

Brenda Cleary, Health Care Consultant

Mary Sue Gorski, Consultant, Center to Champion Nursing in America

Francie Halderman, Board of Directors Chair-Elect, American Holistic Nurses Credentialing Corporation

Kristin Jimison, Director of Communications, Virginia Nurses Association

Tara Koslov, Deputy Director, Office of Policy Planning, Federal Trade Commission

Susan Kosman, Chief Nursing Officer, Aetna

Ruth Lubic, Founder, Developing Families Center

Linda MacIntyre, Chief Nurse, American Red Cross

Sheila Melander, President, National Organization of Nurse Practitioner Faculties

Erica Mobley, Director of Communications and Development, The Leapfrog Group

Susan Moyer, Assistant Program Director, Colorado Center for Nursing Excellence

Frank Purcell, Senior Director, Federal Government Affairs, American Association of Nurse Anesthetists

4:15 p.m.   ADJOURN OPEN SESSION

BOX A-2
PUBLIC SESSION AGENDA

National Academy of Sciences Building
2101 Constitution Avenue, NW
Room 125
Washington, DC 20418

Monday, July 27, 2015

9:00 a.m. Welcome and Introductions

Stuart Altman, Ph.D., Chair, Committee for Assessing Progress on Implementing the Recommendations of the Institute of Medicine Report *The Future of Nursing: Leading Change, Advancing Health*; and Sol C. Chaikin Professor of National Health Policy, The Heller School for Social Policy and Management, Brandeis University

9:15 a.m. Toward a More Highly Educated Nursing Workforce

Moderator: *Jack Needleman, Ph.D., FAAN,* Professor of Health Policy and Management, Fielding School of Public Health, University of California, Los Angeles
Panelists:
Rhonda Anderson, R.N., FAAN, FACHE, Chief Executive Officer, Cardon Children's Medical Center *(by phone)*
Darlene Curley, M.S., R.N., FAAN, Executive Director, Jonas Center for Nursing and Veterans Healthcare
Linda C. Lewis, M.S.A., R.N., NEA-BC, FACHE, Executive Vice President and Chief ANCC Officer, American Nurses Credentialing Center (ANCC), and Director, ANCC Magnet Recognition Program®
Terri E. Weaver, Ph.D., R.N., FAAN, Dean and Professor, University of Illinois at Chicago College of Nursing *(by phone)*

10:15 a.m. BREAK

10:30 a.m. Models of Academic Progression

Moderator: *Paula Gubrud, Ed.D., R.N., FAAN,* Associate Professor, Oregon Health & Science University School of Nursing
Panelists:
Catherine Alicia Georges, Ed.D., R.N., FAAN, Professor and Chairperson of Nursing, Lehman College
Tina Gerardi, M.S., R.N., CAE, Deputy Director, Academic Progression in Nursing (APIN)

continued

BOX A-2 Continued

Jean Giddens, Ph.D., R.N., FAAN, Dean, Virginia Commonwealth University School of Nursing
Beth Hagan, Ph.D., Executive Director, Community College Baccalaureate Association
Jenny Landen, R.N., M.S.N., FNP-BC, Dean, School of Fitness Education; School of Health, Math, Computer Science, Engineering and Science, Santa Fe Community College

11:30 a.m. Nursing Education and Workforce Data

Moderator: *Ed Salsberg, M.P.A.,* Director, Health Workforce Studies, George Washington University Health Workforce Institute and School of Nursing
Panelists:
Maryann Alexander, Ph.D., R.N., FAAN, Chief Officer, Nursing Regulation, National Council of State Boards of Nursing
David Auerbach, Ph.D., Deputy Director for Research and Cost Trends, Massachusetts Health Policy Commission
Patricia L. Moulton, Ph.D., President, National Forum of State Nursing Workforce Centers, and Executive Director, North Dakota Center for Nursing
Marsal P. Stoll, Ed.D., M.S.N., Chief Executive Officer, Accreditation Commission for Education in Nursing
Deborah E. Trautman, Ph.D., R.N., Chief Executive Officer, American Association of Colleges of Nursing
George Zangaro, Ph.D., R.N., FAAN, Director, National Center for Health Workforce Analysis, Health Resources and Services Administration *(by phone)*

12:30 p.m. LUNCH

1:15 p.m.   **Toward Establishing Nurse Residency Programs**

         Moderator: *Carmen Alvarez, Ph.D., R.N., CRNP, CNM,* Assistant Professor, Department of Community-Public Health, Johns Hopkins University School of Nursing

         Panelists:

         Margaret Flinter, APRN, Ph.D., FAAN, c-FNP, Senior Vice President and Clinical Director, Community Health Center, Inc.

         Stuart Gilman, M.D., M.P.H., Director, Advanced Fellowships and Professional Development, Office of Academic Affiliations, U.S. Department of Veterans Affairs

         Debra McElroy, M.P.H., R.N., Senior Director, Nursing Leadership, University HealthSystem Consortium

         Benjamin Murray, M.P.A., Director of Accreditation Services, Commission on Collegiate Nursing Education

2:15 p.m.   **Recruiting and Retaining a Diverse Nursing Workforce**

         Moderator: *Ed Salsberg, M.P.A.,* Director, Health Workforce Studies, George Washington University Health Workforce Institute and School of Nursing

         Panelists:

         Adriana Perez, Ph.D., R.N., ANP-BC, FAAN, Assistant Professor, College of Nursing and Health Innovation, Arizona State University

         Norma Martinez Rogers, Ph.D., R.N., FAAN, Professor, Family and Community Health Systems, University of Texas Health Science Center at San Antonio

         Deborah Washington, Ph.D., R.N., M.S., Director of Diversity for Patient Care Services, Massachusetts General Hospital, and Co-Chair, Diversity Steering Committee, Future of Nursing: Campaign for Action *(by phone)*

3:15 p.m.   **ADJOURN**

BOX A-3
PUBLIC SESSION AGENDA

National Academy of Sciences Building
2101 Constitution Avenue, NW
Room 125
Washington, DC 20418

Tuesday, July 28, 2015

9:00 a.m. Welcome and Introductions

Stuart Altman, Ph.D., Chair, Committee for Assessing Progress on Implementing the Recommendations of the Institute of Medicine Report *The Future of Nursing: Leading Change, Advancing Health*; and Sol C. Chaikin Professor of National Health Policy, The Heller School for Social Policy and Management, Brandeis University

9:15 a.m. Impact of Health Care System Changes on the Culture of Care Delivery

Moderator: *Richard A. Berman, M.H.A., M.B.A.,* Professor, Institute for Advanced Discovery & Innovation, University of South Florida
Panelists:
Nancy Gagliano, M.D., Chief Medical Officer, CVS/MinuteClinic, and Senior Vice President, CVS Health
Gerri Lamb, Ph.D., R.N., FAAN, Associate Professor and Director for the Center for Advancing Interprofessional Practice, Education and Research, Arizona State University College of Nursing and Health Innovation; Chair, American Interprofessional Health Collaborative (AIHC); and Liaison, Arizona Nexus Innovation Incubator to the National Center for Interprofessional Practice and Education
Scott W. Lamprecht, D.N.P., APRN, FNP-BC, R.N., Chief Clinical Educator and Family Nurse Practitioner, Complete Medical Consultants *(by phone)*
Diane Skiba, Ph.D., FACMI, ANEF, FAAN, Professor and Specialty Director, Health Care Informatics, University of Colorado College of Nursing
Julie A. Sochalski, Ph.D., FAAN, R.N., Associate Professor of Nursing; Interim Associate Dean for Academic Programs, University of Pennsylvania School of Nursing

10:30 a.m. BREAK

10:45 a.m. Roundtable on Culture Change in the Health Professions and Health Care Delivery

Moderator: *George E. Thibault, M.D.,* President, Josiah Macy Jr. Foundation

Panelists:

Lawrence "L.B." Brown, Pharm.D., Ph.D., FAPHA, Associate Dean of Student Affairs, and Professor of Pharmacoeconomics and Health Policy, Chapman University School of Pharmacy, and President, American Pharmacists Association

Rebecca S. Etz, Ph.D., Associate Professor, Family Medicine and Population Health, and Co-Director, Ambulatory Care Outcomes Research Network, Virginia Commonwealth University School of Medicine

Thomas Graf, M.D., National Director for Population Health, The Chartis Group

Diana J. Mason, Ph.D., FAAN, R.N., President, American Academy of Nursing, and Rudin Professor of Nursing, Hunter College-Bellevue School of Nursing, City University of New York

Josef Reum, Ph.D., M.P.A., Professor Emeritus, Milken Institute of Public Health, George Washington University

12:00 p.m. Public Testimony

Stephanie Ahmed, President, Massachusetts Coalition of Nurse Practitioners

Britney Broyhill, Nurse Practitioner Fellowship Director, Center for Advanced Practice, Carolinas HealthCare System; and Founding Board Member, Association of Post Graduate APRN Programs (APGAP)

Marci Farquhar-Snow, Nurse Practitioner, Program Director, Cardiology NP Fellowship, Mayo Clinic

Renee Franquiz, Doctor of Nursing Practice student, University of Maryland

Ann Kurth, Professor, New York University College of Nursing

Ruth Lubic, Founder, Developing Families Center

Frank Purcell, Senior Director, Federal Government Affairs, American Association of Nurse Anesthetists

Diana Ruiz, Medical Center Health System (video)

Elaine Ryan, Vice President, Government Affairs, AARP

Susan Stone, President, Frontier Nursing University

1:00 p.m. ADJOURN

Appendix B

The Future of Nursing:
Leading Change, Advancing Health
Key Messages and
Report Recommendations

KEY MESSAGES

1. Nurses should practice to the full extent of their education and training.
2. Nurses should achieve higher levels of education and training through an improved education system that promotes seamless academic progression.
3. Nurses should be full partners, with physicians and other health care professionals, in redesigning health care in the United States.
4. Effective workforce planning and policy making require better data collection and an improved information infrastructure.

RECOMMENDATIONS

Recommendation 1: Remove scope-of-practice barriers. *Advanced practice registered nurses should be able to practice to the full extent of their education and training. To achieve this goal, the committee recommends the following actions.*

For Congress:

- Expand the Medicare program to include coverage of advanced practice registered nurse services that are within the scope of practice under applicable state law, just as physician services are now covered.
- Amend the Medicare program to authorize advanced practice registered nurses to perform admission assessments, as well as certification of

patients for home health care services and for admission to hospice and skilled nursing facilities.

- Extend the increase in Medicaid reimbursement rates for primary care physicians included in the Patient Protection and Affordable Care Act (ACA) to advanced practice registered nurses providing similar primary care services.
- Limit federal funding for nursing education programs to only those programs in states that have adopted the National Council of State Boards of Nursing Model Nursing Practice Act and Model Nursing Administrative Rules (Article XVIII, Chapter 18).

For state legislatures:

- Reform scope-of-practice regulations to conform to the National Council of State Boards of Nursing Model Nursing Practice Act and Model Nursing Administrative Rules (Article XVIII, Chapter 18).
- Require third-party payers that participate in fee-for-service payment arrangements to provide direct reimbursement to advanced practice registered nurses who are practicing within their scope of practice under state law.

For the Centers for Medicare & Medicaid Services:

- Amend or clarify the requirements for hospital participation in the Medicare program to ensure that advanced practice registered nurses are eligible for clinical privileges, admitting privileges, and membership on medical staff.

For the Office of Personnel Management:

- Require insurers participating in the Federal Employees Health Benefits Program to include coverage of those services of advanced practice registered nurses that are within their scope of practice under applicable state law.

For the Federal Trade Commission and the Antitrust Division of the Department of Justice:

- Review existing and proposed state regulations concerning advanced practice registered nurses to identify those that have anticompetitive effects without contributing to the health and safety of the public. States with unduly restrictive regulations should be urged to amend them to allow advanced practice registered nurses to provide care to patients in all circumstances in which they are qualified to do so.

Recommendation 2: Expand opportunities for nurses to lead and diffuse collaborative improvement efforts. *Private and public funders, health care organizations, nursing education programs, and nursing associations should expand opportunities for nurses to lead and manage collaborative efforts with physicians and other members of the health care team to conduct research and to redesign and improve practice environments and health systems. These entities should also provide opportunities for nurses to diffuse successful practices.*

To this end:

- The Center for Medicare & Medicaid Innovation should support the development and evaluation of models of payment and care delivery that use nurses in an expanded and leadership capacity to improve health outcomes and reduce costs. Performance measures should be developed and implemented expeditiously where best practices are evident to reflect the contributions of nurses and ensure better-quality care.
- Private and public funders should collaborate, and when possible pool funds, to advance research on models of care and innovative solutions, including technology, that will enable nurses to contribute to improved health and health care.
- Health care organizations should support and help nurses in taking the lead in developing and adopting innovative, patient-centered care models.
- Health care organizations should engage nurses and other front-line staff to work with developers and manufacturers in the design, development, purchase, implementation, and evaluation of medical and health devices and health information technology products.
- Nursing education programs and nursing associations should provide entrepreneurial professional development that will enable nurses to initiate programs and businesses that will contribute to improved health and health care.

Recommendation 3: Implement nurse residency programs. *State boards of nursing, accrediting bodies, the federal government, and health care organizations should take actions to support nurses' completion of a transition-to-practice program (nurse residency) after they have completed a prelicensure or advanced practice degree program or when they are transitioning into new clinical practice areas.*

The following actions should be taken to implement and support nurse residency programs:

- State boards of nursing, in collaboration with accrediting bodies such as the Joint Commission and the Community Health Accreditation Program, should support nurses' completion of a residency program after they have completed a prelicensure or advanced practice degree program or when they are transitioning into new clinical practice areas.

- The Secretary of Health and Human Services should redirect all graduate medical education funding from diploma nursing programs to support the implementation of nurse residency programs in rural and critical access areas.
- Health care organizations, the Health Resources and Services Administration and Centers for Medicare & Medicaid Services, and philanthropic organizations should fund the development and implementation of nurse residency programs across all practice settings.
- Health care organizations that offer nurse residency programs and foundations should evaluate the effectiveness of the residency programs in improving the retention of nurses, expanding competencies, and improving patient outcomes.

Recommendation 4: Increase the proportion of nurses with a baccalaureate degree to 80 percent by 2020. *Academic nurse leaders across all schools of nursing should work together to increase the proportion of nurses with a baccalaureate degree from 50 to 80 percent by 2020. These leaders should partner with education accrediting bodies, private and public funders, and employers to ensure funding, monitor progress, and increase the diversity of students to create a workforce prepared to meet the demands of diverse populations across the lifespan.*

- The Commission on Collegiate Nursing Education, working in collaboration with the National League for Nursing Accrediting Commission, should require all nursing schools to offer defined academic pathways, beyond articulation agreements, that promote seamless access for nurses to higher levels of education.
- Health care organizations should encourage nurses with associate's and diploma degrees to enter baccalaureate nursing programs within 5 years of graduation by offering tuition reimbursement, creating a culture that fosters continuing education, and providing a salary differential and promotion.
- Private and public funders should collaborate, and when possible pool funds, to expand baccalaureate programs to enroll more students by offering scholarships and loan forgiveness, hiring more faculty, expanding clinical instruction through new clinical partnerships, and using technology to augment instruction. These efforts should take into consideration strategies to increase diversity of the nursing workforce in terms of race/ethnicity, gender, and geographic distribution.

- The U.S. Secretary of Education, other federal agencies, including the Health Resources and Services Administration, and state and private funders should expand loans and grants for second-degree nursing students.
- Schools of nursing, in collaboration with other health professional schools, should design and implement early and continuous interprofessional collaboration through joint classroom and clinical training opportunities.
- Academic nurse leaders should partner with health care organizations, leaders from primary and secondary school systems, and other community organizations to recruit and advance diverse nursing students.

Recommendation 5: Double the number of nurses with a doctorate by 2020. *Schools of nursing, with support from private and public funders, academic administrators and university trustees, and accrediting bodies, should double the number of nurses with a doctorate by 2020 to add to the cadre of nurse faculty and researchers, with attention to increasing diversity.*

- The Commission on Collegiate Nursing Education and the National League for Nursing Accrediting Commission should monitor the progress of each accredited nursing school to ensure that at least 10 percent of all baccalaureate graduates matriculate into a master's or doctoral program within 5 years of graduation.
- Private and public funders, including the Health Resources and Services Administration and the Department of Labor, should expand funding for programs offering accelerated graduate degrees for nurses to increase the production of master's and doctoral nurse graduates and to increase the diversity of nurse faculty and researchers.
- Academic administrators and university trustees should create salary and benefit packages that are market competitive to recruit and retain highly qualified academic and clinical nurse faculty.

Recommendation 6: Ensure that nurses engage in lifelong learning. *Accrediting bodies, schools of nursing, health care organizations, and continuing competency educators from multiple health professions should collaborate to ensure that nurses and nursing students and faculty continue their education and engage in lifelong learning to gain the competencies needed to provide care for diverse populations across the lifespan.*

- Faculty should partner with health care organizations to develop and prioritize competencies so curricula can be updated regularly to ensure that graduates at all levels are prepared to meet the current and future health needs of the population.

- The Commission on Collegiate Nursing Education and the National League for Nursing Accrediting Commission should require that all nursing students demonstrate a comprehensive set of clinical performance competencies that encompass the knowledge and skills needed to provide care across settings and the lifespan.
- Academic administrators should require all faculty to participate in continuing professional development and to perform with cutting-edge competence in practice, teaching, and research.
- All health care organizations and schools of nursing should foster a culture of lifelong learning and provide resources for interprofessional continuing competency programs.
- Health care organizations and other organizations that offer continuing competency programs should regularly evaluate their programs for adaptability, flexibility, accessibility, and impact on clinical outcomes and update the programs accordingly.

Recommendation 7: Prepare and enable nurses to lead change to advance health. *Nurses, nursing education programs, and nursing associations should prepare the nursing workforce to assume leadership positions across all levels, while public, private, and governmental health care decision makers should ensure that leadership positions are available to and filled by nurses.*

- Nurses should take responsibility for their personal and professional growth by continuing their education and seeking opportunities to develop and exercise their leadership skills.
- Nursing associations should provide leadership development, mentoring programs, and opportunities to lead for all their members.
- Nursing education programs should integrate leadership theory and business practices across the curriculum, including clinical practice.
- Public, private, and governmental health care decision makers at every level should include representation from nursing on boards, on executive management teams, and in other key leadership positions.

Recommendation 8: Build an infrastructure for the collection and analysis of interprofessional health care workforce data. *The National Health Care Workforce Commission, with oversight from the Government Accountability Office and the Health Resources and Services Administration, should lead a collaborative effort to improve research and the collection and analysis of data on health care workforce requirements. The Workforce Commission and the Health Resources and Services Administration should collaborate with state licensing boards, state nursing workforce centers, and the Department of Labor in this effort to ensure that the data are timely and publicly accessible.*

- The Workforce Commission and the Health Resources and Services Administration should coordinate with state licensing boards, including those for nursing, medicine, dentistry, and pharmacy, to develop and promulgate a standardized minimum data set across states and professions that can be used to assess health care workforce needs by demographics, numbers, skill mix, and geographic distribution.
- The Workforce Commission and the Health Resources and Services Administration should set standards for the collection of the minimum data set by state licensing boards; oversee, coordinate, and house the data; and make the data publicly accessible.
- The Workforce Commission and the Health Resources and Services Administration should retain, but bolster, the Health Resources and Services Administration's registered nurse sample survey by increasing the sample size, fielding the survey every other year, expanding the data collected on advanced practice registered nurses, and releasing survey results more quickly.
- The Workforce Commission and the Health Resources and Services Administration should establish a monitoring system that uses the most current analytic approaches and data from the minimum data set to systematically measure and project nursing workforce requirements by role, skill mix, region, and demographics.
- The Workforce Commission and the Health Resources and Services Administration should coordinate workforce research efforts with the Department of Labor, state and regional educators, employers, and state nursing workforce centers to identify regional health care workforce needs, and establish regional targets and plans for appropriately increasing the supply of health professionals.
- The Government Accountability Office should ensure that the Workforce Commission membership includes adequate nursing expertise.

Appendix C

Committee Biographies

Stuart H. Altman, Ph.D. (*Chair*), is Sol C. Chaikin professor of national health policy at Brandeis University. Dr. Altman was dean of the Florence Heller Graduate School from 1977 to July 1993 and interim president of Brandeis University from 1990 to 1991. He is an economist whose research interests are primarily in the area of federal and state health policy. From 2000 to 2002, he was co-chair of the Legislative Health Care Task Force for the Commonwealth of Massachusetts. In 1997, he was appointed by President Clinton to the National Bipartisan Commission on the Future of Medicare. He served as chairman of the congressionally legisled Prospective Payment Assessment Commission for 12 years. In addition, Dr. Altman has served on the board of the Robert Wood Johnson Clinical Scholars Program. He holds M.A. and Ph.D. degrees in economics from the University of California, Los Angeles (UCLA), and taught at Brown University and the Graduate School of Public Policy at the University of California, Berkeley. Dr. Altman is a member of the National Academy of Medicine.

Carmen Alvarez, Ph.D., R.N., CRNP, CNM, is an assistant professor in the Department of Community-Public Health at the Johns Hopkins University School of Nursing. Her research focuses on health promotion among underserved populations, particularly the role of patient–provider communication in preventive behaviors and health outcomes among underserved young adults. For the past 7 years, she has practiced in community health centers, serving mainly uninsured and underinsured Latino immigrants. During her postdoctoral fellowship in community health center policy, she collaborated with an array of researchers examining women's experiences with family planning services in community health centers, patient–provider communication about preventive services, and provider attitudes and subsequent communication behavior regarding support for patient self-management. In addition, Dr. Alvarez has been involved in projects highlighting the unique needs of the community health center population. She received her M.S.N. from Emory University and her Ph.D. from the University of Michigan School of Nursing. She also completed a postdoctoral fellowship at the George Washington University School of Public Health.

Cynthia C. Barginere, D.N.P., R.N., FACHE, is senior vice president and chief operating officer at Rush University Hospital in Chicago, Illinois. Previously, she served as president for clinical nursing and chief nursing officer at Rush University Medical Center, and as associate dean for nursing practice and chair of advanced practice nursing at the Rush College of Nursing. Dr. Barginere spent nearly 13 years of her career at the University of Alabama, Birmingham (UAB) Hospital, a 908-bed major academic and level-one trauma center. At UAB, she served as associate vice president and then chief nursing officer, with responsibility for quality/performance improvement and Joint Commission accreditation. During her tenure as chief nursing officer, UAB received the American Nurses Credentialing Center Magnet redesignation for nursing excellence. Dr. Barginere received her undergraduate degree from the University of Alabama, her graduate degree from UAB, and her doctorate from Samford University in Birmingham, Alabama.

Richard A. Berman, M.H.A., M.B.A., is interim director of the Patel College of Global Sustainability, a professor in the Institute for Advanced Discovery and Innovation, and visiting professor for social entrepreneurship in the Muma College of Business at the University of South Florida. He has held health care, educational, housing, and community development leadership positions around the world. In the public sector, Mr. Berman has worked with several foreign governments, the United Nations, the U.S. Department of Health and Human Services, and the U.S. Food and Drug Administration, and as a cabinet-level official for the State of New York. In the private sector, he has worked with Manhattanville College, McKinsey & Company, New York University Medical Center, Westchester Medical, EmblemHealth, and numerous start-ups. Mr. Berman served as co-founder and CEO of LICAS and as an entrepreneur in residence at Georgia Tech's Advanced Technology Development Center. He serves on several boards. He attended the University of Michigan, receiving his bachelor of business administration degree, M.B.A., and M.H.A. Mr. Berman is a member of the National Academy of Medicine.

Karen Donelan, Sc.D., Ed.M., is a senior scientist at the Mongan Institute for Health Policy at Massachusetts General Hospital in Boston, Massachusetts, and an associate professor of medicine at Harvard Medical School. She was previously founding managing director of the Harvard Opinion Research Program at the Harvard School of Public Health and co-founder and senior vice president of Medrock, Inc., a company that provided support to patients confronting critical and complex illnesses. Dr. Donelan is a prominent survey scientist who has conducted numerous national and international surveys of the experiences of patients and health professionals concerning the impact of changes in health policy and health services in health systems. Her recent collaborative interprofessional research involves surveys of patients, nurses, students and faculty, physicians, military personnel, health care executives, and thought leaders, all focused on nurse and physician recruitment, retention, and diversity and the impact on access to and quality of care. Dr. Donelan holds degrees in English and American literature (A.B.), education (Ed.M.), and health policy and management (Sc.D.), all from Harvard University.

Suzanne Ffolkes, M.A., is vice president of communications at Research!America. Previously, she served as director of media advocacy for the American Heart Association, leading media and communication activities for the association's policy initiatives. She also has served as senior media outreach specialist for the American Federation of Labor and Congress of Industrial Organizations (AFL-CIO) and as senior communications specialist for the United Negro College Fund. Ms. Ffolkes has been a journalist for the Associated Press Broadcast News Center and for various broadcast and print media outlets around the country, including CNN. She received a bachelor's degree in journalism and a master's degree in public communication from The American University in Washington, DC.

Paula Gubrud, Ed.D., R.N., FAAN, is an associate professor and special assistant to the dean at the Oregon Health & Science University (OHSU) School of Nursing. She is a founding leader of the Oregon Consortium for Nursing Education (OCNE) and is currently a director for this nationally recognized statewide collaboration. Dr. Gubrud was an Associate Dean at OHSU School of Nursing from 2009 to 2014. Dr. Gubrud consults on the development of community college and university consortiums and has assisted several states in developing shared competency-based curriculum similar to the OCNE model. She frequently leads national workshops on nursing education redesign, simulation, and clinical education. Dr. Gubrud has more than 20 years of experience in community college education. She served as nursing faculty, nursing program director, dean of Nursing & Allied Health, and special assistant to the president for strategic initiatives at Mt. Hood Community College. She also served on several statewide committees and councils through the office of the Oregon Board of Education's Community College and Workforce Development Department. She earned a B.S.N. from Walla Walla University, an M.S.N. from OHSU, and an Ed.D. from Portland State University.

Jack Needleman, Ph.D., FAAN, is a professor and chair of the Department of Health Policy and Management at the UCLA Fielding School of Public Health. His research interests include the impact of changing markets and public policy on the quality of and access to care, and the responses of health care providers and insurers to market and regulatory incentives. For the past decade, Dr. Needleman's research has focused on studies of quality and staffing in hospitals and on the evaluation and design of performance improvement activities. Quality measures he developed have been adopted by the Agency for Healthcare Research and Quality, Medicare, The Joint Commission, and the National Quality Forum, and his expertise in developing, testing, and refining quality measures has been tapped by these and other organizations. He was lead evaluator for the Robert Wood Johnson Foundation initiative Transforming Care at the Bedside. He also has directed projects on a wide range of topics, including studies of for-profit and nonprofit hospitals, the impact of community health centers on hospitalizations for ambulatory care-sensitive conditions, and changes in access to inpatient care for psychiatric conditions and substance abuse. Dr. Needleman received his Ph.D. in public policy from Harvard University. He is a member of the National Academy of Medicine.

Michele J. Orza, Sc.D., serves as senior advisor to the executive director of the Patient-Centered Outcomes Research Institute (PCORI). Prior to joining PCORI, she was a principal policy analyst at the National Health Policy Forum, focused on evidence-based health practice and policy, public health infrastructure and systems, global health, and health science and technology. Previously, Dr. Orza was a scholar at the Institute of Medicine (IOM) with the Board on Global Health and was acting director of the Board on Health Care Services. Prior to that, she had served as assistant director of the Health Care Team at the Government Accountability Office, where she was responsible for managing study teams evaluating a wide range of federal programs. Before coming to Washington, DC, Dr. Orza worked as a research assistant in the Technology Assessment Group at the Harvard School of Public Health on a wide variety of methods for and applications of systematic reviews and meta-analysis and other tools to promote and support evidence-based public health. She has served as a member of the Advisory Board to the Johns Hopkins Center for Health Policy and Healthcare Transformation. Dr. Orza received both her master's degree in health policy and management and her doctorate in program evaluation from the Harvard School of Public Health and received the first B.A. in women's studies from Harvard/ Radcliffe University.

Robert L. Phillips, Jr., M.D., M.S.P.H., is vice president for research and policy at the American Board of Family Medicine. He currently practices part-time in a community-based residency program in Fairfax, Virginia, and holds faculty appointments at Georgetown University, George Washington University, and

Virginia Commonwealth University. From 2004 to 2012, Dr. Phillips served as director of the Robert Graham Center, a center for policy studies in family practice and primary care, in Washington, DC. He has expertise in health services and health policy research, focused mainly on the primary care setting. He also has interests in health workforce research and policy and social determinants of health. Dr. Phillips served on the American Medical Association's Council on Medical Education and as president of the National Residency Matching Program. From 2006 to 2010, he was vice chair of the U.S. Council on Graduate Medical Education. Dr. Phillips is a graduate of the Missouri University of Science and Technology and the University of Florida College of Medicine. He completed training in family medicine at the University of Missouri, after which he completed a 2-year fellowship in health services research and public health. Dr. Phillips is a member of the National Academy of Medicine.

Edward Salsberg, M.P.A., is director of health workforce studies at the George Washington (GW) University Health Workforce Institute and is on the faculty at the GW School of Nursing. He has successfully established and managed three health workforce research centers. He was the founding director of the National Center for Health Workforce Analysis in the U.S. Department of Health and Human Services, which was authorized by the Affordable Care Act. Mr. Salsberg previously established and directed the Center for Workforce Studies at the Association of American Medical Colleges and the Center for Health Workforce Studies at the School of Public Health at the University at Albany of the State University of New York. All three health workforce centers have been leaders in providing information on the supply, demand, distribution, and use of the health care workforce, and they have pioneered approaches to collecting health workforce data. From 1984 to 1996, Mr. Salsberg was a bureau director at the New York State Department of Health. He received his master's degree in public administration from the Wagner School at New York University.

George E. Thibault, M.D., is president of the Josiah Macy Jr. Foundation. Immediately prior to that, he served as vice president of clinical affairs at Partners Healthcare System in Boston and director of the Academy at Harvard Medical School (HMS). He was the first Daniel D. Federman professor of medicine and medical education at HMS and is now Federman professor, emeritus. Dr. Thibault previously served as chief medical officer at Brigham and Women's Hospital and as chief of medicine at the Harvard-affiliated Brockton/West Roxbury Department of Veterans Affairs (VA) Hospital. For nearly four decades at HMS, Dr. Thibault played leadership roles in many aspects of undergraduate and graduate medical education. He had a central role in the New Pathway curriculum reform and was a leader in the New Integrated Curriculum reform at HMS. In addition to his teaching, his research has focused on the evaluation of practices and outcomes of medical intensive care and variations in the use of cardiac technologies. Dr. Thibault graduated summa cum laude from Georgetown University and magna cum laude from HMS. He completed his internship and residency in medicine and fellowship in cardiology at Massachusetts General Hospital. He is a member of the National Academy of Medicine.